The Ultimate Self Care Book

Clara Seeger,
Patrick Forsyth,
Dena Michelli and
Stephen Evans-Howe

The Teach Yourself series has been trusted around the world for over 75 years. This book is designed to help people at all levels and around the world to further their careers. Learn, from one book, what the experts learn in a lifetime.

Clara Seeger is a neuroleadership coach, corporate facilitator, speaker and author, specializing in mindfulness and emotional intelligence. Oxford-educated (MA, M.Phil.) and with a Ph.D. in German literature, she worked in investment banking before training as a coach. Clara works with international companies across many sectors and countries, delivering mindfulness interventions, leadership development courses and coach training.

Following her completion of an M.Sc. in 'Mindfulness: Neuroscience and clinical applications' (Distinction) at King's College London, Clara developed her own mindfulness-based coaching methodology and is passionate about introducing the benefits and neuroscience of mindfulness to the corporate world, both theoretically and practically. She has written several articles on neuroleadership and banking as well as *Investing in Meaning: An alternative approach to leveraging your portfolio* (Completely Novel, 2012), a coaching book for helping professionals maximize their sense of meaning at work.

For my parents and my brother, my husband Marco, and my children, Alexis and Philippos, for all their love and encouragement.

Patrick Forsyth runs Touchstone Training & Consultancy and has worked, widely and internationally, as a trainer specializing in marketing and communications skills. He writes extensively on business matters and is the author of many successful books for managers and executives, all designed to offer proven, practical guidance on the skills required for job and career success.

Dena Michelli is an executive coach and leadership development specialist who works across cultures in business school and organizational settings. She is particularly interested in how people move through transition and change and undertook research to map this process for her PhD.

Stephen Evans-Howe is a Chartered Safety Practitioner and has held a number of senior management and executive roles in a variety of engineering and service environments: petrochemical, aviation, theme parks and defence. He continues to work in industry, leading the implementation of people-based programmes, supporting safety and organizational culture change.

The Ultimate Self Care Book

Improve Your Wellbeing, Build Resilience and Confidence, Master Mindfulness

Clara Seeger, Patrick Forsyth, Dena Michelli and Stephen Evans-Howe

First published in Great Britain in 2020 by Teach Yourself, an imprint of John Murray Press, a division of Hodder and Stoughton Ltd. An Hachette UK company.

Based on original material from *Mindfulness at Work In A Week*; *Outstanding Confidence In A Week*; *Managing Stress at Work In A Week*; *Assertiveness In A Week*

Database right Hodder & Stoughton (makers)

The *Teach Yourself* name is a registered trademark of Hachette UK.

British Library Cataloguing in Publication Data: a catalogue record for this title is available from the British Library.

Library of Congress Catalog Card Number: on file.

Paperback ISBN: 978 1 473 68942 8

Ebook ISBN: 978 1 473 68939 8

1

The publisher has used its best endeavours to ensure that any website addresses referred to in this book are correct and active at the time of going to press. However, the publisher and the author have no responsibility for the websites and can make no guarantee that a site will remain live or that the content will remain relevant, decent or appropriate.

The publisher has made every effort to mark as such all words which it believes to be trademarks. The publisher should also like to make it clear that the presence of a word in the book, whether marked or unmarked, in no way affects its legal status as a trademark.

Every reasonable effort has been made by the publisher to trace the copyright holders of material in this book. Any errors or omissions should be notified in writing to the publisher, who will endeavour to rectify the situation for any reprints and future editions.

Typeset by Cenveo® Publisher Services.

Printed and bound in Great Britain by CPI Group (UK) Ltd., Croydon, CR0 4YY.

John Murray Press policy is to use papers that are natural, renewable and recyclable products and made from wood grown in sustainable forests. The logging and manufacturing processes are expected to conform to the environmental regulations of the country of origin.

Carmelite House
50 Victoria Embankment
London EC4Y 0DZ
www.hodder.co.uk

Contents

**Part 1: Your Mindfulness
at Work Masterclass**

Part 2: Your Confidence Masterclass

PART 1
Your Mindfulness at Work Masterclass

Introduction

There is an increasing awareness of, and appetite for, mindfulness across the corporate world, mostly mediated through mindfulness-trained coaches and leadership facilitators, as well as an increasing body of neuroscientific research, which has underpinned this ancient contemplative practice with solid scientific inquiry and proof of its innumerable benefits. With chronic stress taking its toll, leading to burnout and impaired decision-making, many employees and corporate executives have realized that a new approach to working life is needed. Mindfulness is a tool that helps calm the mind through the conscious and intentional directing of one's attention. It can enhance focus, reduce stress, improve performance, facilitate decision-making, increase self-control and raise your level of wellbeing.

Mindfulness is a quality of our consciousness, a particular relationship to our experience that anybody can adopt at any time while going about one's daily life. This makes it an ideal practice for busy employees and managers.

Mindfulness does not need to be studied theoretically for it to work. It does need to be *practised*, however. Even a few minutes of regular practice are beneficial and can easily be integrated into your work.

CHAPTER 1

What is mindfulness?

Before we delve into the different aspects of working life to explore how they can be enhanced through mindfulness, we need to understand what mindfulness really is. We will introduce you to the best-known definition of mindfulness by the 'father' of mindfulness in the West, Jon Kabat-Zinn, and unpack it to reveal its three central tenets. Further, we will learn about different types of mindfulness practices, both formal and informal, as well as their purpose, and identify their wide-ranging benefits that have been established through scientific studies in different contexts, not just clinical research but also work that has been conducted in the workplace.

Next, we will look at the mechanisms through which mindfulness exerts its effects and review the main changes in brain structure and function that have been established through scientific studies so far.

To conclude, you will be introduced to a basic breath meditation as well as some tips for informal practices that you can start integrating into your day as you set off on your path towards increased mindfulness, greater wellbeing and inner peace.

A definition

So what do we mean by the term 'mindfulness', which has become so ubiquitous these days, yet remains somewhat elusive and more multi-dimensional than most definitions suggest? The most widely used definition stems from Jon Kabat-Zinn who is to be credited for making this ancient Buddhist practice widely accessible to mainstream society.

Having adapted mindfulness from its spiritual roots to the needs of chronic-pain patients in the form of a structured eight-week Mindfulness-Based Stress Reduction (MBSR) programme back in the late 1970s, Kabat-Zinn describes the practice as a form of 'paying attention in a particular way: on purpose, in the present moment, and non-judgementally' (Kabat-Zinn 1994). Unpacking this definition, three key elements of mindfulness can be identified:

1 Mindfulness is something you do **intentionally** rather than by accident.
2 Mindfulness is about paying **attention** in the **present** moment.
3 Mindfulness requires a certain **attitude** towards what you are doing.

These three central axioms of mindfulness have been captured diagrammatically in the following conceptual model by Shapiro *et al.* (2006):

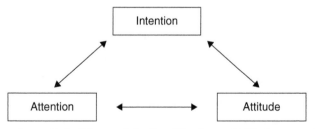

The three axioms of mindfulness – Intention, Attention and Attitude – are not separate stages. They are interwoven aspects of a single cyclic process and occur simultaneously. Mindfulness is this moment-to-moment process.

Let's look at these three elements in more detail.

Intention

Paying attention does not simply occur; it is a purposeful activity, driven by the powerful intention to inhabit the realm of awareness and to be fully present for one's experience, whatever this may be. Before each 'formal' practice it is important to set an intention, which is different from a goal: it is not about reaching a certain outcome (in fact, you are explicitly urged to let go of any such attachments to outcomes!) but about committing oneself to practising in a certain way; this could be anything from focusing on the breath, to being open to whatever may arise, to being kind to oneself for losing focus for the umpteenth time (because you will!). Intentions drive the practice and give it purpose, coherence and meaning.

Attention

In terms of attention, this is widely considered to be the central component of mindfulness, which is often, somewhat reductively, seen as nothing more than attention training. It is undoubtedly a crucial aspect of mindfulness and one that is trained in all forms of mindfulness exercise, particularly when practising breath meditation. It involves directing one's focus and sustaining it on the desired object of attention (usually the breath), while renouncing other stimuli.

The important part about paying attention is that it necessarily occurs in the present moment. This may sound banal, but how often do you really practise this? Our mind tends to wander, casting itself back to some episode in the past that is still lingering and usurping mental space, or it is consumed by plans and to do lists that take us far away into the future. Being present for all of our experience, which, after all, only ever unfolds in the present moment, is the greatest gift that we can learn to give ourselves through practising mindfulness. Present-moment awareness is very simple in principle, but, in practice, it goes against many years of hardwired mental habits of 'time travelling', as it has facetiously been called in the literature. Paying attention in the present moment entails noticing what is going on both within us, our thoughts, feelings and physical sensations, as well as in the outside world.

Attitude

When you notice what is going on inside and around you, it is important to do so non-judgementally, without criticizing yourself for whatever arises in your mind or wishing things to be different. It is entirely normal to experience difficulties when trying to pay attention in the moment as the mind's natural state is to wander and engage in daydreaming, fantasizing, reminiscing, planning and so on, and to switch seamlessly and often erratically from one mental excursion to another, something that the Buddhists call 'monkey mind'. As one has set an intention to sustain the focus on the breath or any other object of attention in the present moment, it is easy to get frustrated and engage in self-critical and judgemental thinking, condemning oneself for failing to follow the instructions to the letter. Yet, unlike any other new practice that you may decide to take up, an accepting attitude is part of the very instructions and an essential ingredient in what you are asked to follow. And this is how mindfulness practice is very different from any other skill you may have learned: rather than aiming at perfect execution, it is content with remaining a 'practice', insisting that you make your peace with imperfection and do so with a kind and self-compassionate attitude.

What you do

Broadly speaking, mindfulness can be practised in two mutually enhancing ways: first, by way of **formal practices** where you sit, stand, lie or walk mindfully for a predetermined length of time and follow the instructions from your teacher, a tape or even your own, and second, **informally**, by integrating mindfulness into your everyday life and activities, doing what you do anyway, but doing so in a non-habitual, mindful fashion.

Formal practices

The two most common formal practices are breath meditation where the breath is used as the anchor and object of attention (**shamata**), aimed at steadying the mind, practising narrow-focus concentration and calming the nervous system, and the more advanced insight meditation (**vipassana**), which aims at eliciting deeper insights into the nature of impermanence and the interconnectness of all phenomena and thus at attaining wisdom. Shamata is considered a prerequisite for wisdom and insight – only a steady mind can achieve enlightenment. The most common posture is sitting, either on a cushion on the floor or on a straight-back chair, the spine erect but not stiff, the eyes closed or cast downwards, the posture signalling alertness and dignity, rather than pure relaxation. In shamata meditation, the breath is used as a tool to steady the mind and to ground it in present-moment awareness. The breath has the advantage of being easily available to us at all times and being intimately connected to the present: you can only ever breathe in the present moment, which makes the breath ideally suited as an object of mindfulness meditation.

Observing your breath means following it for the duration of each in-breath, as well as each out-breath, without wanting to change it in any way or making it different from what it is. You can focus on the sensations of the air on your upper lip as it moves in and out of your nostrils or feel your abdomen rising with each in-breath and falling with each out-breath, wherever you feel it most strongly. When you notice your mind wandering away from the breath, as it inevitably will, gently but firmly bring it back to the breath, remembering to maintain a non-judgemental attitude towards yourself. Learn to treat the realization that the mind has wandered as an achievement, rather than a failure, a sign that you have woken up and become aware.

In addition to this basic sitting meditation you can practise a so-called 'body scan' meditation lying down, where you shine the spotlight of attention on each part of the body in turn, gradually working up from your feet to the top of your head. Furthermore, you can practise mindful movement where you engage in gentle stretches or subtle yoga movements, exploring your physical edge in a non-competitive and accepting manner. Finally, mindful walking is a practice that brings present-moment awareness into each and every aspect of walking and thus constitutes a transitional practice between formal and informal practices.

Informal practices

By informal practices we mean practices that bring mindfulness into your everyday life, for example making your tea mindfully or taking a mindful shower, brushing your teeth or doing the dishes mindfully. The idea here is to transfer what you have learned from the formal practices and integrating this firmly into your daily life, making you fully aware of all aspects of your experience in the present moment and thus creating a richer and more consciously experienced reality than normally tends to be the case. We rarely register seemingly banal details such as the sensation of the toothbrush's bristles against our gums, and, by extension, we may overlook more significant moments: a smile, a kind word, the sound of our children's laughter or the warmth of the sun on our skin. We are so used to mentally fast-forwarding our life to the next important milestone that we often miss the richness of our everyday moments in the process. Yet these moments are all we ever have as the past and future only exist in our imagination and are ultimately insubstantial. As Kabat-Zinn reminds us, we have only moments to live. In other words, if these moments right here, right now, are all we ever have, they are precious – we might as well turn up and live them to the full!

Benefits

The impact of mindfulness practice on a wide variety of different aspects of human functioning has been firmly established in an enormous body of academic studies, which is growing exponentially. The list of salutary effects on our physical, mental and intellectual wellbeing is seemingly endless, impacting on virtually every aspect of life:

Physical	Emotional	Intellectual/mental
Lower blood pressure	Better emotional regulation	More mental clarity
Stronger immune system	More calm	Better focus and concentration
Slower ageing (telomere lengthening)	More wellbeing/ happiness	Better memory
Improved cardiovascular health	Enhanced emotional intelligence	Increased attention span
Quicker recovery time from surgery, illnesses	Less reactivity	Improved decision-making
Faster healing of wounds	Increased resilience	Better problem-solving
Less inflammation	More self-compassion	Enhanced cognitive flexibility
Lower stress levels	Reduced depressive relapse	Less rumination
	Less emotional volatility	More creativity
	Less anxiety	Less mental proliferation
		More self-awareness

Workplace benefits

It is easy to see how this ever-growing list of beneficial effects can also be of great service in the workplace, and a number of specific workplace benefits have already been identified in the academic literature:

- better focus and concentration
- lower stress levels
- better self-control and emotional regulation
- higher empathy and emotional intelligence
- improved relationships
- better decision-making

- improved job satisfaction and engagement
- lower absenteeism due to sickness
- improved creativity and innovation
- enhanced productivity and performance.

The evidence is so strong that a number of mindfulness-based interventions and training courses have been created or adapted for workplace requirements and numerous books have been written on the subject of mindfulness in the workplace. As mindfulness is becoming increasingly mainstream, a growing number of CEOs and high-profile business figures are 'coming' out as being long-term meditators, many of whom we will encounter in the course of this book.

> *'When I went on holiday with my family recently, I wasn't afraid to switch on my out-of-office email message. When was the last time you did the same? If you can't recall, then maybe it's time to slow down, switch off your phone and focus on the present. Your business will benefit as a result.'*
>
> Richard Branson, Founder of Virgin

Mindfulness shapes our brain

So how does mindfulness produce such countless beneficial effects on human functioning? The last 20 years have seen immense advances in the field of neuroscience, and mindfulness has attracted considerable interest from scientists, keen to explain its mechanisms of change. The discovery of neuroplasticity – the capacity of the brain to rewire itself and produce new neurons even in adults (neurogenesis) – has opened our eyes to the fact that the specific content of our consciousness (external stimuli plus our thoughts, emotions and body sensations) as well as the quality of attention that we bestow on it, can all exert a lasting influence on our brain. What and how we think literally changes our brain! Mental connections are strengthened and embedded through repeated or prolonged use, while others that are no longer needed will eventually atrophy. Through mindfulness we can thus change the way our brain is wired – for the better. In the famous words of the neuroscientist Donald Hebb, 'neurons that fire together, wire together.' But before we explore how mindfulness changes and shapes our brain, let us have a brief look at what it is precisely about mindfulness that effects these changes.

A review by neuroscientist Britta Hoelzel and colleagues (2011) has identified four key mechanisms acting on the brain – attention regulation, body awareness, emotion regulation and a change in perspective on the self – all of which interact closely to bring about an entire range of benefits, as outlined above.

1 Attention regulation

The first mechanism can be split into attention on internal states and attention on external states. Meditators who are trained in focused attention (i.e. attention on a single object such as the breath, sounds, etc.) have an improved capacity to concentrate on a single task for longer, enabling them to renounce distraction and reduce ineffective multitasking.

2 Body awareness

Body awareness describes the ability to notice subtle physical sensations. Attention to internal states increases interoception: the ability to attend to and be perceptive of sensory and emotional information and cues from within, creating greater self-awareness and as a corollary, self-management – two of the cornerstones of emotional intelligence. The ability to notice your emotional and physical state without reacting to it in the usual automatic and often dysfunctional way enables you to regulate such states, which is especially important if they are somewhat unpleasant or difficult. You learn just to 'sit with them', let them be, focusing your attention on their specificity rather than on how to avoid them, fight them or fix them. This non-reactivity in itself is healing and can be very liberating – freeing yourself from the perennial tendency to solve problems, overcome obstacles and strive for achievements, which has been defined as the 'doing mode'. Whatever the situation is and however you may find it, if it is already there, it would be unwise to spend any energy on feeding a state of inner resistance or resentment to it. If there is any skilful action to be taken to alleviate or change such a state, you are more likely to identify what needs to be done if you first accept the reality of what is happening as it is happening, in all its dimensions. Such increased alertness can thus contribute to more conscious and wiser decision-making.

It has been argued that internal awareness of one's own experience is a prerequisite for empathy. The brain regions associated in interoception (most notably the insula and the temporo-parietal junction) are also implicated in social cognition and empathic responses. It is through this mechanism that mindfulness can thus improve social awareness and relationship management, the other two building blocks of emotional intelligence, as measured by the Emotional Competence Inventory, published by The Hay Group.

3 Emotion regulation

By emotion regulation we mean the modification of emotional responses through the intervention of regulatory processes. Evidence suggests that even mindfulness novices show a reduction in emotional interference (the delay in reaction time after being shown emotive pictures, which indicates less emotional reactivity) after just seven weeks of training. Physiological studies have also found decreased emotional reactivity as measured by reduced skin conductance in response to negative stimuli, as well as a quicker recovery time from emotional upsets. We will explore the topic of emotion regulation in more depth in Chapter 5.

4 Change in perspective on the self

One of the key mechanisms of mindfulness is its promotion of metacognitive awareness and insight: when you practise mindfulness you are not only paying attention or being mindful but you *know* that you are being mindful. As you are observing your thoughts, emotions and body sensations you are not only aware of these as specific *contents* of your consciousness but aware of yourself as the consciousness in which these phenomena can arise. Mindfulness is thus a *quality* of consciousness rather than being tied to specific contents of mind – these only serve as the training ground through which the mind becomes aware of itself.

The practice of mindfulness is thus not only the act of paying attention itself but the awareness of this act. When you are mindful you are no longer the protagonist in your personal drama but the omniscient observer who watches the drama unfold, can see the big picture as well as the details, and can remain disinterested and dispassionate, not carried away in the ebb and flow of ever-changing experiences. This dis-identification from the contents of your consciousness, based on the observation of their constant state of flux, ultimately leads to the dissolution of the sense of self in the narrow sense of a stable, unchanging, separate entity.

The mechanism of metacognitive awareness has far-reaching benefits, most notably in the clinical context where it has been identified as the key mindfulness element in the prevention of recurrent depressive relapse, and has made it into the UK's National Institute for Health and Care Excellence (NICE) guidelines as mindfulness-based cognitive therapy (MBCT). In this, an adaptation of MBSR for depression, people with three or more previous depressive episodes learn to nip the onset of ruminative thinking in the bud by recognizing their negative thoughts as merely 'mental events' of no real substance. This process of 'decentring' or 'reperceiving' is a useful skill even beyond the condition of depression and can foster emotion regulation, clarity of mind and inner peace.

Brain changes

Based on the four components outlined above, neuroimaging studies have established that mindfulness promotes neuroplasticity in areas of the brain that are repeatedly engaged during formal practice. Here is an overview of the major scientific findings, testifying to the structural and functional brain changes detected in experienced meditators:

- Meditators have greater cortical thickness (i.e. more cortical tissue on the outer shell of the brain) compared to non-meditators in areas associated with
  - **sustained attention and cognition–emotion integration** (right prefrontal cortex, Brodmann Areas 9/10). In 40- to 50-year-old meditators, the cortical thickness of this area was found to be comparable to that of 20- to 30-year-old meditators and controls, suggesting that regular meditation practice may slow down the rate of neural degeneration in prefrontal areas where it is most pronounced.
  - **interoception**, the awareness of internal body states (right anterior insula)
  - **sensory processing** (somatosensory cortex)
  - the **connection between self and others** (right inferior occipito-temporal cortex). This area has been shown to correlate most strongly with the amount of meditation experience of practitioners.
- Meditators have significantly higher grey matter concentration and volume in the **hippocampus** (a region important for learning and memory processes which also puts things in perspective by down-regulating the alarm bell in the brain, the amygdala), particularly in a sub-region involved in stress regulation.

In terms of functional changes, the following effects have been identified in long-term meditators by the use of functional magnetic resonance imaging (fMRI):

- reduced activation in the default mode network, which is involved in mind wandering and self-referential thinking

- less mental fixation and elaboration, evident in faster disengagement of brain areas during semantic processing, suggesting that meditators are better able to control the automatic proliferation of thinking
- more openness to negative experience (e.g. pain), demonstrated by activation of the pain network (thalamus, insula, amygdala) but deactivation of areas involved in pain reactivity and distress (prefrontal and anterior cingulate cortex)
- Increased activation on the left side of the prefrontal cortex, which is associated with positive emotion, better mood and creativity.

Mindfulness on the job

One of the reasons people are sometimes reluctant to take up a regular mindfulness practice is because they are pressed for time. We all are. It is a sign of our times not to have time to spare. The good news about mindfulness practice is that it does not necessarily require much time. Beneficial as it is to have a daily sitting practice of 20 minutes, this is not always practical in periods of high pressure, when you are working to tight deadlines, are on a business trip or have to work incredibly long hours as well as having a family to look after when you get home.

However, the good news is that mindfulness is a quality of mind, a lifestyle choice, if you will, to live your life fully and consciously. You do not necessarily need to take time out or practise in a dedicated area (although having a regular space for your formal practice can indeed be helpful). Mindfulness needs to be practised in daily life, not just on the cushion or the chair. You can practise on the job, as it were. In fact, the real litmus test for the effectiveness of your mindfulness practice is to be able to integrate it into your life.

Here are some tips on daily opportunities for mindful awareness of the breath that can easily slot into your daily work without the need to sit cross-legged on the office floor.

Mindful breathing

Throughout the working day, return to your breathing, becoming aware that you are breathing, without changing it in any way. Notice when your breathing is deep and slow and when it speeds up or becomes shallow. As the Zen Buddhist teacher Thích Nhât Hanh suggests, it may help to say to yourself the following words while you are following your breath:

'Breathing in, I am aware of my in-breath. Breathing out, I am aware of my out-breath. Breathing in, I am aware of my body. Breathing out, I release the tension in my body.'

You can do this at any time, for example in the following situations:

- as you travel to work by car, train or bus
- as you enter your office and walk up to your desk
- as you greet or engage with colleagues
- as you wait for the kettle to boil or the water to fill your glass
- as you walk to the bathroom
- as you eat your lunch
- as you have a drink
- as you sit and work at your computer
- on your journey home.

'Just watch this moment, without trying to change it at all. What is happening? What do you feel? What do you see? What do you hear?'

Jon Kabat-Zinn, Professor of Medicine Emeritus and creator of the Stress Reduction Clinic and the Center for Mindfulness in Medicine, University of Massachusetts Medical School

Summary

In this chapter we learned what mindfulness is: a form of present-moment awareness, practised intentionally and with an open and non-judgemental attitude. We looked at the history of how this ancient practice was introduced to Western culture through the work of Jon Kabat-Zinn, and distinguished between formal practices to help you build your 'mindfulness muscle' and informal practices to apply and integrate this quality of consciousness into your daily life. Further, we identified some of the manifold physical, emotional and mental benefits that have been established through scientific experiments, as well as their impact on the workplace.

We then outlined the four mechanisms through which mindfulness exerts its beneficial influence. We also learned how mindfulness practice can change both the structure and function of the brain in beneficial ways, leading to larger volume in areas associated with attention, learning and memory, interoception and a smaller fear centre, as well as more activation on the left side of the prefrontal cortex, associated with positive emotions and creativity. Finally, we shared a simple breath meditation and some tips on where and when mindfulness can be practised on the job.

Fact-check (answers at the back)

1. Which of the following elements is *not* part of the definition of mindfulness?
   a) Relaxation ❏
   b) Intention ❏
   c) Attitude ❏
   d) Present-moment awareness ❏

2. Mindful attention entails a focus on
   a) The past ❏
   b) The future ❏
   c) The present moment ❏
   d) Time travelling ❏

3. Your meditation posture should embody
   a) Relaxation ❏
   b) Alertness ❏
   c) Fun ❏
   d) Happiness ❏

4. What is the purpose of informal practices?
   a) To entertain you in everyday life ❏
   b) To practise meditation in a more relaxed way ❏
   c) To get better at your daily tasks ❏
   d) To live consciously ❏

5. Neuroplasticity denotes
   a) The brain's plastic-like texture ❏
   b) The brain's ability to change and rewire itself ❏
   c) The neurons' similarity to plasticine ❏
   d) Brain surgery ❏

6. Which benefits does attention training yield?
   a) A longer attention span ❏
   b) More multitasking ❏
   c) Fewer distractions ❏
   d) More interesting work ❏

7. What does a reduction of emotional interference suggest about mindfulness?
   a) It helps you experience fewer upsetting emotions ❏
   b) It makes you no longer care about your experience ❏
   c) It helps you regulate your emotions better ❏
   d) Emotions will not interfere with your daily life ❏

8. What is meant by metacognitive awareness?
   a) Awareness of all phenomena ❏
   b) Awareness of internal states ❏
   c) Awareness of our cognitions ❏
   d) Awareness of our self ❏

9. How can metacognitive awareness help with depression?
   a) It leads to less negative thinking ❏
   b) It lifts your mood ❏
   c) It helps you focus on something else ❏
   d) It helps you 'decentre' from your thoughts and feelings ❏

10. Which change in brain structure or function has *not* been identified as a result of mindfulness practice?
    a) A larger amygdala ❏
    b) A larger hippocampus ❏
    d) More activation of the left frontal area ❏
    d) A stronger insula ❏

CHAPTER 2

Paying attention mindfully

Attention may not be a topic one expects to find in a book teaching workplace skills, yet attention is absolutely fundamental to so many different aspects of working life that it deserves pride of place in this book: it is essential to learning, storage and retrieval of information, professional effectiveness, cognitive flexibility and adaptability, decision-making and cultivating a positive mental attitude.

Nevertheless, the modern workplace makes impossible demands on our attention: working in an open-plan office is the norm, multitasking is an unwritten expectation in most job descriptions, as is juggling the constant stream of emails, phone calls, around-the-clock availability, endless meetings and relentless business trips as part of the working week. Today's employees are expected to possess inexhaustible attentional resources and to switch the focus of their attention between processes and interactions at the drop of a hat.

As we will see, both expectations are entirely unrealistic and many corporate employees suffer from what has been termed **attention deficit trait** (ADT) due to too much input and a hyperkinetic working environment. Now we will explore what attention is, why it is so crucial to develop, why it can be tricky to achieve and how mindfulness might help us to train this muscle.

What is attention and why is it crucial in the workplace?

We live in an information age brought about by the digital revolution. Our economy is based on information computerization and a large proportion of our modern workforce is employed by the information industry. Even in our free time, information is ubiquitous, freely available and often overwhelming. The difficulty is no longer the availability or even reliability of the information but the filtering out of what is inappropriate and irrelevant, while ensuring that we do not miss potentially vital information.

Information processing and information overload

This is where attention comes in: it is a crucial part of information processing. It helps us select relevant and discard irrelevant information. There are numerous different and, at times, contradictory theories of attention but most of them agree on the premise that attention is **selective** and in **limited supply** due to our finite pool of attentional resources. Many early researchers have proposed so-called 'bottleneck' theories of attention, which are centred around the notion that the processing of information is conducted via a single channel, meaning that we can only process information sequentially rather than simultaneously (Pashler & Johnston 1998). Later theorists stress the idea of attention as a 'selective distribution of a limited amount of cognitive resources' (Smith & Kosslyn 2013) in a dynamic process by which the selection of information for further processing goes hand in hand with the inhibition of other information.

Top-down versus bottom-up processing

Out of the countless items of incoming stimuli our brain only ever selects a small fraction of information for further processing. This selection process is driven both from the '**top down**' by our goals at any one time (not just the bigger goals in our life but also small, daily objectives such as searching for a particular news item on the Internet or browsing through a set of charts to find the most relevant one to include in your report), and from the '**bottom up**' by salient sensory stimuli in our environment (e.g. a sudden fire alarm or the sound of breaking glass that automatically grabs our attention). Neuroscientists have discovered that two distinct neural networks are at play when we engage our attention in a goal-oriented versus a stimulus-driven fashion. While top-down attentional networks involve frontal and dorsal parietal areas, stimulus-driven attentional networks engage a more ventral system (Corbetta & Shulman 2002). The two networks are functionally independent but interactive.

This combination of goal- and stimulus-driven information processing enables us to function and make decisions from day to day, to achieve our goals while safeguarding our wellbeing, and to deal with the uncertainty that would otherwise paralyse us.

Having said this, useful and necessary as it is, the selectivity of our perception may also lead to problems and even distress as we inevitably distort and misconstrue sometimes vital signs or clues, leading to misconceptions and a more or less unconscious bias in our decision-making. This can have potentially dangerous consequences in the corporate world.

Corporate challenges on our attention

The limitations of our attentional capacity in combination with individual differences in our ability to pay attention pose several challenges within a corporate context, which all pertain to our capacity for attentional control – the deliberate directing of attention to the specific task at hand or the rapid shifting of attention from one task to another. The normal, innate challenges to our attention are often exacerbated in a corporate environment due to the specific external, non-conducive conditions outlined above and can be summarized as follows:

- remaining focused on the job at hand for a prolonged period of time (e.g. finishing a report or presentation, conducting a meeting, creating a spreadsheet)
- managing external distractions (e.g. phone calls, unscheduled conversations, meetings, emails, office noise)
- disengaging from the source of external distractions back to the task at hand
- managing our internal appetite for stimulation (e.g. the urge to be part of a conversation, surfing the web, looking for a new task/challenge)
- switching of attention from one task to another, driven by external demands beyond one's control.

The cost of divided attention

These common attentional challenges may all lead to a potentially perilous impairment of the quality of our attention – divided attention – that impacts on our effectiveness and efficiency in the daily handling of our job responsibilities but which, in the worst-case scenario, can also have serious consequences for decision-making. Divided attention severely compromises not only the speed at which we accomplish our tasks (Shapiro *et al.* 1994) but also, most importantly, their quality (Neisser & Becklen 1975). Our brain is simply not designed to do more than one thing at a time without paying a price. In cognitive neuroscience this impairment caused by the simultaneous handling of two tasks is labelled 'dual-task interference'. Translated into the business context, this price is called 'performance' and no employee or business can afford to pay it in the long term.

Moreover, in business we are usually not just faced with interference from dual tasks but from (the clearly misguided expectation of) multitasking. One obvious area where performance will suffer from divided attention is learning and memory, as the brain will encounter problems encoding and subsequently retrieving information that has not been properly attended to. The problem is, however, that employees as well as organizations often only become aware of this compromise in the quality of attention when there is a serious problem.

Given our brain's capacity to change as a result of paying focused attention, it is thus extremely important to be conscious of, and intentional about, what we pay attention to. Both good and bad habits are a product of the attention economy in the brain. By focusing on the 'right' object and in the 'right' way (i.e. with awareness) we can influence how our brain may change in response to our attentional habits.

Key learning points about attention

- Attention shapes the brain (neuroplasticity) – what you attend to will become hardwired.
- Attention is limited and selective.
- Attention can occur from the top down (goal-driven) and from the bottom up (stimulus-driven).
- Focused (i.e. undivided) attention is needed for sustainable learning and memory – you can retain only what you attend to.
- Focused attention is needed for performance accuracy and speed – focus on one task at a time to ensure top performance.

TIP *Divided attention is poor attention. Multitasking, while still expected and glorified in the corporate world, has been exposed as a myth by modern neuroscience.*

How mindfulness trains attention

One central aspect of mindfulness, as well as one of its major benefits, is the control of attention. Roughly speaking, we can distinguish between two types of practice:

1 the practice of **focused attention**, which, as the name suggests, focuses attention on a single object, usually the breath
2 **open presence** (also called choiceless awareness) where attention is directed to anything that arises from within or the outside, without preference.

In the beginning we learn to train our attention to stay focused on one particular anchor, most commonly the breath. This practice of focused attention addresses all the challenges to our attention encountered in the workplace, as identified above:

● We train our mind to be able to remain focused on the object of attention for as long as we intend to, as well as notice when it strays from it.
● We learn to deal with external distractions (e.g. noises or sounds in our environment) without losing focus: we simply register them and gently escort our mind back to the breath, without reactivity.
● We manage our internal thirst for more stimulation by committing ourselves to stay focused on the object of attention, without judgement.
● Finally, we learn to shift our attention from one object to another at will (e.g. from our thoughts, emotions, body sensations to the breath and then to the body as a whole).

'The ability to concentrate on one thing, and not get distracted. There's no point in getting stressed about things you can't control, the key is learning to understand that. It's focusing, and realizing what's important in your business, and not getting distracted by the things that aren't important.'

Guy Blaskey, CEO of luxury dog-food brand Pooch and Mutt

Practising the art of paying attention in this way will inevitably increase our expertise and skill in doing this, not just while meditating but in real life – and at work. Not only will we perform our roles better but we will be more in touch with the state of our mind and body through paying attention to thoughts and feelings as well as the quality of our breath, thus noticing much earlier than otherwise when we need to take a break, a holiday or even seek help.

Furthermore, the experience of focusing our attention 'on purpose' will make us more conscious of where our attention is placed at any one moment and give us more choices on how we want to deploy this incredible gift mindfully, to serve our business as well as life needs.

Paying attention is a voluntary act that leads to higher performance, fewer mistakes, less bias, better encoding and sustainable learning.

Ideas for training mindful attention

● Set the timer on your phone for one minute and form an intention to observe your breath as it unfolds naturally, for the whole duration of the in-breath and the out-breath. If one minute is easy for you, gradually increase the time.

● Using top-down goal-setting and engaging the language centre of your brain, count each full breath (one complete cycle of in-breath and out-breath) until you reach ten breaths, then start over. When your mind wanders and you lose track of your counting, start again.

● Focus your attention on a particular sensation of your breath, wherever you feel it most intensely: the sensation of the cold air coming into your nostrils and the warm air coming out, or the rising and falling of your belly during the breath.

What to try at work:

Whenever you need to work on a particular task requiring focused attention **set an intention** to remain focused on this for the duration of the time you have set aside, consciously letting go of anything else.

When **distractions** occur, **acknowledge** them and consciously decide to deal with them later, if need be.

To prevent yourself looking elsewhere for more stimulation **notice as many features of your current task** as you can. Acknowledge and appreciate all aspects of what you are doing or who you are with.

Be mindful of **where** you focus your attention – if you notice any unhelpful thoughts or comments, make a conscious decision not to dwell on them; instead, gently escort your mind back to whatever you intended to be doing.

Summary

In this chapter we explored why attention is such a crucial skill for the workplace as a way to process information and prevent information overload. Having established selectivity as a common feature of several models of attention we distinguished between goal- and stimulus-driven attention. Subsequently, we identified some of the common challenges on our attention in the workplace.

Further, we dispelled the most common myth around attention and revealed that there is no such thing as multitasking as information is processed sequentially by our brain. Only undivided or focused attention ensures full encoding of information, which is a prerequisite for sustainable learning. Performance – accuracy as well as speed – is impaired when we multitask.

Lastly, we explored how mindfulness can help us overcome the common challenges to our attention in the workplace by giving us a choice of where to focus our attention and how to sustain it.

Fact-check (answers at the back)

1. Attention requires a balancing act between
   a) What to do now and what to do later ❏
   b) The big picture and the detail ❏
   c) Your goals and your tasks ❏
   d) Selecting and inhibiting information ❏

2. Which adjectives best describe attention?
   a) Inexhaustible ❏
   b) Unlimited ❏
   c) Limited and selective ❏
   d) Undiscerning ❏

3. What does top-down information processing mean?
   a) Attending to goal-relevant information ❏
   b) Attending to what senior management expects ❏
   c) Attending to the big picture rather than the details ❏
   d) Processing information in chronological order ❏

4. The ultimate purpose of stimulus-driven processing is to
   a) Be more mindful ❏
   b) Notice the details in your environment ❏
   c) Keep you interested and engaged ❏
   d) Alert you to events that may be relevant to your survival ❏

5. What is meant by 'dual-task interference'?
   a) Multitasking ❏
   b) When two tasks disturb your working day ❏
   c) The impairment of performance when two tasks are accomplished simultaneously ❏
   d) The preference for one task over another ❏

6. How is attention relevant to learning and memory?
   a) Only information attended to can be encoded and retrieved successfully ❏
   b) You have to pay attention to your memories ❏
   c) You need a good memory in order to learn ❏
   d) If you pay attention, you will enjoy learning more ❏

7. Which mindfulness practice contributes most to overcoming attentional challenges in the workplace?
   a) Open presence ❏
   b) Focused attention ❏
   c) Choiceless awareness ❏
   d) Informal practices ❏

8. What is the main benefit of training our attention?
   a) Overcoming multitasking ❏
   b) Prioritizing the right thing ❏
   c) Better concentration ❏
   d) Giving us more choice about where and how to focus ❏

9. How does training attention affect the brain?
a) It changes it
b) Not at all
c) It makes it smarter
d) It helps it think

10. For which function is attention *not* crucial?
a) Decision-making
b) Performance
c) Learning and memory
d) Teamwork

CHAPTER 3

Enhancing your performance

In most organizations there is naturally a lot of talk about performance, often at the expense of deeper principles such as meaning, purpose and happiness. Sadly, the overriding preoccupation with performance more often than not seems to be at odds with employees' wellbeing. As a result, and in an effort to maximize performance, managers often push themselves and their teams hard and beyond the call of duty: employees work 12- to 15-hour days, they plough away through weekends or even sleep at their desk, often with disastrous consequences for their own physical, mental and emotional health.

In this chapter we will uncover some of the myths behind performance that companies and employees often fall prey to. Following on from this we will define performance as a state of optimal mental arousal. We will look at the neuroscience of performance and establish which conditions in the brain enable peak performance. You will have the opportunity to explore when and how often you are operating under such conditions and what changes you might want to make to amplify these. Finally, we will share some tips on using mindfulness to help you get 'into the zone' more often.

Myths around performance

There is a myth that is being perpetuated through the ethos of many companies who wish to remain competitive. This myth seems to suggest that increased input will lead to increased output and that performance and productivity are therefore the direct result of the hours you put in. But is this really true? Research has shown that our attention span is exhausted within minutes rather than hours, and that if you do not take regular breaks your brain will eventually take an involuntary break in the form of disturbed attention, leading to errors and bad decisions, as well as ill health. According to an article in the *Harvard Business Review* (Hallowell 2005), this has reached epidemic proportions in today's organizations. Hallowell names this condition, caused by 'brain overload', and accompanied by symptoms such as 'distractibility, inner frenzy, and impatience', as well as 'difficulty staying organized, setting priorities, and managing time', **attention deficit trait** (ADT).

The neuroscience of optimal performance

So how much sense does it make to keep pushing further through the barriers of pain and to defy one's body's and brain's need for a break, food, sleep and overall balance? Not much, according to recent neuroscience research. In fact, you will do yourself some serious damage and compromise your performance along the way.

To help us understand optimal performance it is useful to explore the neuroscience behind it. You may be familiar with the fairy tale of 'Goldilocks and the Three Bears'? Goldilocks needed everything to be 'just right': the porridge she ate, the chair she sat on, the bed she slept in. According to neurobiologist Amy Arnsten (2004), the part of our brain in charge of higher executive functions (decision-making, planning, abstract thinking), the prefrontal cortex (PFC), is the 'Goldilocks of the brain'. It needs a very precise environment of the brain's chemicals (known as neurotransmitters) to function at its best.

This 'sweet spot' of peak performance is easily compromised: as you can see in the inverted U-curve diagram below. If the brain does not release sufficient amounts of noradrenalin and dopamine, we tend to be lethargic and sleepy, unfocused, bored and distracted. This may be the case when you are lacking motivation or have disengaged from your work because you are no longer stimulated or because you may have become disenchanted with your boss, colleagues or other working conditions.

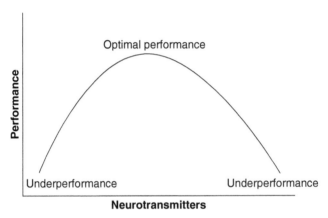

Optimal performance curve

If the neurotransmitters are, on the other hand, over-activated, as is the case with many busy managers and employees in today's fast-paced adrenalin-packed workplace, stress ensues and the brain goes into overdrive. In this over-aroused state, performance of your executive brain is compromised and starts declining rapidly. This can ultimately lead to burnout or cognitive shutdown. **In other words, too much stimulation is just as counterproductive and detrimental to your performance as insufficient chemical arousal.** In order to perform at your personal peak you need to work in alignment with your ideal level of neurotransmitters that regulate your thinking brain.

The consequences of too little mental activation

- boredom
- lack of concentration and focus
- sleepiness, lethargy
- apathy
- lack of motivation
- disengagement

The consequences of too much arousal

- stress
- tension
- restlessness
- anxiety
- burnout
- depression
- hyper-reactivity to perceived threat

Although the consequences of too little mental arousal look diametrically different from those of too much activation, they have something very fundamental in common:

- They both impair cognitive functioning, memory encoding and retrieval.
- They both compromise rational and responsible decision-making.
- They both subvert emotional intelligence and regulation.
- They both disable healthy relationships.

In short, they severely lower performance.
Conversely, when you hit your sweet spot:

- You are optimally positioned for higher cognitive functioning, goal pursuit, abstract thinking and planning, organizing and communicating.

- You find it easier to commit information to memory and remember it later.
- You are capable of greater focus, deeper empathy, better impulse control, clearer communication and wiser decision-making.

It is thus essential to maintain an ideal chemical environment for the executive centre to perform at its best, which is something that varies from person to person.

Looking at the inverted U-shape of the optimal performance curve, where would you position yourself overall, 80 per cent of the time? At work, do you tend to be under- or over-stimulated? Does your position on the arousal curve vary from day to day or from morning, midday to evening? Does it vary according to the task? Depending on the time of the week? Take a moment to write down your insights from your reflections.

The importance of dopamine

As discussed, the sweet spot of peak performance is hit when the two key neurotransmitters in your PFC, dopamine and noradrenalin, are perfectly in sync. Neurotransmitters are the chemical signals that relay information from neuron to neuron via synapses, the connections between neurons. Communication in the brain is essentially a chemical process.

Dopamine is the key driver of the reward response and is at the heart of any feeling to do with 'approach' states (e.g. motivation, curiosity, interest, desire). The dopamine level also signals the expected reward or pleasure from future events and is therefore a decisive factor in decision-making. Furthermore, dopamine levels also rise with novelty, giving you a rush of dopamine when new connections are formed in the brain. Unsurprisingly, dopamine is therefore one of the key neurotransmitters that is released when people have insights, those euphoric 'eureka' moments. And, lastly, dopamine is central to initiating physical movement.

In the PFC, dopamine is crucial, in conjunction with noradrenalin, for optimal functioning, mental focus and efficiency. Too little can be just as damaging as too much. The PFC needs just the right amount of both neurotransmitters to function at its optimum, as demonstrated in the inverted U-shape of the optimal arousal curve.

As a key excitatory neurotransmitter connected to all approach-related emotional states, dopamine is of central importance to the corporate world in terms of our goal-setting and goal-pursuit capabilities, as well as motivation, learning and the management of expectations.

> **'A few years ago, people took multitasking to be a great virtue. But it's about finding that quiet, centred place within so you're functioning at a much higher level of performance.... It's not just about stress reduction but having a capacity for insight and awareness, and engaging on a whole new level.'**
>
> Qua Veda, Intel

Mindfulness and performance

But how can we empower ourselves to achieve peak performance? This is where mindfulness comes in. While mindfulness naturally takes care of our mental wellbeing, and of all the other benefits outlined in this book, it can also – crucially for the workplace – enhance performance and therefore productivity in several direct and indirect ways.

> **'[Mindfulness] can help employees be more productive and make better decisions for the organization, which helps improve the bottom line of a business. Research from the mindfulness program we now offer to**

all Aetna employees shows that participants are regaining 69 minutes per week of productivity. This increase in productivity equates to an 11:1 return on investment.'

Mark Bertolini, CEO of Aetna

Direct ways of improving performance

- By fostering a wide attentional focus on external phenomena, mindfulness can thus help prevent costly mistakes that occur when employees miss crucial cues in their environment.
- Its external attentional focus enables people to take notice of emotional and social cues from the people they interact with. A field study of trial lawyers showed the key role of mindfulness in permitting lawyers to take into account a wide range of courtroom phenomena, including the facial expressions and reactions of the judge, jury members, and opposing lawyers, which were instrumental for judging when and how to argue their case and employ other persuasive tactics (Dane 2008).
- Mindfulness supports executive functioning, essential for good performance, by aiding clarity of mind. Research has shown that there is a negative relationship between mindfulness and cognitive failures (Herndon 2008).
- In its honing of narrow-focus attention, mindfulness helps sustain focus on the task at hand and block out distractions.
- Mindfulness increases employees' attention span, enabling them to work in a focused way for longer.

Indirect ways of improving performance

- Mindfulness reduces stress, which, as we saw in Chapter 2, impairs performance.

- Mindfulness can increase job satisfaction, which is conducive to performance.
- Mindfulness increases general wellbeing – happy workers perform better!
- Mindfulness decreases psychological distress by fostering acceptance – that is, being 'OK with' whatever is happening, facilitating mood-independent performance.
- Mindfulness reduces health-related absenteeism, removing one of the major drains on productivity.

> **'This is a tough economy. Stress reduction and mindfulness don't just make us happier and healthier, they're a proven competitive advantage for any business.'**
>
> Arianna Huffington, founder of the *Huffington Post*

Mindfulness and routine tasks

We all have certain routine tasks at work which we need to do as part of our job description but which do not really excite us as they may be repetitive, mechanical, uninspiring – in short, boring. You may need to do some bookkeeping, log calls, update spreadsheets, compile information, send standardized emails or something similar every day, every week, every month. As we have already seen, 'neurons that fire together, wire together', and the more we repeat a specific task the more it becomes hardwired in a subcortical region of the brain called the basal ganglia. This is where the implicit process of the task is embedded, ensuring that it becomes a habit, something we can do without thinking about it, a bit like riding a bike.

It is extremely useful that the brain is able to form such deep mental grooves through repetition, allowing you to perform this action routinely – that is, on autopilot. It helps conserve precious resources from the energy-intensive prefrontal cortex that does all the thinking.

However, the benefits of this ingenious performance economy in the brain are also its pitfall, which may affect your performance: while you go through the motions with the help of your basal ganglia, giving your easily depleted PFC a break to recharge its batteries, your executive centre goes on annual leave! If your mind is not focusing on the task, lost in thought or daydreaming, mistakes can happen as you may fail to detect slight changes or details, either in the task itself or with something else happening in your immediate environment.

Another caveat is that while you execute something in a perfunctory manner your conscious mind disengages and gets bored, leading to a drop in dopamine, which is also detrimental to your performance, as we have seen.

Optimizing dopamine levels through mindfulness

One of the ways in which mindfulness can help us achieve optimal performance is by regulating and optimizing the dopamine levels in our brain, which are so crucial for the chemical balance in our PFC.

More specifically, dopamine is associated with two essential functions involved in paying attention (see Chapter 2):

1 maintaining focus on the task at hand
2 'updating' the mental sketchpad that is our working memory with new, incoming information, as and when necessary.

A steady supply of this neurotransmitter ensures that the gate to working memory remains firmly closed. This mechanism supports our focus on the task at hand by blocking out any stimuli that may divert our attention. If dopamine levels plunge, or, indeed, if they rise further, this gate to our working memory will open, letting new information enter and throwing us off course.

Thus, the key to keeping the gate to your working memory closed, enabling a steady focus that will keep you operating around your sweet spot of optimal mental arousal, is to ensure that your dopamine supply remains steady and high as much as possible.

One way that mindfulness can help you experience more reward from whatever you are working on is by enabling you to place your full attention on the task at hand – no matter how tedious, tiring or challenging you may find it – and approach it with an attitude of openness, acceptance and curiosity; in other words, with **'beginner's mind'**, setting aside any expectations or previous experience you may have. Beginner's mind will serve you by keeping the novelty and hence the reward value of the task high (as novelty is intrinsically rewarding for the brain): by noticing all of its different and hitherto unnoticed aspects and features, as well as any reactions to it that may arise (e.g. resistance, resentment, frustration, boredom, disengagement, as well as tendencies to rush, avoid or resort to doing it mindlessly). Being fully present in mind and body will help you enjoy even the least enjoyable activities – after all, they will not last for ever!

Tips for increasing novelty and reward through beginner's mind at work

Be curious: really notice as many new aspects of what you are doing, no matter how small or insignificant they may seem. Imagine showing and explaining them to a curious child – what would you say to them to engage their attention and interest? Doing this will increase your presence in the moment, make you more alert and increase your enjoyment of the task.

Do things differently: resolve and practise doing things slightly differently from the way you normally would, especially for routine tasks: sit in a different chair or position, possibly in another room, if available, and tackle the task in a new way, as if you have never done it before, even if there seems to be only a subtle difference. This could be about the preparation, the execution or the attitude in your mind. Have fun experimenting with this and operating 'out of character': for example, create a mind map or make a list; use a different font or colour, a different choice of words, greeting, structure or layout; work in a more intuitive or a more linear, sequential way; engage your reason or your emotion more than you normally would in this situation. This unfamiliarity or novelty effect will wake up your executive centre and keep dopamine levels high!

Appreciate: start cultivating an appreciation for the importance of what you are doing, see its necessity and place in the bigger scheme of things, the value it adds to your team, your customers, the organization as a whole or, in a small way, even society at large. As well as increasing your appreciation of your work, this will also make you feel the interconnectedness of all things.

'We have a wellbeing portal on our intranet which provides resources to staff on a range of topics to do with health and wellbeing. These include mindfulness podcasts which we have promoted to staff since May 2014. As an employer we believe improving employees' ability to maintain their health and wellbeing, handle pressure and balance work and home life is common sense, because ultimately it leads to improved individual and organizational performance.'

A spokesperson for the London Mayor's Office

Summary

In this chapter we uncovered the myth that performance is a direct product of the working hours we invest, proposing instead an inverted U-curve as a more adequate model of performance. We defined performance as a state of optimal mental arousal in the brain's prefrontal cortex, which necessitates a very precise chemical environment of the two key neurotransmitters dopamine and noradrenalin in our executive centre.

We explored the detrimental effects of an under-aroused as well as an over-stimulated brain, which, while bearing different signatures, both lead to a state of underperformance. We then identified direct ways in which mindfulness can help improve performance through both its narrow and its wider attentional focus. We also explored several indirect ways in which mindfulness may enhance performance by reducing some of the factors that can compromise the quality of our work.

We subsequently had a closer look at the role of dopamine and its links to novelty and reward and learned how mindfulness can ensure high and steady levels of this neurotransmitter in support of optimal performance through approaching tasks with 'beginner's mind'. Finally, we shared three practices that will help you embed this approach into your working day.

Fact-check (answers at the back)

1. Which label has been given to the condition of brain overload in organizations?
   a) Attention deficit disorder ❏
   b) Attention deficit trait ❏
   c) ADHD ❏
   d) Performance anxiety ❏

2. Why has our PFC been likened to the fairy-tale character Goldilocks?
   a) It is curious to discover new things ❏
   b) It rules over areas of the brain similar to the three bears ❏
   c) It grabs resources without asking ❏
   d) It needs everything 'just right' ❏

3. What are the brain's chemicals called?
   a) Neurotoxins ❏
   b) Neurons ❏
   c) Neurotransmitters ❏
   d) Neurodegeneration ❏

4. Which two of the following chemicals determine peak performance?
   a) Serotonin ❏
   b) Noradrenalin ❏
   c) Oxytocin ❏
   d) Dopamine ❏

5. If you are to the left of your 'sweet spot', you may be feeling
   a) Alert ❏
   b) Excited ❏
   c) Stressed ❏
   d) Lethargic ❏

6. Over-arousal may lead to
   a) Over-performance ❏
   b) Disengagement ❏
   c) Burnout ❏
   d) Boredom ❏

7. High levels of dopamine are associated with
   a) Insomnia ❏
   b) Attention and motivation ❏
   c) Avoidance ❏
   d) Loss of voluntary movement ❏

8. Which part of the brain is associated with habit formation?
   a) The prefrontal cortex ❏
   b) The amygdala ❏
   c) The basal ganglia ❏
   d) The hippocampus ❏

9. From a brain perspective, what is the purpose of habits?
   a) To strengthen certain connections in the brain ❏
   b) To stimulate your executive centre ❏
   c) To help you perform better ❏
   d) To conserve precious resources of your PFC ❏

10. How can mindfulness help you keep dopamine levels high?
   a) Through the cultivation of beginner's mind ❏
   b) Through relaxing your mind ❏
   c) Through new meditation practices ❏
   d) Through clearing your thoughts ❏

CHAPTER 4

Controlling your stress levels

Stress nowadays seems to be accepted as a natural corollary of corporate life, with a large proportion of all employees considering themselves stressed, a label that has lost its threatening connotations and has almost gained the character of a status symbol. One is expected to have a high threshold for stress, which rises with increasing responsibility and seniority at work. Having said this, thanks to the advances of neuroscience, we are becoming increasingly familiar with the detrimental effects of chronic stress on our health, our brain and our wellbeing.

Part 4 discusses stress in greater depth, but in this chapter we will explore some facts and figures about the global stress epidemic in the workplace and its concomitant costs to the economy. We will learn what stress means from a brain perspective and what damage it does, explore the origins and physiology of the stress response, and learn how to reduce the stressful activation of the nervous system through mindfulness practice.

What is stress?

Many employees complain about stress. Yet before we look at different ways of reducing our stress levels we need to understand what we mean by stress. There is no clear consensus on this. Stress is a blanket term, widely used, and possibly overused, to describe a wide range of different situations. It is highly subjective and does not present in a uniform manner. Rather, it manifests in many different ways in different people, whose thresholds for what they find stressful also varies strongly.

For the purpose of this chapter, we propose a working definition of stress as the activation of the mind and the body in response to a situation (whether real or imagined) that is experienced as threatening in some way. It is a mechanism to help the organism cope with challenges or onslaughts to its equilibrium. To be more precise, we can distinguish among the following aspects of stress:

- the stimuli that trigger stress (stressors), classified into different types of stressors
- the individual's subjective feeling of stress (perceived stress)
- stress-related cognitions (e.g. threat appraisal, anxiety, worry, rumination, negative thinking)
- stress arousal (physiological responses).

We will look at what such stressors may be in the workplace and what the stress response entails physically and mentally later in this chapter. First, it is crucial to understand the severity of stress as a major challenge for employees' health and wellbeing and its concomitant cost to organizations.

The extent and cost of workplace stress

Workplace stress has become something of a global epidemic, as evidenced by the following stress-related facts and statistics from around the world, compiled by the Global Organization for Stress

- 80 per cent of workers feel stress on the job and nearly half say they need help in learning how to manage stress; 42 per cent say their co-workers need such help (American Institute of Stress).
- Stress levels in the workplace are rising, with six in ten workers in major global economies experiencing increased workplace stress. China (86%) has the highest rise in workplace stress (The Regus Group).
- Australian employees are absent for an average of 3.2 working days each year through stress. This workplace stress costs the Australian economy approximately $14.2 billion (Medibank).
- An estimated 442,000 individuals in Britain, who worked in 2007/08 believed that they were experiencing work-related stress at a level that was making them ill (Labour Force Survey).
- Approximately 13.7 million working days are lost each year in the UK as a result of work-related illness at a cost of £28.3 billion per year (National Institute for Health and Clinical Excellence).

'Mindfulness and yoga-based programs can also help reduce stress, which is a universal issue that can damage people's health. Our research found that employees reporting the highest stress level had nearly $2,000 higher medical costs for the preceding year than those reporting the lowest stress levels. These programs were successfully proven to reduce stress, which can help reduce associated health care costs.'

Mark Bertolini, CEO of Aetna

The neuroscience and physiology of stress

The stress response has its roots in our evolution. Our ancestors needed to ensure their survival and safety from various predators. Over millions of years those individuals who were skilful at fighting, fleeing or freezing in the face of a life-threatening situation passed on this 'fight or flight' response to the next generation. Those who failed to do so perished.

So what happens during stress? When we feel threatened or under pressure in any way, our mind and body are on heightened alert, sounding alarm bells and mobilizing for the fight or flight response. This is executed by the autonomic nervous system (ANS), which regulates our internal organs (viscera) such as the heart, the stomach and the intestines as well as some of our muscles.

'Fight or flight'

There are two parts of the ANS that are of interest in the context of stress: the sympathetic wing and the parasympathetic wing. When we feel stressed, the sympathetic wing of the nervous system (SNS) kicks into action in combination with the hypothalamic–pituitary–adrenal axis, getting you ready to fight that threat!

When you enter fight or flight mode, the thalamus signals to the brain stem to flood your brain with the excitatory neurotransmitter noradrenalin. Your adrenal glands are instructed by the hypothalamus (the brain's controller of the endocrine system) via the pituitary gland to release the stress hormones adrenalin, noradrenalin and the steroid hormone cortisol. This makes your pupils dilate, your heart rate and blood pressure increase, the bronchioles of your lungs enlarge and your digestive system temporarily grind to a halt in order to be able to perform under pressure and fight off the stressor – you need to be able to see better, run faster, breathe more easily and block out any low-priority functions (e.g. digestion) that may get in the way of this battle.

A short-term release of cortisol can be beneficial as it has an anti-inflammatory effect (designed to help heal wounds more quickly), but if it becomes chronic it is detrimental for the immune system and can lead to a decline in the function or structure of brain cells (neurodegeneration), which may ultimately result in neuronal death. Cortisol also stimulates the amygdala, which instigated these changes in the first place, by further ringing the alarm bell, which can lead to hyper-vigilance (an exaggerated sensitization to threat) and further cortisol production. The prefrontal cortex is tipped beyond the sweet spot of optimal performance and becomes severely compromised, as does the hippocampus, which is essential for learning and memory as well as for modulating the amygdala – altogether a toxic combination in terms of healthy functioning.

You can see why such extreme physical and mental reactions are designed as short-term mechanisms against stressors but not as a permanent state of affairs. The problem with our modern-day stress epidemic is that a great proportion of workers are under chronic mild to moderate stress, which takes its toll on the brain and the body, compromising the immune system and cognitive functioning, lowering mood, increasing the risk of depression and leading to emotional hyper-reactivity.

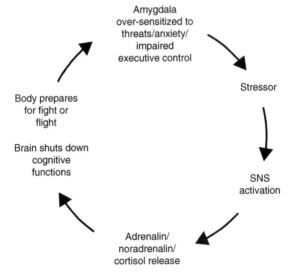

'Fight or flight' cycle

'Rest and digest'

The parasympathetic wing of the ANS works in the opposite way. Also dubbed the 'rest and digest' system, it is active when we are feeling calm, relaxed, happy and safe. With no threats to fight our pupils can constrict, the heart can slow down, the lungs can revert to their normal size and the internal organs can resume their function. This is and should be our default state, albeit somewhat elusive in today's workplace. Let us explore what we can do to redress the balance, bringing both body and mind back into a state of equilibrium.

Social threats – workplace stressors

Nowadays, we are no longer in acute physical danger of being attacked by wild animals – today's threats in the workplace are of a more social kind: our standing within our team may come under threat, our role may be cut, we may feel excluded from our team or department, unfairly treated in the annual bonus round, or not given as much information or control to determine our own workload, job description or working hours. Social threats abound.

As neuroscientists Matthew Lieberman and Naomi Eisenberger (2008) have demonstrated in experiments using fMRI, the networks in our brains that activate in response to physical pain or danger also do so during social pain. As far as our brain is concerned, social threats are as much an issue of life or death as physical ones.

The main areas where stress can be felt and a threat or 'away' response may be triggered at work (as well as elsewhere) have been identified by David Rock (2008) as:

● Status – your place in the social hierarchy
● Certainty – your ability to make predictions about the future
● Autonomy – your control over what happens
● Relatedness – your sense of belonging to a group
● Fairness – being treated in an equitable manner.

These social areas also respond to rewards, in which case they mobilize a sense of 'toward' or approach. However, for reasons we will explore later, threats weigh more heavily than rewards.

Explore which of the five factors trigger the strongest stress response in you by ranking these in order of severity, starting with the strongest:

- Does it bother you most when you feel diminished in your standing at work? (*Status*)
- Do you react with worry, insecurity or even anger when you are not provided with the full picture of what is going on in your team or the organization as a whole? (*Certainty*)
- Is not being in control of your own destiny most stressful to you? (*Autonomy*)
- Do you feel insecure and upset when your sense of belonging and acceptance by others is under threat? (*Relatedness*)
- Are you most bothered when your sense of justice and fairness come under fire? (*Fairness*)

How mindfulness alleviates stress

There is a growing scientific evidence base demonstrating the beneficial effects of mindfulness on cellular, hormonal and immune markers associated with a reduced physiological stress response. In addition, it has been shown to reduce perceived stress, which may be just as important in terms of the distress and detrimental effects on mind and body.

As we explored in Chapter 1, mindfulness in the West started off as a stress reduction intervention (MBSR) for chronically ill patients and has proven hugely beneficial in managing their distressing symptoms and their perceived stress. Subsequently, several studies in therapeutic contexts (e.g. on cancer patients) have demonstrated a significant reduction in cortisol levels when assessed before and after the MBSR programme. These improvements often proved sustainable in the longer term, as participants showed reduced cortisol levels even at the six or twelve-month follow-up (Carlson *et al.* 2007).

Interestingly, there is also some evidence to suggest that mindfulness may have a positive effect on stress on the cellular level and may play a role in slowing down cellular ageing, as measured by increased telomere length. Telomeres are protective 'caps', stretches of DNA at the end of our chromosomes, which protect our genetic material. Each time a cell divides, telomeres become shorter, until they are so short that cells can no longer divide, leading to cellular death. The shortening of telomeres is associated with ageing, cancer and a higher risk of death.

What makes mindfulness an ideal practice to reduce stress are the following factors:

- Mindfulness practice stimulates the parasympathetic nervous system through its calming emphasis on the breath. Although not primarily aimed at relaxation, relaxation surely is a pleasant and beneficial side effect.
- Activation and sensitization of the fear centre of the brain (amygdala) are drastically reduced.
- The volume of the hippocampus, which can dampen down limbic responses, increases.
- Mindfulness increases bodily awareness (interoception) and mental self-awareness through the close observation of thoughts, feelings and sensations. This alerts us to any stressful activation right from the beginning and gives us a choice on how to deal with it (e.g. by doing more mindfulness!) before we are sucked into the downward spiral of stress reactivity.
- Metacognitive awareness: being aware of the stress signals in your mind and body you are more able to dis-identify from them, holding them in a vast space of awareness, letting them be.

Mindfulness exercises to calm the nervous system on the job

Here are some tips on how you can use mindfulness while you are sitting at your desk to reduce the stressful activation of the nervous system and to stimulate your parasympathetic system:

- Take three calming breaths: breathe in for five counts, breathe out for seven (a longer outbreath has a calming effect).

- Work with a smile: rather than sitting or walking around the office with a grim expression on your face make a habit of smiling. This sends the message to your brain that you are safe and will relax the nervous system as well as induce a state of wellbeing.

- Try laughing out loud at the next mildly funny thing you see or hear (laughter relaxes you and lifts your mood, which also reduces stress levels).

- Indulge yourself with a long yawn, deliberately initiating a relaxed, almost drowsy state.

- Take a mindful minute (or two!) when you are feeling very stressed or anxious.

Summary

In this chapter we explored the ever-present topic of stress in the workplace. We started off by defining what we mean by stress and identified different categories of stress. We established some key facts about the extent and cost of workplace stress globally to quantify its detrimental effect.

Further, we explored what happens during stress in our brain and our body, driven by the sympathetic wing of the autonomic nervous system. We honed in on the damaging effects of too much cortisol on brain cells and the negative stress spiral into which it can escalate. We also identified the antidote to stressful 'fight or flight' activation, which lies within the remit of the 'rest and digest' parasympathetic nervous system.

Subsequently, we explored how stress nowadays plays out in the modern workplace and how mindfulness practice can reduce stressful activation of the nervous system.

Fact-check (answers at the back)

1. What is the original purpose of the stress response?
a) To alert us to the fact that we are working too hard ❑
b) To ensure our survival in response to threat ❑
c) To help us stay competitive ❑
d) To help us perform better ❑

2. Which system in the body is responsible for the stress response?
a) The central nervous system ❑
b) The digestive system ❑
c) The cardiovascular system ❑
d) The autonomic nervous system ❑

3. When we are stressed we activate the
a) Sympathetic nervous system ❑
b) Parasympathetic nervous system ❑
c) Prefrontal cortex ❑
d) Blood pressure ❑

4. Which of the following hormones is not associated with stress?
a) Cortisol ❑
b) Noradrenalin ❑
c) Adrenalin ❑
d) Testosterone ❑

5. What is the effect of too much stress on executive function?
a) It stimulates thinking and performance ❑
b) It impairs performance ❑
c) It has no impact ❑
d) It increases alertness ❑

6. Cortisol can lead to
a) Neuroregeneration ❑
b) Neurotoxicity ❑
c) Neurodegeneration ❑
d) Inflammation ❑

7. Why can social factors trigger a fight or flight response?
a) Social situations are naturally threatening ❑
b) They may compromise your safety ❑
c) You may be hypersensitive ❑
d) Social threats activate the same brain networks as physical threats ❑

8. Which social need can trigger threat?
a) Competence ❑
b) Certainty ❑
c) Comprehension ❑
d) Creativity ❑

9. Evidence of telomere lengthening suggests that mindfulness
a) May contribute to better genetic material ❑
b) May contribute to a better immune system ❑
c) May counteract cellular ageing ❑
d) May contribute to a more youthful look ❑

10. How does mindfulness reduce the stress response?
a) By stimulating the parasympathetic nervous system ❑
b) By triggering the sympathetic nervous system ❑
c) By avoiding the triggers of stress ❑
d) By facing up to the causes of stress ❑

CHAPTER 5

Regulating your emotions

Contrary to the prevalent ethos of many companies and corporate executives, organizations are emotional hot houses. It is neither realistic to leave your emotions at home when you come to work, nor should you have to. Emotions are a normal and even desirable part of working life and an integral, enabling part of decision-making, professional or otherwise – but they need to be managed. Unfortunately, more often than not, emotions are managed poorly and relationships at work can be just as dysfunctional as they may be beyond the workplace.

In this chapter we will look at the two ways the brain processes emotions – the fast and automatic way of emotional reactivity and the slow and considered way of emotion regulation – explore different emotion regulation strategies and introduce you to mindfulness as an alternative and constructive way of managing how you feel. We will review the current evidence from neuroscience on mindfulness as an emotion regulation strategy, which can help us manage emotions from the top down and from the bottom up. To conclude, drawing on Buddhist wisdom on emotions we will learn how to 'sit' with emotions in a mindful way, allowing them to arise without reactivity.

Emotional processing: low road or high road?

So, what are emotions and why are they so important? Literally meaning 'movements', emotions originate in physical sensations and can be described as responses to internal or external events, which are of particular significance to the individual. According to neuroscientist Antonio Damasio, emotions are an important part in the organism's equilibrium and intimately related to reward and punishment mechanisms. They both represent and regulate the body state. Emotions occur automatically and change the body, brain and mental state in profound ways.

Emotions have a huge impact in the workplace, just as everywhere else. They affect employees'

- mood and attitude
- wellbeing
- stress levels
- productivity
- performance
- working relationships
- decision-making
- job satisfaction.

No employee or executive can afford to ignore their emotions (or other people's, for that matter) or take them lightly. Scientists have distinguished two distinct pathways of processing emotions in the brain, which have been dubbed the low road versus the high road of emotional expression.

Steps involved in emotional processing

As can be seen in the diagram, emotions arise in response to a specific event or stimulus. It is our assessment of this stimulus – which may be more or less conscious – that ultimately leads to the emotional response. This response may be regulated to a larger or lesser degree.

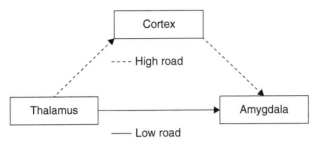

The low road and high road of emotional processing

As it is essentially a stress response, the **low road** of emotional expression is the 'fight or flight' response we explored in the previous chapter, also known as emotional reactivity, 'acting out' or 'mindless emoting' (Teasdale 1999). As discussed, this involves the direct route between the thalamus that receives the input and the amygdala as the seat of emotional reactions. In this pathway, emotions are activated before our cognitive faculties have a chance to intervene and regulate (Wager 2003). Being a short cut in the brain, this route is fast and automatic, requiring no conscious effort.

The **high road** is that of emotion regulation. Here, the thalamus acts as the sensory gateway to the cortex, which orchestrates higher cognitive processes, thus enabling emotion regulation from the top down. As we will see in the next section, such regulation can take different forms. Emotional regulation from the top down is slower as it constitutes an indirect pathway and, as such, it requires considerable conscious mental effort. Emotions can be down-regulated to lessen the impact of negatively perceived stimuli or up-regulated to increase the impact of positive ones.

Emotional regulation strategies

There are a number of different ways to regulate emotions in order to avoid mindless emoting. As the executive centre and the limbic system work in a kind of seesaw effect, where activation of one suppresses the other, we can use insights into emotion regulation to help ourselves get a grip on our amygdala.

Limiting exposure

A proactive way of regulating emotions is to intervene *before* strong and predictable emotions arise in the first place: limit your exposure to situations that elicit threat responses, and avoid, if possible, those that you already know will make you 'go limbic'. For example, if you keep volunteering to present at meetings and then you drive yourself crazy with stage fright you may decide not to keep putting yourself through this.

Tips to try

- Be discerning about what additional workload you take on.
- Only expose yourself to challenges you will benefit from tackling.
- Avoid taking on last-minute commitments.
- Schedule meetings well in advance.
- Set realistic deadlines.
- Avoid exposure to dysfunctional working relationships.
- Choose to work more closely with colleagues with whom you have a better working relationship.

Adjusting exposure

When situations cannot be entirely avoided, which will often be the case in a corporate environment, you may be able to tweak certain aspects in order to avoid strong emotional reactions and ensure maximum 'safety', convenience, flexibility and certainty for yourself or the other people involved.

Tips to try

- Keep your cool by preparing yourself well in advance for meetings.
- Exercise any freedom you may have about setting the time/day/length/agenda of a meeting.

> ● Make sure that you have some refreshments/snacks before any important or emotionally charged decisions, meetings, or encounters to avoid low blood sugar or hunger throwing you off course.

Attention focusing

When you come across situations that can neither be avoided nor adjusted you still have an important choice: to decide where to place your attention. You do not have to let yourself be hijacked by maladaptive emotions that make you miserable. Train yourself to focus your attention on *other* aspects of the situation – constructive outcomes, positive features – any consensus within your team, rather than remain stuck in negativity bias. Before important events or situations, prime your brain to pay attention to positive aspects and outcomes. As we have seen, directing your attention on purpose is a crucial skill and focus of mindfulness.

Verbal labelling

Neuroimaging studies have shown that the act of verbal labelling – that is, attaching a name to an affective state – can help down-regulate emotional processes through the activation of the right ventro-lateral part of your PFC, which exerts an inhibitory function on the amygdala, dampening down limbic responses (Creswell *et al.* 2007).

Cognitive reappraisal

In this emotion regulation strategy you consciously manipulate the *input* into what is called the emotion-generative system from the top down, again using the executive centre of your brain. Here, you actively reinterpret emotional stimuli in a way that modifies their emotional impact. An example of this would be when you reframe some disappointing feedback on a piece of work in the light of the opportunity for self-improvement that it presents. Functional neuroimaging studies have shown that during reappraisal prefrontal regions of the brain are active while the amygdala shows decreased activation (Ochsner 2008). Similar to verbal labelling, reappraisal down-regulates and inhibits the limbic system.

Suppression

Suppression is a regulation strategy that suppresses the behavioural *output* of the emotion-generative system from the top down. By contrast to cognitive reappraisal, which leads to decreases in limbic area activity, suppression may diminish the acting out of negative emotions but studies have found increased activation of the brain's emotional centre in the long term. While you may be able to prevent acting out your negative emotional experience for a short while, suppression is not a good idea in the long run as it will come at the cost of greater emotional turmoil later.

Managing emotions mindfully: top-down versus bottom-up processing

If you want to handle your emotions in a more constructive way, mindfulness may well be your best bet. There is substantial scientific evidence that, the more you practise, mindfulness will lead to more effective emotion regulation and reduced emotional reactivity. Neuroscientists have found that long-term mindfulness practitioners show less activation and sensitization in limbic regions such as the amygdala. Practitioners learn an alternative way of relating to present-moment experience where both pleasant and unpleasant emotions are allowed to surface but are not acted or dwelled upon with habitual reactivity. Instead, practitioners are encouraged to accept how they feel with self-compassion and be curious about the bodily manifestation of the emotion. This is reflected in the increased activation of the insula, which tracks sensory experiences and thus enables a more vivid and direct experience of reality through the senses while emotions are kept in check.

A review of existing neuroimaging studies by Chiesa *et al.* (2013) suggests a distinction between novice practitioners who are undergoing initial mindfulness training (e.g. an eight-week MBSR course) and experienced long-term practitioners with several years of regular practice under their belt: while meditation novices tend to display more top-down activation, mindfulness experts show an increased ability to regulate their emotions without the involvement of executive brain areas, thus requiring less conscious effort. This suggests that the more you practise, the less you need to work on actively regulating your emotions, and the more you will become adept at managing your emotions non-cognitively and from the bottom up.

To sum up: mindfulness enables more adaptive emotional processing and the switch from emotional reactivity to emotional responsiveness in a way that can become second nature with increasing practice and skill.

> **'[Meditation] gives me a centeredness, it gives me an ability to look at things without the emotional hijacking, without the ego, in a way that gives me a certain clarity.'**
>
> Ray Dalio, Bridgewater Associates

Try this: mental noting and depersonalizing

When you start off on the mindfulness path, it can be extremely useful to practise top-down regulation. A traditional way of doing this in the light of the evidence on affective labelling presented above, is to engage in a practice, common in the 'insight' meditation tradition, called **mental noting.** When you notice feelings coming up for you, make a soft mental note of what is arising: for example 'There is anger/disappointment/irritation etc.' Do not spend too much time trying to identify the right word and getting embroiled in semantics. The effect of this practice is that you engage the executive centre of your brain, which, through the seesaw effect mentioned above, attenuates the limbic centre, dampening down the emotional charge of the feeling.

Taking the self out of the equation (by favouring noting such as 'there is frustration', rather than 'I feel frustrated'), you also depersonalize the feeling and thus make it less salient to yourself and your survival – a subconscious fear that is often triggered when we experience negative feelings, which then activates the stress response. The key to using this technique effectively is to keep the label neutral and short so that you are not taken hostage by the emotion or become too emotionally involved with it.

A Buddhist perspective

How do experienced mindfulness practitioners manage their emotions without resorting to either mindless emoting or cognitive control from the top down? The answer lies within the foundations of Buddhist philosophy, a brief foray into which will provide a context for an alternative perspective on emotions than we are used to in Western societies.

Emotions as passing phenomena

Unlike in Western psychology where emotions are taken extremely seriously and tend to be seen as integral to who we are and what defines us, Buddhist philosophy does not attach the same importance to emotions. Here, emotions are seen as mental phenomena that arise and fade away just like anything else, for example thoughts. They have their origin in bodily sensations and have ultimately no real substance or defining power over us. Buddhism explicitly warns against constructing an identity out of our transient emotions as it does not believe in a stable and separate self in the sense that we tend to do in the West, where we become so identified with, say, our anger, that we are completely consumed by it, unable to distinguish ourselves from it. In other words, in Buddhism, you are not your emotions – your anger, your disappointment, your sadness – but can, and should, dissociate from them, holding them in a vast space of awareness.

The 'feeling tone' of experience

Yet Buddhism does not deny the existence of emotions, nor their power. Quite the contrary, it encourages allowing and accepting them as they are, but without becoming sucked into them, and proposes three ways of describing what it calls the 'feeling tone' of each experience, classifying it as either pleasant, unpleasant or neutral. So far, so good. There is nothing wrong with experiencing situations or feelings as having a positive or negative emotional valence. The problem only arises once you start *reacting* to a pleasant feeling tone with wanting or clinging and to unpleasant feeling tones with aversion. This grasping for the pleasant and pushing away of the unpleasant creates and perpetuates suffering, due to the ever-changing nature of our experience.

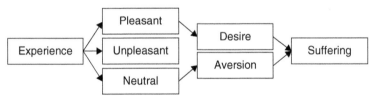

The origins of suffering

Mindfulness practice for emotion regulation

Before we have a go at a four-step practice for working with feelings mindfully, let us have a look at what each of the steps involves and what it does. This process will help you manage your emotions more constructively, and increasingly from the bottom up, the more you practise.

1 Take notice of the feeling tone

The first step towards regulating your emotions is to become more aware of them. This may sound obvious but we often do not notice the initial stirrings of an emotion until it has snowballed into a personal drama, catastrophe or other emotional roller coaster. Make a habit of registering the emotional charge of all stimuli you encounter during your working day. Here's a checklist to help you get started but do add your own situations or emotional trigger points to it.

How do you feel when...

- You first walk into your office in the morning?
- You walk out of the door in the evening?
- You see or talk to your boss/colleagues/direct reports?
- You sit in a meeting?
- You interact with clients/other stakeholders?
- You meet with a challenge or difficult situation?
- You are working to a deadline?
- Your workload is overwhelming?
- You go on your lunch break?
- You do not have time to take a break?

The list is endless. Whatever situation or experience you encounter during your working day, there will be a feeling tone attached to it, whether you realize that at the time or not. Practise noticing it. **Is it pleasant, unpleasant or neutral?** Avoid conventional value judgements such as good or bad and stick to these more neutral labels to avoid triggering strong likes and dislikes. This part of the exercise is merely about strengthening the power to *notice* the nature of experience as having a specific feeling tone *before* a cascade of emotions are set in motion and hold you hostage.

2 Label your feelings

The second step involves applying a mental label to your emotions by using just one or two words. Here are some examples to help you get started:

- anticipation
- frustration
- excitement
- anger
- trepidation
- satisfaction
- fear
- resentment
- worry
- anxiety
- stress
- elation
- relief
- joy
- pride.

Again, the list goes on. Feel free to add to it and choose the labels that most accurately describe what you feel. Caveat: this is not about 'getting it right' or finding the most accurate description, it is about the power of awareness. Remember to take yourself out of the equation. Rather than 'owning' the feelings, as we are encouraged to do in Western culture, see yourself as the witness, the observer of whatever arises.

3 Allow yourself to feel your feelings

The third step is about allowing yourself to feel whatever arises. As we have seen, regulating emotions mindfully is not about avoiding or suppressing them; it is about changing your attitude or relationship to them: allowing them to arise and fade without reacting to them, whether that is wishing them away or chasing after them.

Now comes the crucial step, the one that will help you get out of the relentless wheel of emotional reactivity and help you process emotions from the bottom up: rather than reacting to your emotions in your usual, habitual way, 'drop' into your body – where do you feel it? Is there a lump in your throat? A queasy feeling in your belly? Does your heart pound? Is your head throbbing? Do you have butterflies in your stomach? A heavy weight on your chest? Bring to this investigation a sense of openness, acceptance and curiosity, and, most importantly, do not judge yourself for feeling what you feel. Practise consciously suspending your value judgements. Tell yourself that it is OK to feel like this, liking or disliking your experience; there is no need to censor it in any way, let alone judge yourself. Your experience is your experience. Yet there is no need to invest any energy in perpetuating, fighting or chasing such feelings. For better or worse, they will arise and pass on their own, much more quickly than you might wish (in the case of the pleasant ones) and much less slowly than you fear (in the case of the unpleasant ones)! So when you explore your feelings, try noticing as many details as possible, focusing on the sensations inside and outside of your body and mentally record them like an impartial scientist would record his or her findings.

4 Dis-identify from your feelings

The last step is crucial. It has to do with the fact that emotions, like all other phenomena, are transient – they come, they go, and you may even come to wonder how you could possibly have felt a certain way only an hour later. How could I have got so worked up about something that does not seem so bad right now? Was it really worth going out of my way to run after this award? While it is important to experience your feelings fully when they arise, it is also vital not to take them for something more substantial or permanent than they actually are.
Do not get too attached to them. Your emotions are nothing but momentary, situational representations of your physical and mental responses to certain events. You do not have to construct an identity for yourself out of what and how you feel at any one time.

Look at the following train of thought that may snowball from a feeling of fear: 'I am so scared of this presentation, I'm no good at public speaking, nobody will take me seriously, I'm such a loser.' This is as unnecessary as it is dysfunctional, yet many of us will indulge in such faulty reasoning as part of our daily emotional routine. A better way of relating to such emotions, especially the unpleasant ones, is to notice them in an impersonal way. 'Ah, there is anxiety again, rearing its ugly head' or simply 'I notice frustration.' This holds emotions at bay, forcing them to keep their distance, and takes you out of the equation. Emotions are just phenomena that arise, not your personal creation. They can lose their power to threaten you and throw you off course. They are nothing more than changing neural weather formations.

' "Meditation is not about thinking about nothing," he said. "It's about accepting what you think, giving reverence to it and letting it go. It's losing the attachment to it. Same thing with pain." '

Mark Bertolini, CEO of Aetna

Try this!

To help you manage your emotions mindfully, have a go at the following practice on a regular basis, particularly if you are suffering from strong emotional reactivity, triggered by specific, recurrent situations. First of all, spend a few minutes reflecting on what your personal triggers are: What are the things that drive you crazy? What gets your blood boiling? Set an intention to do this practice every time you encounter these.

1 **Notice** the feeling tone: categorize the situation/event as pleasant, unpleasant or neutral. You may find that there are many more neutral events than you ever thought!

2 **Label** your feelings as and when they arise. Practise finding short and snappy adjectives for what you feel ('concerned', 'anxious', 'cheerful'). Do not spend too long worrying about finding the best possible description; this step is about acknowledging your feelings rather than diagnosing them with clinical precision!

3 **Allow** your feelings without judgement. Tell yourself gently 'It is OK to feel like this; no need to judge or do anything about it.' Avoid the temptation to react by finding pleasant feelings or rejecting those you find unpleasant.

4 **Dis-identify** from your feelings, be careful not to get sucked into them and any drama that may be brewing under the surface. You are not your feelings!

You can practise this both formally, in a moment of calm at home, and also informally when the situation arises. When you practise it on a chair or cushion at home, just see what emotions come up and work with these. The more you practise formally, the stronger your non-reactivity muscles will become and the better you will be able to nip any strong reactions in the bud.

'Between stimulus and response there is a space. In that space is our power to choose our response. In our response lies our growth and our freedom.'

Viktor Frankl, Austrian neurologist

Summary

In this chapter we discussed the nature of emotions and their importance in the workplace. We learned about two distinct ways of emotional processing – the fast, automatic and energy-saving 'low road' of amygdala reactivity to a stimulus versus the slower, conscious, energy-consuming 'high road' where emotions are processed via the executive centre of the brain.

We explored a number of different emotion regulation strategies including the two top-down strategies of verbal labelling and cognitive reappraisal that both involve executive control via the PFC. We also discussed suppression as a counterproductive strategy.

Furthermore, we explored neuroimaging findings suggesting that with growing expertise mindfulness practitioners shift from actively managing their emotions from the top down to an increasingly bottom-up regulation without cognitive intervention. We learned from Buddhist philosophy how emotions can lead to suffering to help us understand how mindfulness can support emotion regulation. In addition, we shared the techniques of mental noting and depersonalizing emotions. You were then introduced to a four-step practice for working with emotions that will over time help you regulate them from the bottom up.

Fact-check (answers at the back)

1. Which of the following statements is *not* true about emotions?
   a) Emotions occur automatically ❏
   b) Emotions arise from conscious thinking ❏
   c) Emotions reflect and regulate the state of the body ❏
   d) Emotions occur in response to internal and external events ❏

2. The low road of emotional processing is also called
   a) Mindfulness ❏
   b) Rest and digest ❏
   c) Emotion regulation ❏
   d) Mindless emoting ❏

3. The high road of emotional processing occurs via the
   a) Amygdala ❏
   b) Prefrontal cortex ❏
   c) Thalamus ❏
   d) The limbic system ❏

4. In what way is attention key to emotion regulation?
   a) It helps you focus on the emotions ❏
   b) It strengthens your attentional capacities ❏
   c) It inhibits negative emotions ❏
   d) It gives you the choice not to dwell on unhelpful emotions ❏

5. How does verbal labelling help regulate emotions?
   a) By reappraising them ❏
   b) By amplifying them ❏
   c) By dampening down the amygdala ❏
   d) By suppressing them ❏

6. Why should you be cautious about using suppression as an emotion regulation strategy?
   a) It eventually backfires ❏
   b) It makes you repressed ❏
   c) It is cathartic to act your emotions out ❏
   d) It is maladaptive ❏

7. In what way is mindfulness a bottom-up strategy?
   a) It does not require cognitive intervention ❏
   b) It activates the amygdala ❏
   c) It allows you to identify with your emotions ❏
   d) It does not suppress emotions ❏

8. Which aspect of their emotional experience do mindfulness practitioners tend to focus on?
   a) How it affects their executive centre ❏
   b) The moral ramifications ❏
   c) The deeper meaning of the emotion ❏
   d) The sensations in the body ❏

9. How does mental noting help alleviate painful experiences?
   a) By 'owning' your emotions ❏
   b) By identifying exactly what they are ❏
   c) By depersonalizing them ❏
   d) By using language to capture their meaning ❏

10. In Buddhist thinking, suffering is created by
    a) Negative emotions ❏
    b) Reacting to emotions with desire or aversion ❏
    c) The feeling tone of experience ❏
    d) Immoral emotions ❏

CHAPTER 6

Mindful decision-making

Decision-making is a key part of corporate life. Each employee from a junior clerk to a senior executive is faced with numerous opportunities for decision-making on a daily basis. The higher the rank, the more momentous and far-reaching the decision is likely to be. Often, it is only when decisions incur disastrous consequences that we are alerted to the significance of decision-making in the workplace.

In this chapter we will review some of the underlying causes of unethical workplace behaviour, outline the key components of major decision-making models and explore why and how mindfulness can enhance ethical decision-making. Finally, we will offer some suggestions for using mindfulness to support ethical decision-making, which can pave the way towards more considered and socially responsible corporate behaviour.

Unethical decision-making in the workplace

KPMG Forensic's latest Integrity Survey (2013) into corporate fraud and misconduct, based on the experiences and perceptions of more than 3,500 US employees across all industries, demonstrated that unethical behaviour and misconduct in the workplace are shockingly widespread. According to the survey, 73 per cent of all employees nationally reported that they had observed misconduct in the 12-month period preceding the research. Moreover, 56 per cent of participants stated that what they had witnessed could cause 'a significant loss of public trust if discovered'. This prevalence of unethical behaviour holds true across industries, ranging from 61 per cent in the Media & Communications sector to 82 per cent in the Consumer Market sector (with Banking roughly in the middle at 71 per cent) and makes bleak reading.

Alarmingly, this percentage has risen by 10 per cent since the previous survey in 2009, driven largely by a staggering 26-per-cent increase in reported unethical behaviour in the Electronics, Software and Services industry, followed by a 20-per-cent rise in Consumer Markets and in Chemicals and Diversified Industrials, a 19-per-cent increase in Aerospace and Defence, a 15-per-cent rise in Real Estate and Construction and a 14-per-cent rise in Banking and Financials.

The nature of the specific misconduct, ranging from issues of financial reporting fraud, to a broader set of potential misconduct, was split into 42 different types of offences, distributed among six broad categories of fraud and misconduct, deemed to compromise trust on many levels and affecting different groups, spanning customer or market place trust, supplier trust, shareholder/organizational trust, public or community trust, employee trust or general trust.

Ironically, when asked, employees reported that they were reasonably familiar (77–78%) with the acceptable standards of conduct, as outlined in policies, laws and regulations specific to the employees' job function, as well as the organizational code, values and principles. They also gave positive feedback (over 90%) on the communication and training employees received with regards to those standards.

So what causes employees to act unethically? According to the KPMG survey, the most commonly reported cause was pressure to meet business targets (64%), and, in fact, another three causes were tightly related to this organizational emphasis on meeting targets: the belief that achieving results was rewarded above the means to achieve them (59%), the fear of losing their job if they failed to meet targets (59%) and the lack of resources to get the job done without resorting to unethical means (57%). Selfish motives of self-advancement and disregard for ethical standards played a smaller part in such behaviour (49%).

Ethical traps

A deeper analysis of these and other ethical entanglements that employees and managers of organizations can get caught in have been outlined by Hoyk and Hersey in *The Ethical Executive* (2010), which identifies 45 psychological traps (including biases, justifications and conflicts of interest) that might distort managers' perceptions and entrap them in unethical behaviour that may subvert their desire and intention to act ethically. The authors distinguish between primary traps that are mainly external stimuli that can derail us, defensive traps, which constitute mental manoeuvres to deal with the shame and guilt that ethical transgressions cause us, and personality traps, which are internal traits that make us more prone to wrongdoing.

Evidence also suggests that unethical actions may be caused by self-delusion as a result of subconscious and automatic psychological or cognitive processes, including biases and rationalizations (Carlson *et al.* 2002). What makes matters worse is the fact that, according to Epley and Caruso (2004), self-serving judgements are effortless and almost immediate, in contrast to effortful and time-consuming perspective-taking, required to develop an unbiased opinion. In addition, Chugh *et al.* (2005) argue that people have a favourable view of themselves as moral and are often unable to appreciate the extent of their own biases and conflicts of interest, which makes them unable to overcome them.

Moreover, research has established that employees might at times violate their own moral framework in order to fit in with their company's culture. Due to the impact of group and organizational cultures, staff are frequently oblivious to the impact that group pressure may be having on their behaviour. The motivation for unethical acts is often driven by social factors such as conformism (Asch 1951), the impact of authority (Milgram 1963) and social roles (Zimbardo 1974), as well as by group thinking, bystander apathy and dispersed responsibility, among other factors.

In a nutshell, it looks as though, when it comes to acting ethically, we are completely up against it, with a plethora of threats and dangers lurking around us as well as inside us to throw us off course.

Mindfulness and decision-making

As we have established, what is expected of you as employees or managers in the service of corporate profitability may at times be at odds with your own ethical imperatives, disconnecting you from your true intentions and values. By drawing attention to such discrepancies between people's values and their behaviour at work, mindfulness can facilitate moral convergence through its facilitation of insight and direct experience.

Moreover, it is crucial to understand that, although this is not part of its narrow definition, mindfulness needs to be more than just attention training, if one wishes to honour the origins and spirit of its ancient tradition. In its Buddhist context, mindfulness is embedded in a whole system of philosophy and ethics, and constitutes only one part, albeit an important one, of what is called the Noble Eightfold Path, which the Buddha realized at his enlightenment. This path, which is postulated to lead to happiness, includes elements that enable the attainment of wisdom, ethical conduct and mental discipline. While 'right mindfulness' (together with 'right effort' and 'right concentration') is listed as one of the three attributes facilitating mental discipline, ethics is taken care of by 'right speech', 'right action' and' right livelihood'. In other words, when looking at ethical decision-making, mindfulness needs to be steered in the right direction by our values and virtues. Without these, mindfulness is a like a ship without a rudder.

Mindfulness encourages socially responsible behaviour

Research by INSEAD has shown that traditional executive training approaches, based on cognitive moral reasoning and didactic top-down teaching, are not effective in increasing the likelihood of 'socially responsible behaviour' (SRB; Schneider *et al.* 2005) in corporates, as they have little or no impact on the three psychological attributes that enable such behaviour: first, the cognitive capacities, manifest in, among others things, moral reasoning and decision-making; second, personal values and, third, emotional dispositions. There is, however, compelling evidence that non-cognitive interventions such as introspection and meditation practices have a significant positive impact on SRB and can succeed in shifting psychological traits and changing personal values towards an increased level of social consciousness among corporate executives (Zollo *et al.* 2007).

Awareness is key to decision-making

Recent research has indeed demonstrated a strong relationship between mindfulness and ethical decision-making. Mindfulness, in its key sense of being attentive to and aware of one's current experience or present reality (Brown & Ryan 2003), can be seen as a central element of the ethical decision-making process, as illustrated by various decision-making models where awareness of an ethical issue constitutes the crucial first step in a four-stage process (Rest 1986; Jones 1991) before moral reasoning/judgement, forming an intention and taking action can follow:

91

The four-stage process of ethical decision-making

Emotional awareness is thus integral to ethics and has been advocated as an essential contributor to enhanced clarity in ethical decision-making.

A 2010 study by the Wharton Risk Management and Decision Processes Center has established that the correlation between mindfulness and ethical decision-making manifests in three ways: according to self-report measurement scales, mindful individuals are more likely:

- to act ethically
- to value upholding ethical standards
- to use a principled approach to ethical decision-making.

In addition, the researchers also found that more mindful individuals cheated less in a behavioural experiment on unethical behaviour.

How mindlessness can promote unethical behaviour

The same study on the impact of mindfulness on ethical awareness and ethical decision-making also demonstrates how a lack of mindfulness can compound various causes of unethical behaviour, for example through what Tenbrunsel and Messick have called 'ethical fading' (2004): in the presence of certain cues in the environment (for example, when they feel observed by a surveillance system, ironically installed to safeguard ethical behaviour) people may lose sight of the ethical dimensions of their actions, and start reframing their decisions as business decisions rather than ethical ones. In such situations, people tend to deceive themselves by the use of justifications and euphemisms in order to protect themselves from facing up to their unethical actions.

Another example is Bandura's model of 'moral disengagement' (1999), where individuals disengage from their moral convictions and justify unethical behaviour by using various strategies to abnegate responsibility and to make their actions palatable to themselves. This process operates below the level of conscious awareness and is hence also exacerbated by a lack of mindfulness.

How mindfulness supports ethical decision-making

But what are the mechanisms by which mindfulness may further ethical decision-making? The pathways via which mindfulness may have a beneficial influence on the decision-making process are outlined below:

Allowing and non-judging lead to less censoring of uncomfortable truths

Mindfulness encourages openness to whatever arises in the mind, including difficult thoughts and emotions that may be potentially detrimental or threatening to one's self-image. For example, if your ego is dented by the fact that your sales record this month has not been up to the expected standard, this painful truth can be held in mindful awareness, overcoming the need to avoid, suppress or mask it. This accepting, non-judging quality of mindfulness can help us be more willing to consider all – even those personally uncomfortable or inconvenient – ethical aspects of a decision rather than find strategies to avoid, ignore or justify them. In this way, mindfulness helps us face up to the possibly more challenging aspects of all ethical considerations and can heighten moral awareness.

Metacognitive awareness and honesty reduce self-delusion

The type of self-awareness honed through mindfulness encompasses awareness of one's own thoughts (metacognitive awareness), which in turn can help curtail unethical behaviour by leading to an increasing dis-identification from one's thinking. Practitioners learn to observe their thoughts increasingly as mental events without becoming embroiled in the story created by their thinking. A common analogy used to illustrate the nature of thoughts is to see them as 'clouds in the sky'; no matter whether they are white and fluffy or dark and menacing, all clouds are ultimately insubstantial in nature and impermanent, destined to arise and pass away. The sky of one's mind, however, or pure awareness, always remains blue, untainted by whatever weather formation may arise at any given moment. This type of metacognitive awareness may thus heighten one's recognition of any deluded or self-serving judgements on ethically ambiguous situations, thereby reducing both their occurrence (to some extent) and their hold over one's mind, opening up a choice of whether to act on them or not. In this way, mindfulness may inhibit unethical behaviour. Research has indeed established that those high in mindfulness value honesty and integrity more highly than external rewards and may thus be more likely to act ethically.

Internal focus can raise alarm bells

Highly mindful individuals tend to be strongly in touch with their current internal experience, closely observing their thoughts, emotions and body sensations. They are hence more likely to notice their internal 'alarm bells', alerting them to the fact that something does not feel right because it may be at odds with their personal values. As a result this internal focus encourages greater alignment with their moral compass. This has indeed been borne out by recent, hitherto unpublished research I and colleagues conducted in the workplace, following a short mindfulness induction.

Being mode

Just as we make a shift from the so-called doing mode towards the domain of 'being' with increasing mindfulness practice, the emphasis of decision-making also moves from the preoccupation with reaching a swift outcome to the increased importance of the process itself. With mindfulness one is more inclined to take one's time and consider the decision carefully and consciously rather than rushing towards making it, while falling prey to the many pitfalls inherent in decision-making. Mindfulness thus minimizes the risk of 'the end justifies the means' type of reasoning, a frequent contributing factor to unethical behaviour.

Compassion

Compassion, and its flip side of loving kindness, is a practice that often goes hand in hand with mindfulness, although it is not strictly speaking part of it. Based on a belief in the connectedness of all creatures (as it includes the animal world, too), who are all linked in their desire to be happy and free from suffering, this practice facilitates perspective-taking and connecting with others, not just with the people close to us but also with those we tend to overlook or ignore and even with potentially 'difficult' people whom we may otherwise dehumanize in our minds. In this way, by making us mindful of our shared humanity, compassion practice can substantially reduce the likelihood of our acting in ways that harm others and thus promote more ethical decision-making.

Emotion regulation

As we saw in the previous chapter, mindfulness lets us reduce or overcome the automaticity in our reactions, leading to less proneness to short-circuiting (taking the low road) and impulsive decision-making out of anger, revenge or just habit, while being more conducive to emotion regulation, both from the top down (which includes moral reasoning) and, more importantly, from the bottom up, from an increasing ability to practise non-reactivity and mindful choice.

Try this: acting out of virtue

There are two aspects to the concept of virtue: on the one hand refraining from causing harm, both to yourself as well as others, and, on the other hand, actively promoting positive values.

1 Bring to mind some key words or phrases that sum up the virtues you wish to live by.

2 Notice what these feel like in your body by letting them sink into your heart. How does it feel in your body to 'act with integrity', to 'be compassionate' or whatever else you chose as your virtue? Do not *think* about these concepts – just connect with how they *feel* physically and emotionally from the inside.

3 Choose one of your virtues and visualize what would happen if you acted by this precept at all times, irrespective of other people's behaviours. What would happen if you operated in alignment with your own moral code, even when others do not or when they trigger your reactivity? See whether you can connect with this sense of freedom that can arise when you are no longer acting with predictable automaticity but out of true and virtuous choice.

4 Now bring to mind a decision you need to make, sit with it, checking in with the feelings and sensations this gives rise to. If you acted purely in accordance with your own moral compass, how would that feel in your body? What would it look like? What effect would this have on your team, your company, your customers? Let the felt sense of this sink into you, absorbing the effects of this practice.

Summary

In this chapter we explored the nature, extent and the causes of unethical behaviour in the workplace. We established that misconduct is widespread in the corporate world and, to a large extent – but not exclusively – due to the pressure to meet business targets. A review of the scientific literature shed light on deeper causes of unethical behaviour, including subconscious psychological and cognitive biases leading to self-delusion and self-serving judgements, as well as several factors to do with group and organizational cultures.

Subsequently, we explored the role of mindfulness in raising our awareness of any discrepancies between our personal and company values and highlighted the importance of seeing mindfulness as embedded in a larger ethical framework beyond the narrow confines of attention training. We outlined the many different ways in which mindfulness may further socially responsible behaviour and ethical decision-making, most notably through enhanced awareness as a crucial part of several decision-making models and an element often missing in unethical behaviour.

To conclude, we introduced a practice to help us reconnect with our virtues from a felt sense in the body rather than as a top-down decision, which will support us in acting with awareness, intentionality and in accordance with our own values.

Fact-check (answers at the back)

1. According to the KPMG Forensic Integrity Survey (2013), the biggest cause of workplace misconduct was due to
   a) Lack of awareness of acceptable standards of conduct ❏
   b) A lack of communication and training ❏
   c) Pressure to meet business targets ❏
   d) Selfish motives of self-advancement ❏

2. Unethical actions are often based on self-serving judgements because
   a) People are selfish ❏
   b) Such judgements require less conscious effort ❏
   c) People refuse to consider other perspectives ❏
   d) Unbiased opinions will not get them very far in the workplace ❏

3. Mindfulness best supports ethical decision-making when
   a) It is practised with the 'right effort' ❏
   b) It is narrowly defined as attention training ❏
   c) It is seen as a stand-alone tool ❏
   d) It is embedded in our value system ❏

4. Evidence suggests that meditation can facilitate socially responsible behaviour by
   a) Shifting psychological traits and changing personal values ❏
   b) Facilitating cognitive moral reasoning ❏
   c) Implementing top-down training ❏
   d) Influencing emotional dispositions ❏

5. Which step precedes moral reasoning in Rest's decision-making model?
   a) Moral intention ❏
   b) Moral action ❏
   c) Moral recognition ❏
   d) Moral judgement ❏

6. In terms of the links between mindfulness and ethical decision-making which of the following statements is *not* true?
   a) Mindful individuals cheat less ❏
   b) Mindful individuals value upholding ethical standards ❏
   c) Mindful individuals tend to be more principled in their decisions ❏
   d) Mindful individuals always act ethically ❏

7. Ethical fading and moral disengagement are
a) Conscious strategies to obscure unethical behaviour ❏
b) Subconscious processes ❏
c) Attributes of unethical people ❏
d) Excuses to justify unethical behaviour ❏

8. The fact that mindfulness encourages openness towards all experiences
a) Can lead to amorality ❏
b) Makes it more difficult to choose the right action ❏
c) Gives us the courage to face up to difficult truths about ourselves ❏
d) Makes ethical decisions easy ❏

9. Metacognitive awareness helps inhibit unethical behaviour by
a) Giving us a choice on how to act due to dissociation from our thoughts ❏
b) Improving the knowledge of our cognitions ❏
c) Connecting us with our morals ❏
d) Making us more aware of the power of our thoughts ❏

10. A focus on inner experience can facilitate ethical behaviour by
a) Making us focus on how good it feels ❏
b) Stressing the importance of the experiencing subject ❏
c) Making us more aware of internal warning signs ❏
d) Helping us concentrate on our emotions ❏

CHAPTER 7

Don't worry, be happy

You may be surprised to find a chapter on happiness in a workplace skills book. We all know that we need to manage stress, be productive, make savvy decisions, perform well and get along with our colleagues. But happiness? Why is happiness important at work? Is that not a luxury that may be nice to have but ultimately not essential in order to hold down a job? However, research has shown that happy people perform better, are more creative and innovative, cope better with stress, have better physical health (so they take fewer days off due to illness!) and are more immune to mental illness. Most managers would agree that this is a compelling business case for encouraging staff to maximize their levels of happiness.

In this chapter we will explore a different understanding of happiness, based on insights into our three in-built causes of suffering, identify when people tend to be at their happiest and explore how mindfulness can help us increase our levels of wellbeing. We will learn some techniques based on these insights to help us practise internalizing happiness in order to hardwire it in the implicit memory of our brain.

What is happiness?

It is safe to say that we all want to be happy. Yet very
few people would probably lay claim to this label for any
sustainable length of time. By extension, how many people
do you know who are happy in their jobs or would rate their
job satisfaction a ten out of ten? More likely than not, even if
you land your dream job – if there is such a thing – you will
most probably end up not being continuously happy either.
I would argue that this is due to the fallacy in the very way
we tend to define happiness in the first place, namely as a
proliferation of pleasant experiences.

First cause of suffering: the brain's negativity bias

For evolutionary reasons, humankind developed a brain
that is governed by one overriding principle: to minimize
danger and to maximize reward. As we explored earlier,
this avoidance of threat and pursuit of rewards has served a
powerful purpose in the evolution of humanity: to ensure our
survival. While recognizing a genuine threat was a matter
of life and death, seeking rewards, while important, was
somewhat less critical. If you lived to see another day, you
could try your luck again tomorrow to secure your dinner!
So over millions of years our brains evolved to be hyper-
vigilant with regard to danger and less perceptive of potential
rewards. This inherent negativity bias tilted our brains
towards detecting possible threats, which are sensed and
suspected behind every corner, so to speak, even though
today's threats tend to be social ones.

By contrast, positive experiences may seem scarce and,
what is worse, the brain's negativity bias means that you
may not even notice them when they do occur (Baumeister
et al. 2001). Moreover, unless you make a special effort to
dwell on them, they are less likely to leave a trace in your
implicit memory, which colours how you feel about your
life. So, in order to find happiness, we need to overcome

our inherent prioritizing of the negative and shift the focus consciously and deliberately towards the positive. Happiness is so much more elusive than unhappiness!

 TIP *To see whether this is true for you challenge yourself to make a list of ten good things that happened to you this week and ten things that went wrong. Which events were easier to recall? Which left a stronger imprint on your memory?*

Second cause of suffering: grasping

As if this innate imbalance in the way our brain is wired has not made it difficult enough to be happy, human beings compound their own misery by two fundamental and entirely natural, but ultimately dysfunctional and counterproductive, tendencies of the mind: desperately to hold on to pleasures and rewards and anxiously to push away any pain, danger or discomfort. Whether it is praise and positive feedback, a lucrative sale, a good working relationship, a successful pitch or a delicious meal, we are rarely content with these isolated incidents and rewards; we quickly expect and even demand more, and when things do not work out we are disappointed.

There is nothing wrong with liking the good things and disliking the unpleasant ones; of course, this is entirely normal. But there is a problem inherent in such likes and dislikes when they turn into clinging or aversion, to use the Buddhist terminology, or greed and fear, to use the jargon of the financial markets. Pleasure and pain, gain and loss, fame and disrepute, praise and blame – they arise and pass and alternate due to circumstances (other people's psychology, events, etc.) beyond our control. Attachment to the pleasant side of this equation and the delusion of permanence are doomed to failure and hence breed suffering. Similarly, the misconception that unpleasant experiences will persist makes you vulnerable to depression as you lose the perspective of the changing fortunes inherent in life, not being able to imagine that better days may eventually come. It may sound banal but how often do we get sucked into catastrophizing thoughts, just because one presentation or phone call did not go according to plan, visualizing and anticipating our professional downfall?

Redefining happiness

So, what if the secret to our happiness were this: to be able to enjoy and relish all the pleasant experiences in our life and work without grasping for more, without getting attached to an erroneous expectation of their never-ending proliferation, and, by the same token, the capacity to face up to the unpleasant situations without the inner fight and resistance that create suffering?

If you redefine happiness in this way, as a form of what in Buddhism is called equanimity and non-reactivity, rather than viewing it as the predominance of positive emotions, it is indeed within your grasp to be happy a great deal more, if not most of the time. Why? Because happiness no longer depends on unrealistic conditions that are impossible to fulfil or control in any sustainable way. Pleasant experiences are transient, just like everything else, and making your sense of happiness contingent on them is like building a house of cards. Yet being open to all events and situations, by and large making your peace with whatever arises, is an attitude and habit of the mind that you can learn and achieve when you practise mindfulness. The benefits are life changing and can transform the way you view your job in the process.

 TIP *When you no longer react habitually to pleasant and unpleasant experiences you can nourish a sense of equanimity – of no longer wishing for things to be different from what they are. Incline your mind to think 'It's OK as it is.' However, if there are changes to be made to make things better, do not hesitate to initiate them! Notice any resistance to doing this practice and see whether you can consciously let go of it. It does not serve you.*

When are we happiest?

One way to achieve such equanimity is to immerse yourself fully in the present moment with an attitude of openness and curiosity. In other words, not having an agenda in terms of your experience. You need to ensure that you are not just physically going 'through the motions' of whatever you are engaged in; a difficult client call, a boring meeting, a daunting presentation, the dreaded admin tasks that only seem bearable when you engage in pleasant daydreaming, while fantasizing about your upcoming holiday or reminiscing about the big party you went to last weekend – no, to become fully immersed in the present moment means rooting your mind and not just your body in the here and now, rather than time-travelling to a better place, a nicer time...

Third cause of suffering: the wandering mind is an unhappy mind

Recent research has indeed established that people are happiest when their mind does not wander from whatever they are doing at any given time (Killingsworth & Gilbert 2010). Through the use of an iPhone app, participants from over 80 occupational categories were contacted randomly several times during the day as they went about their life, and asked about their thoughts, feelings and actions. These were recorded on a database in order to establish how often people engaged in mind wandering and to what extent this affected their level of happiness. The results were astounding, establishing that:

1 Mind wandering occurs very frequently and almost half of the time people drifted into this state, confirming that mind wandering indeed seems to be our default state, as established by previous neuroscience research. Interestingly, the pleasantness or otherwise of people's current activity had little bearing on the occurrence of daydreaming.

2 People reported being happier when their mind did *not* wander from what they were currently doing, even when the activity was not considered particularly enjoyable and even when their mind wandered to pleasant topics.

3 Happiness levels depended disproportionately more on people's *thinking* rather than on their doing – in other words, thoughts were a better predictor of people's happiness levels than the activities they were engaged in.

Our brain's default mode network

So what insights can we gain from this? Mind wandering is indeed our natural, default state, as neuroimaging studies have also established. We have two distinct networks in the brain: a task-positive network that is active when we engage in an activity, and a task-negative, so-called default mode network (DMN), which is active at all other times. In other words, rather than ever being truly 'at rest', our brain's natural baseline is to indulge in mind wandering, from which it departs only when our attention is summoned elsewhere. Whenever we are not specifically working on something, the DMN kicks into action and hijacks our mind with thoughts about the past, the future, other people and ourselves, creating narratives that take us away from experiencing our lives fully and making us unhappy, as, more often than not, the stories we create are made up of worries, concerns, anxiety, regrets, guilt, shame and pending catastrophes.

In other words, rampant mind wandering often is the *cause* of unhappiness, as well as a symptom of it. They say that actions speak louder than words but it seems that the reverse is true! What you think is even more decisive than what you do in terms of your chance of happiness. You may be engaged in a job or activity which you do not find that enjoyable and still have a better chance of being happy if you focus on it entirely than when you indulge yourself in daydreaming about an exotic holiday on a white, sandy beach. According to the researchers, a 'wandering mind is an unhappy mind' as the cognitive feat of self-projection into past or future brings with it an emotional cost.

> *'The present moment is filled with joy and happiness. If you are attentive, you will see it.'*
>
> Thích Nhất Hạnh, Vietnamese Buddhist monk

Try this: staying present

1 Identify a specific task that you do regularly and that leads to feelings of boredom, frustration or resistance of some sort. This may be something like doing the accounts, writing a report, preparing a presentation, creating an Excel spreadsheet, cold-calling, leaving voicemails for clients or any other aspect of your job description that may in some ways dampen your mood or lower your energy.

2 Set an intention to 'stay with' the experience, however unpleasant you find it, and detect your mind's tendency to wander. When it does, as it will inevitably do, note where it has gone and gently bring it back to the present moment. Noticing that your mind has wandered is an indication that you are becoming more mindful and is thus a reason to rejoice rather than beat yourself up!

3 Notice whether there is any sense of aversion to the task in the background of your mind. Without judging yourself in any way, see whether you can gently release this feeling and relax into the experience, noticing its feeling tone without reacting to it.

4 To help your mind focus on the present moment, bring to the experience a sense of curiosity or beginner's mind, as we have already practised. Noticing details about the task will help you enjoy it more as your mind will settle into the present moment.

How mindfulness promotes happiness

How can we expect to be happy when we do not even turn up for our experience as we time-travel to the past or the future and, when we finally do, we refuse to accept the constant flux that is part of the human condition and wish for things to be different from what they are? Having grasped the key sources of human unhappiness and distress it is easy to see how mindfulness might support us in reducing, if not removing, them.

Direct experience versus mental narratives

Living and valuing the present moment and direct experience for their own sake naturally reduces mind wandering and hence tendencies to get hijacked by the narratives we create in our head through the DMN, featuring rumination on negative thoughts and feelings, as well as worry and anxiety.

Absorbing the positive

By encouraging us to notice, appreciate and absorb the often neglected positive, as well as neutral, aspects of our experience rather than focus solely on the negative, mindfulness can help us redress our brain's in-built negativity bias.

Equanimity

At the same time we learn to notice and hence transcend the slavish pursuit of pleasant experiences and the avoidance of unpleasant ones and instead to open to and be more at peace with the whole gamut of our experience.

Being versus doing

Mindfulness takes us out of 'doing mode', our habitual way of living by which we constantly diagnose what is missing or wrong and strive to fix or improve the current situation. Our obsession with closing the gap between what is and what we would like there to be (discrepancy-based processing) is an integral part of our distress. This tendency, at the heart of our Western culture, is a major driver of our unhappiness. Mindfulness stops us from perceiving our life and work from the perennially dissatisfied perspective of such processing and teaches us that we are complete and whole, just as we are, allowing us to let go of any such striving. Relating to experience mindfully means to reside in the realm of being.

Gratitude

Mindfulness can foster a sense of gratitude, allowing you to appreciate, not just cognitively with your mind, but as a feeling in your heart, all the pleasant and positive things that have been offered to you at and through your work. These may be:

- a kind and supportive attitude by your boss or colleagues
- a decent salary to enable you to live comfortably
- a safe and pleasant working environment
- interesting work
- opportunities to develop yourself
- your own talent, skills and resilience.

Raising the happiness set point

Neuroimaging research has confirmed that mindfulness can indeed raise what has been termed the happiness set point, the biologically determined average level of happiness around which our emotional range converges. According to research dating back to the 1970s, this has been shown to remain relatively stable throughout people's lives, irrespective of their specific experiences, returning to the individual base level a short while after either happy or distressing events have been digested. Apparently, whether you win the lottery or you become paraplegic, within one year you will end up back at your personal set point of happiness! Such individual differences have been confirmed by brain scans that have demonstrated that people with more baseline activation of the left versus the right prefrontal areas tend to be happier than those where the right side of the PFC is more active. Yet it has also been shown that mindfulness can incrementally raise this set point: the more hours of mindfulness practice you have under your belt, the more the activation ratio in your brain tilts towards the left. These results are apparent even after only eight weeks of mindfulness training, as a study by Davidson and Kabat-Zinn at the biotech company Promega (2003) has found: compared to a control group, course participants showed a shift of the happiness ratio towards the left PFC after the training, coupled with a reported reduction in stress and anxiety levels and an increase in energy. Moreover, the study also demonstrated a strengthening of participants' immune system, as evidenced by the amount of flu antibodies in their blood after a flu jab. After only eight weeks, mindfulness had improved both their health and their happiness!

Try this: mindfulness for increasing happiness

To redress the brain's negative bias and increase your experience of happiness, practise absorbing the good things that happen to you in the following way. This is not about chasing positive experiences – as we have seen, this is futile and hence more likely to make you miserable. However, it is about appreciating what is already there and allowing it to increase your happiness set point:

1 **Notice**: make a habit of noticing the good things that happen to you. This could be your colleague, boss or client thanking you for a piece of work you have done or a compliment you receive, something you achieve or complete at work, a gesture of kindness towards you or just the fact that it's a sunny day or that you are having a nutritious meal. Give yourself permission to let this event register as a positive experience in your heart and mind, rather than mentally moving on to the next thing and letting it evaporate straight away. See how this feels.

2 **Attend**: place the spotlight of your attention on this positive experience for half a minute or so, really resting on it and giving your brain a chance to make some new connections (remember: 'Neurons that fire together, wire together')!

3 **Absorb**: Soak up and absorb the positive experience consciously, letting it infiltrate your body and become part of your felt sense of reality at that moment. By repeating this step every time you have even a small positive experience, you will start lifting your felt sense of happiness bit by bit.

TIP

Make this exercise a daily staple. If you want to give happiness a fighting chance, you need to counteract the in-built negativity bias of the brain by an equally, if not more, powerful antidote. Rather than waiting for really life-changing events, which are few and far between, use a steady trickle of small, good daily experiences, to gradually fill your brain with a pervasive sense of wellbeing.

Summary

In this chapter we started off by questioning the conventional understanding of happiness as a proliferation of positive experiences and explored the three causes of human suffering: first, the in-built negativity bias of our brain, which has developed through millions of years of evolution to make us hyper-sensitive to threats and danger; second, our tendency to grasp for pleasant experiences and push away unpleasant ones, which makes us unable to deal with the impermanence of all experiences; and third, the tendency of the human mind to wander away from the present moment, making it challenging for us to live fully in the here and now.

We proposed a definition of happiness as the ability to be at peace with both pleasant and unpleasant experiences without reacting with clinging or aversion. We then explored how mindfulness can help us overcome the three causes of suffering we identified. Mindfulness offers a different, being-based way of relating to experience from our habitual discrepancy-based processing that is aimed at reducing the gulf between 'what is' and what we would ideally like. We shared some tips for practising equanimity and for raising our happiness set point.

Fact-check (answers at the back)

1. The negativity bias in the brain originates in
   a) Our thoughts ❏
   b) Our emotions ❏
   c) Evolution ❏
   d) The brain ❏

2. Negativity bias means that
   a) Negative experiences outweigh positive ones ❏
   b) The brain is more sensitive to negative experiences ❏
   c) We tend to see things negatively ❏
   d) If we expect negative things to happen, they will ❏

3. Which statement is *not* true about the human tendency to cling to the pleasant and push away the unpleasant experiences?
   a) It leads to suffering ❏
   b) It is natural ❏
   c) It is unethical ❏
   d) It compounds the brain's negativity bias ❏

4. Equanimity means
   a) A state of non-reactivity ❏
   b) Being fair in your judgements ❏
   c) Liking everything the same ❏
   d) Being happy ❏

5. Happiness can be defined as
   a) A predominance of pleasant experiences ❏
   b) The absence of negative experiences ❏
   c) A constant state of wellbeing ❏
   d) Being OK with whatever arises ❏

6. Mind wandering occurs
   a) When we are engaged in an activity we do not enjoy ❏
   b) When we are happy ❏
   c) Frequently and for many people ❏
   d) When we are unhappy ❏

7. People tend to be happiest when
   a) They are engaged in pleasant activities ❏
   b) They are thinking pleasant thoughts ❏
   c) Their minds do not wander from what they are doing ❏
   d) Their minds are wandering ❏

8. Which statement is *untrue* about the default mode network?
   a) It is a restful and rejuvenating brain state ❏
   b) It is active when we are not engaged in a task ❏
   c) It creates stories about the past or future ❏
   d) It revolves around other people and ourselves ❏

9. What do we mean by the 'doing mode'?
   a) Being proactive ❏
   b) Being busy ❏
   c) The tendency to improve things through constant doing ❏
   d) Being efficient and getting things done ❏

10. Which of the following statements is false: Discrepancy-based processing is

a) The opposite of the 'being mode' ❏
b) A synonym for 'doing mode' ❏
c) Perceiving experience from a position of finding it lacking ❏
d) A way of making things better ❏

7 × 7

1 Seven key ideas

- **Befriend the present moment:** it is the only one you will ever have.
- **Practise acceptance:** do not fight 'what is'; it is already here.
- **Go beyond thinking:** there is an alternative to being lost in thought; it is called awareness.
- **Keep breathing...** and *know* that you are breathing! The breath is always available to you, to ground you and bring you back to the present moment.
- **Do not take things personally:** if you look closely enough, most unpleasant things that happen to you do not have your name tag on them!
- **Be kind to yourself:** beware of self-critical judgements.
- **Be mindful:** it does not matter what you do or how much you enjoy it, you will feel better if you do it mindfully.

2 Seven best resources

- **Best introduction to mindfulness:** Mark Williams and Danny Penman, *Mindfulness: A practical guide to finding peace in a frantic world* (Hachette, 2011). This book contains the complete eight-week MBCT course developed at Oxford University in an easy-to-follow format, with many simple but powerful practices to integrate into your daily life. It also contains a CD with accompanying meditations.
- **Best free guided meditations:** this web page contains all of the meditations from the book *Mindfulness: A practical guide to finding peace in a frantic world* as well as many other resources. http://franticworld.com/free-meditations-from-mindfulness/

- **Best introduction to mindfulness at work:** Shamash Alidina and Juliet Adams, *Mindfulness at Work for Dummies* (John Wiley & Sons, 2014). This book is a comprehensive guide to mindfulness at work and covers how to practise mindfulness as well as implement mindfulness training in the workplace, including plenty of invaluable resources.

- **Best book on mindful leadership:** Janice Marturano, *Finding the Space to Lead: A practical guide to mindful leadership* (Bloomsbury Publishing USA, 2014). Marturano describes the nature and benefits of mindful leadership and shares a variety of simple ways to cultivate it. Many of the meditations are available in audio at www.FindingtheSpacetoLead.com

- **Best Buddhist wisdom on mindfulness at work:** Thích Nhât Hanh, *Work: How to find joy and meaning in each hour of the day* (Parallax Press, 2013). One of the best-known Buddhist monks adapts Buddhist teachings to the modern workplace, showing how one might apply mindfulness to all aspects of the working day.

- **Best neuroscience book drawing on Buddhist wisdom:** Rick Hanson, *Buddha's Brain: The practical neuroscience of happiness, love, and wisdom* (New Harbinger Publications, 2009). Hanson, a neuropsychologist and meditation teacher, combines neuroscience with contemplative wisdom to explain how to strengthen your brain for more happiness, love and wisdom.

- **Best neuroscience-based guided meditations CD set:** Rick Hanson and Richard Mendius, *Meditations to Change Your Brain: Rewire your neural pathways to transform your life* (Sounds True, 2010). This set contains introductions to how mindfulness works on the brain, as well as neuroscience-based guided meditations.

3 Seven great companies

- **Google:** the technology company introduced a programme called Search Inside Yourself, led by Chade-Meng Tan, its Jolly Good Fellow, to increase emotional intelligence using mindfulness, backed by scientific research. The vision behind this programme is to bring mindfulness and peace to the workplace. The programme is now offered to organizations outside the Googleplex.

- **Aetna:** the health insurer offers its workers meditation classes. Nearly a third of the company's 50,000 employees have taken a class. According to the company, participants show increased productivity and report less stress and pain. More than one-quarter of the company's workforce of 50,000 has participated in at least one class. Participants report a 28-per-cent reduction in their stress levels on average, a 20-per-cent improvement in sleep quality and a 19-per-cent reduction in pain. They also gain an average of 62 minutes per week of productivity each, which Aetna values at $3,000 per employee per year. Demand for the courses continues to rise and all classes are overbooked.

- **Sounds True:** a multimedia company dedicated to disseminating spiritual wisdom, Sounds True is one of the world's largest publishers of spoken words and spiritual teachings and is one of the world's first organizations to operate with genuinely integral principles, with an emphasis on multiple bottom lines of purpose, people, profit and planet.

- **Headspace:** founded in 2010, by Andy Puddicumbe, a former Buddhist monk, and Rich Pierson, who has a background in marketing and new brand development. Based on a mission 'to make meditation accessible, relevant and beneficial to as many people as possible', Headspace created a meditation smartphone app, which teaches simple meditation techniques for improving physical and mental wellbeing. Among its clients are firms such as Credit Suisse, KPMG and Deloitte.

- **Intel:** mindfulness at Intel began when a handful of committed people started meeting regularly in a conference room to practise. The Awake@Intel program was created in an effort to bring the benefits of mindfulness to the company's workforce. The training promotes stress reduction in a culture where employees 'feel that if they weren't stressed it would mean they're not working hard enough'. So far more than 1,500 employees have completed the nine-week, 90-minutes-per-session Awake@Intel programme. According to participant feedback, the benefits include 'improved wellbeing, creativity and focus, reduced feelings of stress and stronger engagement in meetings and projects'.

● **Salesforce:** founded in 1999 by Marc Benioff, this is a cloud computing company headquartered in San Francisco, California. It is renowned for its efforts in philanthropy and social activism and for providing more than just financial benefits to its employees. The Salesforce.com Foundation donates 1 per cent of the company's resources (defined as profit, equity and employee time) to support organizations that are working to 'make the world a better place'.

● **Apple:** Following the example of their late CEO, Steve Jobs, employees of the tech giant are allowed to take 30 minutes each day to meditate at work, where they can access classes on meditation and yoga, as well as have the use of a meditation room.

4 Seven inspiring people

● The Tibetan Buddhist spiritual leader the **Dalai Lama** played a central role in bringing together Eastern contemplative wisdom and the emerging field of Western neuroscience when he asked neuroscientist Richard Davidson in 1992 to explore the effects of meditation on the brain. This started a fruitful and ongoing cross-fertilization of these two hitherto separate fields that has led to important advances in the field of neuroplasticity as well as fuelling interest in the practice of mindfulness in the West.

● Thích Nhât Hanh is a Vietnamese Buddhist monk, teacher, author, poet and peace activist. He has published more than a hundred books, including more than 40 in English. He is active in the peace movement, promoting non-violent solutions to conflict and was nominated for the Nobel Peace Prize by Martin Luther King in 1967.

- **Matthieu Ricard** is a Buddhist monk who has been described as the happiest man on earth, following fMRI brain scans at the Laboratory for Affective Neuroscience in Wisconsin, which recorded an 'off the charts' state of positive emotions (-0.45 on a range where -0.3 is described as 'beatific'). His advice is: 'Being happy is about raising your "baseline". It's not about seeking sudden fireworks or euphoric experiences. The first step to take is to realize that you want to improve – that the world is not a mail-order catalogue for our fantasies and desires and that we have a relatively limited control over those transient, illusory conditions.'
- **Jon Kabat-Zinn** is Professor of Medicine Emeritus at the University of Massachusetts Medical School and founder of its Stress Reduction Clinic and the Center for Mindfulness in Medicine, Health Care, and Society. Through his structured eight-week course in Mindfulness-Based Stress Reduction (MBSR) for patients with chronic pain, stress and illness he introduced mindfulness to the West in the 1970s, taking it out of its Buddhist framework and making its teachings widely available. MBSR is now offered by many hospitals, medical centres and health-maintenance organizations.
- **Eckhart Tolle** is a spiritual teacher and author who, at the age of 29, experienced a deep inner transformation that radically changed the course of his life. He devoted many years to understanding, integrating and deepening that transformation and started working with individuals and small groups as a counsellor and spiritual teacher. Tolle is the author of the number-one *New York Times* bestseller *The Power of Now* (translated into 33 languages) and the highly acclaimed follow-up, *A New Earth*, which are widely regarded as two of the most influential spiritual books of our time.
- **Arianna Huffington** is the co-founder, chair, president and editor-in-chief of the *Huffington Post*, a nationally syndicated columnist and author of 14 books. She believes that mindfulness is at the heart of everything and has been meditating regularly since the age of 13. She is a sought-after

speaker on how mindfulness can be integrated into different aspects of our lives and work, redefining success in her book *Thrive: The third metric to redefining success and creating a life of well-being, wisdom and wonder* (W.H. Allen, 2015).

- The billionaire and founder of hedge fund Bridgewater Associates **Ray Dalio** has been practising transcendental meditation for over 40 years. He famously declared that 'meditation, more than any other factor, has been the reason for what success I've had.'

- **Steve Jobs** is best known as the creative genius behind the innovative and groundbreaking products of Apple. Somewhat less known is the fact that he had been a long-term regular meditator who attributed his creativity to his contemplative practice.

5 Seven great quotes

- 'You can't stop the waves, but you can learn to surf.' – Jon Kabat-Zinn

- 'Don't believe everything you think. Thoughts are just that – thoughts.' – Allan Lokos

- 'Our own worst enemy cannot harm us as much as our unwise thoughts. No one can help us as much as our own compassionate thoughts.' – Buddha

- Whatever the present moment contains, accept it as if you had chosen it. Always work with it, not against it.' – Eckhart Tolle

- 'Pain is inevitable, but suffering is optional.' – Anonymous

- 'Mindfulness isn't difficult, we just need to remember to do it.' – Sharon Salzberg

- 'Life only unfolds in moments. The healing power of mindfulness lies in living each of those moments as fully as we can, accepting it as it is as we open to what comes next – in the next moment of now.' – Jon Kabat-Zinn

6 Seven things to do today

● **Mindful listening:** next time you have a chat with a colleague, a client or your boss, set an intention to give them your full attention, taking in not only their words but also what remains unsaid, their gestures, facial expression, their intentions. Resist the urge to chip in and share your thoughts. Let them speak without interrupting them. Listen from their agenda, from a perspective of wishing them well rather than judging what they say and whether you agree with them. Being fully present without judgement is a great gift to the people around you.

● **Mindful speaking:** be intentional and mindful about what you say and how you say it. Consider the effect it may have and whether it will be harmful or beneficial to others, or whether you are just saying it to make yourself feel better by complaining or judging.

● **Mindful walking:** when you walk to a meeting, to buy lunch or just to the bathroom or the photocopier, do so mindfully. Connecting your breath with the movement, consciously notice the sensations in your feet and legs as you move. Do not rush – rejoice in every step. In the words of Thích Nhât Hanh: 'Walk as if you are kissing the Earth with your feet.'

● **Mindful eating:** experiment with eating one meal or snack mindfully at work. Be intentional about the choice of food and take your time, savouring the experience, the colour, smell, texture and finally the taste of the food. Resist the temptation to read your emails while you eat. They can wait until afterwards. Chew with awareness and notice the urge to swallow. See how this changes your experience of eating.

● **Mindful emailing:** next time you send an email, take a couple of minutes longer to contemplate how it will 'land' with the person receiving it rather than focusing on offloading what you want to say. Before you press the 'Send' button, take three mindful breaths to ensure that this is what you want to say and how you want to say it.

- **Break your routine:** experiment with stepping out of 'automatic pilot', and do a routine task differently. Choose a different route to work or to your desk, sit in a different chair in a meeting, structure your day or even a task differently. See how this gives you a sense of beginner's mind.
- **Mindful breathing:** during the day, find opportunities to practise mindful breathing, even if it is just one to three breaths at a time. Take an external event as your cue – for example every time you take the lift/elevator or when you wash your hands or when the phone rings. As Thích Nhât Hanh suggests, you can treat your ringing phone as a mindfulness bell, reminding you to take a mindful breath before you answer it to ensure your full presence in the ensuing conversation.

7 Seven trends for tomorrow

- **Mindfulness in organizations:** given that the leading cause of sickness absence tends to be mental ill health, mindfulness is well positioned to become an integral part of standard corporate learning and development initiatives. As Sally Boyle, head of human capital management at Goldman Sachs, put it: 'In years to come we'll be talking about mindfulness as we talk about exercise.'
- **Compassion training:** compassion training is rising in popularity as a standalone intervention. Although not strictly speaking part of mindfulness, 'lovingkindness', as it is often called, is often practised alongside mindfulness and has a growing body of evidence supporting its salutary effects on psychological wellbeing as well as positive relationships. In this specific practice, people learn to direct the wish that one may not suffer to oneself and then extend the same wish to others, friends and 'enemies' alike, finally to include all living beings. This practice is based on the Buddhist belief that all beings are interconnected in their experience of suffering and their wish to be happy.

- **Mindfulness in schools:** given encouraging evidence so far, mindfulness may become an integral part of the teaching at schools and other educational establishments. Mindfulness-based interventions may be increasingly employed to help with difficult behaviour as well as conditions such as ADHD.

- **Mindfulness parenting:** there is growing evidence that introducing both parents and children to mindfulness can be beneficial for family life, particularly for parents in socio-economically disadvantaged families who are also at greater risk of stress. This can lead to less dysfunctional and destructive behaviour in parents, stress reduction and better behaviour in children.

- **Mindfulness in health:** although already established in the treatment of depression, mindfulness will continue to be rolled out in the health sector, making it more widely available to people with a long-term physical health condition and a history of recurrent depression. In the UK, latest recommendations include the target of making MBCT for depression available to 15 per cent of people at risk by 2020. To make this possible, 1,200 new MBCT teachers will need to be trained by then.

- **Mindfulness in the criminal justice system:** following encouraging evidence emerging out of the United States, indicating improved self-regulation, reductions in negative emotional states and reduced drug use, mindfulness may become a standard offering for offender populations, not least to deal with the problem of recurrent depression.

- **Mindful executive coaching:** as mindfulness is an essential part of being aware and present in the coaching relationship, and an increasing number of executive coaches are espousing a personal mindfulness practice, this field is bound to experience a gradual shift from the still-prevalent goal- and performance-driven approach of executive coaching, to a more mindful and compassionate, being-based approach. Rigorous training is needed to help coaches integrate mindfulness into the very fabric of their coaching presence as well as their communication with their clients.

PART 2
Your Confidence Masterclass

Introduction

You've no idea what a poor opinion I have of myself – and how little I deserve it.

W. S. Gilbert

It is an old saying, and perhaps a sobering thought, that 'if you think you can, you can, and if you think you can't, you're right'. What often makes the difference between doing something successfully and failing is the level of confidence you bring to the task. The trick is to ensure that you have sufficient confidence to bring.

Feeling fear, uncertainty and a lack of confidence is a position all too easy to find yourself in. There always seem to be a hundred and one good reasons why something will be difficult, impossible or a disaster. Psychologists say that a huge amount of what they call 'self-talk' is instinctively negative. Faced with a task, we naturally think first of the difficulties and too often go on to conclude that we will fail and/or not enjoy the process of trying. All our inner dialogue begins with something like 'I can't'.

Be assured that you are not unusual if you feel like this; you are normal.

Abraham Lincoln said something to the effect that a man obtains the level of happiness he *decides* to obtain. He was implicitly saying that you have to work at it. And obtaining a level of confidence, a useful level that actually acts to help you achieve something, while lessening the fears and discomfort about it, is very much the same. If you feel you currently lack confidence, in general or about some specific task – making a presentation, say – something that can understandably cause apprehension, then, be assured, it is possible to boost it.

CHAPTER 8

What is confidence?

The dictionary says that confidence is 'a feeling of reliance or certainty, a sense of self-reliance; boldness'. We all understand this as the feeling that we can do something. This is not necessarily linked to perfection. With, say, a presentation to make, you may know you are not the best orator in the world but you know that you can do a good, workmanlike job of it that more than meets the needs of the occasion.

Confidence is not just a feeling; it is something that actively works to help you do things. It may not negate the need for study, preparation or whatever but it boosts the likelihood of success in a tangible way. Furthermore, feeling confident can act to make you appear confident – professional, expert, or whatever is appropriate – and that, too, can help the process, in the way that an audience may sometimes already be thinking that your presentation will be good even before you open your mouth.

Some people despair, believing that you are either born confident or not. Certainly, people may have a natural tendency to feel confident, part inherent, part from background – the nurture aspect of their upbringing. But, without a doubt, natural tendency is only one factor, and in any case the most important message of this book is that your level of confidence is *not* fixed. Think about it. There is almost certainly something you can think of that you originally approached with little or no confidence and which you now view more positively, having done it, perhaps repeatedly, and survived.

Of course, there may be things we never learn to love, but which, despite that, we are able to undertake with some equanimity, perhaps after experiment, review, training or practice; or all these things. But usually, whatever we fear doing, we can actually do with less fear if we decide to change our feelings and work at doing so.

Confidence and performance

We need to keep a clear perspective on confidence as we proceed here. It is not a panacea. No amount of confidence will make up for a lack of information or skill that simply prohibits you from doing something. But there are things that you may be perfectly well able to do and yet a lack of confidence reduces your level of performance or, at worst, makes you fail. Furthermore, a lack of confidence can have you avoiding things, things that should not be avoided, and risk you being judged harshly for doing so.

Presenting, mentioned above, makes a good example as there is certainly a level of trauma involved and because of that many people lack confidence in standing up to speak in public. They avoid ever having to get into a position where they must do so. Yet such a task is so important in many jobs, and avoiding such things may be dangerous. I can well remember the Managing Director of a company where I was to conduct a training workshop on making presentations, starting his introduction by reminding people that 'no one gets promoted here unless they can make a good presentation'. True enough, yet not, with hindsight, a phrase to boost participants' confidence.

Consider an example, something I observed at a conference, and which demonstrates the very powerful effect confidence can have on events. One speaker among several, sitting in a line on the platform next to the Chairman, was introduced and rose to speak. He began seemingly in a routine manner: *Ladies and Gentlemen*, he said, *I know time is short, but in the hour I have available I will ....* The Chairman, who sat beside him, looked horrified, tugged his sleeve and pointed to his watch. The speaker glanced in his direction for a second, looked up and continued: *Of course, I am so sorry, in the half hour I am allocated...* As he said this he paused, lifted his notes, in the form of A4 sheets, and tore them in half lengthways down the page, throwing half of them behind him and thus apparently halving the duration of his talk. As the papers fluttered down he then continued – with every member of the group giving him their complete attention. The feeling among every one of the two hundred or so people in the room said, *This should be good.*

What he did had nothing whatsoever to do with his topic. It was a device, what I call a flourish, designed only to indicate that he was confident. It was probably planned with the Chairman, but that did not matter, the effect was palpable and it helped him make a good start. He clearly understood that confidence breeds confidence. He knew that if he displayed confidence, the audience would feel more confidence in what was to come.

It was a simple enough thing to do; though it's possible that even this experienced speaker had to steel himself a little to do it. Now you may well say that such a trick requires a degree of confidence that you do not (as yet) possess. Perhaps. The point is, first, to recognize the effect of such a thing and, secondly, to show that it is actually quite simply achieved. What had to be done took only a moment and a minimal amount of preparation (not least so that the notes actually needed were not destroyed), but it clearly reflected a state of mind – someone determined to be confident and to show confidence.

TIP *Confidence breeds confidence: if you can show your audience that you are confident, they will have confidence in you.*

The results of lack of confidence

Let us be clear here too about the effects of a low level of confidence. First, it is uncomfortable, at worst even crippling, in an overall sense. It is to be avoided as it can be a continual factor reducing any satisfaction your job may provide and giving rise to feelings of stress (which in turn can lead to an ongoing negative cycle: low confidence makes you stressed; being stressed, or rather failing to cope with stress, makes you less able to be analytical and actually tackle and reduce the problem; and so on). It handicaps your operating efficiency and spoils and interferes with everything you try to do and from which you should get satisfaction.

Secondly, it has specific effects: that is, it prevents you getting to grips with individual tasks and executing them as well as you could if your confidence was higher. Have you ever had an interview, for instance, that worried you, went less well than it could have done and which, if you think about it honestly, went by default? In other words, you effectively gave up on it and did not really give it your best shot.

Lack of confidence is a tangible thing. It can be all-pervasive, creating feelings of:

- lack of enthusiasm
- tiredness
- shame, or even guilt or anger
- sickness: headaches or stomach problems
- inappropriate introspection and avoidance of people and situations
- poor self-esteem
- inappropriate compliance
- poor concentration and focus
- stress and anxiety.

All such feelings can affect your performance. Confidence affects your well-being and it cannot be left to find its own level; rather, it must be seen as something requiring active attention. The question is how to address it.

TIP *If you recognize yourself from the list above, then acknowledging that such symptoms may be linked to or stem from an insufficient and, perhaps, inappropriate level of confidence can be a constructive first step to making a positive change.*

The causes of a lack of confidence may be many and varied and range from childhood influences, experiences in the past (however far back) and relationships with others (including such extremes as bullying, harassment or rejection). Even physical personal characteristics may play a part. I once had a participant on a presentation skills course who was convinced their small stature prevented them from making a good job of this task, yet once they had some instruction and some practice, it quickly became apparent that this was no handicap at all and presenting was something at which they could excel. A change of perception may be all that is necessary in such a case.

The psychology of such past influences is rather beyond the brief here. A solution is more likely to be possible through *practical* intervention in the present than in deep analysis of the past. There is an old maxim that 'given oranges, the job is to make marmalade'; the job here is to find ways to boost confidence regardless of such long-term influences. As the presenter described above found, acquiring a sound knowledge of how to go about making an effective presentation was far more important than a deep-seated fear that his shortness of stature would prevent him from doing such things well.

Routes to boosting confidence

Lack of confidence can result, in part at least, from natural human instinct and responses. Boosting it means resisting these pressures and taking steps which lead to you adopting a positive attitude to things. There is sadly no instant magic formula; confidence does not appear in a moment just because you punch the air and shout 'Yes!' On the other hand, there is a formula that does result in increased confidence, even if it needs working at progressively in a number of different ways. Be reassured; the effects of such working are cumulative. Remember the old (Chinese) maxim that a journey of a thousand miles begins with a single step. Each of the many things you can do to help your situation can act to boost your confidence just a little, until you might surprise yourself by the difference you have made.

At this stage it is useful to identify the main areas from which help can stem. Overall there are three:

1 **Consideration, attitude and understanding:** perhaps the foundation to change is to accept that change *can* be made. It is a prime aim of this Part to help you adopt an attitude towards confidence of being able to work to increase it, and for you to see that the route to this is to think the problem through analytically (helping yourself to understand the problem) and select and take practical and specific action that will help.

2 **Focus on the task:** much lack of confidence occurs in relation to specific tasks: a fear that if you lift the telephone to make that call, stand up to make that presentation or whatever, you will be in trouble. As will be made clear, understanding the task, having sufficient knowledge about it and developing a suitable level of skill to do it, is a prime route to boosting confidence. Knowledge is power. So is proven skill, and thus there are some tasks where, realistically, confidence only truly builds with practice. Again, I repeat, confidence may not be raised instantly; some things are best dealt with through a campaign of confidence building. Realism about this helps the process: seeing yourself as taking useful steps, rather than despairing because confidence levels are not yet as you would wish.

3 **Feedback:** this also takes a number of forms. First, there is your own experience. Probably we have all had the experience of doing something for the first time (amid fear and trepidation) and finding it was not so bad after all, or even that it goes well. This certainly means we approach it differently the next time, when we *know* it is not as bad as we first thought. Secondly, there is the input of others, ranging from detailed help and advice about how to achieve

something, to a simple word of encouragement. The latter is a good example of the power of small elements to add positively to the situation; again, surely we can all remember a word of encouragement that helped us in some way. Encouragement, let me say, may be wholly pleasant, but it may also be offered with some authority and insistence (even with some power you may regard at the time as unpleasant). For example, your boss may tell you to get on and do something in no uncertain terms (leaving no possibility to say that you would 'rather not'), yet they may still include a strong element of encouragement, making it clear that they believe you are well able to complete the task successfully.

Another problem can be an overall fear of failure: we focus on the bad result, rather than thinking about how to achieve a good result. Think positive.

We return to these themes as we progress. Here let me add an analogy intended to make it easier to appreciate how a variety of things can help as you read on. Imagine your level of confidence represented by a set of scales. On one side are negative factors that pull your confidence down, on the other are positive things that act in some way to boost it. You want the plus side to weigh heaviest. Making this so can be achieved either by adding things – imagine them represented by plus signs of different sizes and weights – or by removing things from the minus side of the balance. Note, too, that a difference can also be made by reducing the weight of minus factors, rather than removing them, and similarly by increasing factors on the positive side; also note that small changes may affect the overall balance significantly for good or ill. This latter point means that small factors can be significant and must not be overlooked.

If you take just one thing from this chapter, let it be that levels of confidence can be changed, increased, and resolve to do just that, albeit step by step.

Summary

Thus the confidence building game-plan, as it were, is clear: you need to believe you can positively influence your level of confidence and construct an appropriate balance, going about that in a way that allows you both to assess and understand the problem and work to make things better. Another factor helps: that of understanding your starting point; seeing how you approach things now (and how you *are* now) will make the path to progress easier. It is to this we turn in the next chapter.

Fact-check (answers at the back)

1 Our level of confidence is what?
a) Fixed for life ❏
b) Always changeable ❏
c) Rarely changeable ❏
d) Only changeable by chance ❏

2 What is level of confidence most influenced by?
a) Being born confident ❏
b) Early experiences ❏
c) Working at being confident ❏
d) Good luck ❏

3 Which is the greatest influence on your confidence to perform a specific task?
a) Your knowledge of *how* to do it ❏
b) Your feeling about its difficulty ❏
c) The colour of your eyes ❏
d) Your experience of other things ❏

4 What can lack of confidence make you feel?
a) Content ❏
b) Hungry ❏
c) Lacking in concentration and focus ❏
d) Uncaring ❏

5 What are feelings of stress most likely to do?
a) Increase confidence ❏
b) Reduce confidence ❏
c) Not affect confidence at all ❏
d) Affect confidence very little ❏

6 How can overall confidence most easily be increased?
a) By making one massive change ❏
b) By proceeding step by step ❏
c) By doing nothing ❏
d) By making one tiny change ❏

7 Of the three areas from which a positive change can flow, which of the following is *not* the foundation for change?
a) Focusing on the task ❏
b) Seeking feedback ❏
c) Consideration, attitude and understanding ❏
d) Avoiding the full moon ❏

8 What imagined device can help you envisage your state of confidence and how it can be changed?
a) A saucepan ❏
b) A frying pan ❏
c) A kettle ❏
d) Weighing scales ❏

CHAPTER 9

A little judicious self-analysis

In this chapter, we look at the overall influences that affect your level of confidence and see how understanding them can assist you. This book takes a practical approach to boosting confidence, not least because the focus is on the workplace and workplace-related tasks, so we will not get overtly psychological about things, though in a sense psychology is involved here.

Thinking through your situation (and, indeed, contemplating the kind of person you are) may well be helpful, but soul searching is no panacea. There are practical actions to be taken, too, both to influence your thinking and to tackle and change other influences.

Consider first three overall factors that influence how confident you feel:

1 **Your background:** it is possible that attitudes which now dictate how confident you tend to feel (and, indeed, how you view life) link back to childhood and family circumstances. And it is also possible that any significant difficulties you have suffered in the past (and I mean a range of serious issues such as bullying or abuse) influence you too. Substantial problems of that sort are beyond the scope of this book, and some could need serious intervention. At another level such things may simply need leaving behind, and doing so may need only a small degree of resolve or a change to habitual thinking; after all, you may conclude that such matters have little link or relevance to your present–day circumstances and activities.

   Of course there can be serious issues, and I have no wish to suggest such things do not exist, but it is all too easy to allow them to become an excuse (something you quote to yourself to justify your lack of confidence rather than taking a view that can increase it). Writing this reminds me of a T-shirt I saw with the slogan *Yeah, right – move on.* Certainly that is a sobering reminder that other people may not be interested in, or make excuses for, your background problems.

2 **How you think:** a constructive attitude here is important. Faced with difficulty, you need to think positively and you also need to be realistic and practical because you may need to take action to overcome or reduce the problem. As has been said, the first thing here is a resolve to make a difference; more of this anon.

3 **What you do:** leaving a feeling of low confidence unaddressed (perhaps viewing it as inevitable or unchangeable) will achieve nothing. Some, often much, of what you can actually *do* will change how you feel about a task; although all fear of it may not be removed, you can make it possible, manageable, and even enjoyable (well, perhaps enjoyable having *done* it). Subsequent chapters focus on this approach, giving ideas and examples of how you can actively affect matters.

If you aim to change yourself, or at least the way you feel about something, it is helpful to work out what degree of change is necessary. What is the starting position and how do you move from one condition to another? A little self-analysis is useful here.

Reversing negativity

Everyone surely has some inner self-motivation, sufficient to give them enough confidence to get out of bed in the morning and get down to the everyday tasks that face them (if you do not then this is not the book for you and you should seek more radical remedies). But confidence can be stillborn. You could be confident (perhaps you even feel you could be) but any such feeling is constantly overruled by negative thinking. This can take various forms, but all can be reduced or overcome. Consider the following factors.

Setting, and avoiding, 'impossible' tasks

This is characterized by taking an extreme view: feeling something is right or wrong, good or bad and so on. It is thinking that gets you setting your sights too high, believing something is only any good at the extremes, then avoiding getting started because you think *I'll never get there.*

Solution: Do not fix on an unmanageable, whole target. You must do it in stages (manageable stages). Make a start, work progressively through the stages, and congratulate yourself on their successful completion (stage by stage). Right, a reward for me when I finish this chapter!

Allowing negatives to pervade thinking

This is an extreme form of the natural human tendency for negative self-talk. It can certainly be applied to a task like making a presentation, where you dwell on all the difficulties but forget any positives (you have to speak on something people will find interesting, you know the topic well, etc.)

Solution: Form the habit of assessing things in two columns, the plusses as well as less good factors; ask others about things too (perhaps picking the brains of one of your habitually more optimistic colleagues).

Jumping to conclusions

This reflects the term 'self-fulfilling prophecy': you find yourself habitually *sure* you know the key thing about something and that it is negative – like *knowing* the group will hate your presentation (but why should they?).

Solution: Look for evidence of your feeling. Is it a factual point or just a feeling? Again, a conversation with others, asking *What's most important about this?* may help you to adjust your focus.

Underrating your achievements

Belittling your actual achievements (and yes, I bet you have many) can easily be a habit of people with low confidence – and doing so just makes things worse.

Solution: Recognize what you do here and progressively aim to change this habit. Write things down, tell others what you have done (and listen to what they have done too) and mark achievements by giving yourself a metaphorical pat on the back or an actual reward (though not *too* much cake!).

Putting up a sign

Some people label themselves. They pick labels that demonstrate their low confidence: *I'm new to this job* (even after a few years), say, or, worse, labels such as *I'm a disaster* (i.e. expressing the belief that nothing goes right, when surely much does). Psychologically having such descriptions in mind leads to negative thinking and thus to low confidence.

Solution: Ask yourself what you actually mean when you do this. Saying *I'm an idiot* may only mean you have made one minor slip and have nothing to do with the big picture.

Making mountains

... out of molehills. This form of overdramatizing is usually somewhat emotional – distress and drama escalate so that the perceived problem seems to way outstrip reality, and certainly prevents you from thinking logically about something.

Solution: Count to ten before you even begin this process, then you can spot the emotional self-talk as it comes to the fore. Remember that it will all be the same in a hundred years and that even if something is going to be difficult it may not be true to say it is an unredeemable catastrophe.

Making feelings facts

Here you let your feelings influence you, despite the fact that they are just your feelings. Thus being apprehensive about making a presentation does not mean you are less able to make one than other people; that's a view of yourself that *will* make it more difficult.

Solution: This thinking must be replaced by a more factual approach – asking *why* you fear doing something and then addressing the problem; it's another habit to establish in the right way.

Wrongly taking the blame

You should not take the personal blame for every problem or failure. Things can fail for all sorts of reasons. If you miss an important appointment because you let the car run out of fuel, then it may well be your fault. But if someone runs into you through no fault of your own, it may still leave you with problems to sort out but it does not help to blame yourself. Feeling bad about it won't help resolve things.

Solution: If something isn't your fault, don't beat yourself up over it. If blame is really shared (and this may need some assessment), then the responsibility for taking action to sort things out may also need sharing; again, this is something to look at pragmatically.

This, therefore all

Here you allow one thing to be generalized. You make a pig's breakfast of one thing then apply it to everything. Not so. If I write an unintelligible sentence, there is no need for me to feel that the whole chapter is rubbish.

Solution: In my example, the unintelligible sentence needs sorting, but I need to keep this in proportion and not lose faith in the whole text. Again, like all these points, the key thing is to recognize what is happening, resolve to find another, better way and change perspective. There is in fact nothing complicated about the solutions.

If you are to think positively and boost your confidence, then you need to consider how confidence originates. This is influenced in a number of ways.

Not taking the initiative

There is a saying that if we want to do something we do it, and if we don't we make an excuse. If a lack of confidence means we do nothing then, by definition, nothing happens. Allowing fate to guide us – a kind of 'something will turn up, let's wait' attitude – is a recipe for failure.

Solution: A first step is always to resolve not to dwell on something, but rather to actually tackle things (even if in so doing you also resolve to find out the best way of approaching it first).

Attitudes to success (or failure)

Think about something you have done: learning to ride a bike or drive a car perhaps. Almost certainly there was a stage where it just seemed impossible, but a degree of perseverance got you there in the end.

However, if you continued to feel it was impossible, gave up, assumed mistakes or setbacks meant you couldn't do it, blamed something (or someone) else for the difficulty or found endless excuses – then difficult or impossible it no doubt was.

But if you were prepared to invest some time, to try and try again, believed you could learn from your mistakes and get it right in the end, checked the best way to go about it and took responsibility for your actions – then you would likely have found it easier.

Never forget that your attitude directly affects your achievement – and that a positive attitude towards getting things done gives you the confidence to achieve.

Response to failure

Failure may just be finding the first stage of something uncomfortable and then backing off, but bouncing back is a better attitude. Avoid despair – *I'm useless, I'll never do it* – and recognize that the (initial) failure is less significant than your response to it. It is not just a question of try, try again; Henry Ford said that failure was an opportunity to start again *more intelligently.* The moral here is to confront the problem, consider the best way forward and make sure you expect future success. Viewing life as a series of opportunities to learn is an attitude that works well.

Optimist or pessimist?

It is said that some people see a glass as half empty but others, more positively, see it as half full. Maybe a better response is to say that the glass is simply the wrong size! Optimism is an aid to confidence, but it should not be based on unthinking faith in the future, rather on an essential pragmatism and realism. Winston Churchill said: 'A pessimist sees the difficulty in every opportunity; an optimist sees the opportunity in every difficulty.' True enough: the confident approach rejects pessimism – an irrational *I know this will be difficult, I know I can't* approach – and sees success as possible, resolving to make it happen and, if necessary, to find out just how that can be made possible.

 TIP *Most often, lack of confidence persists because no effort is made to change things. Remember that if you always do what you have always done, things will tend to continue in the same old way. Change is inherent to building confidence. If how you are and how you think now leaves you lacking confidence, then you need to think and act differently.*

Summary

The key issue here is how you think about things. Low confidence breeds even lower confidence all too easily. If there is one thing to emphasize about this, it is that many of the things referred to in this chapter are habits. We do not study the situation and then ignore all the positives, thinking this is the best way forward; rather, we act instinctively and from habit that takes us in the wrong direction. Habits are not necessarily easy to change, but easier once you have decided what to aim to stop and what to put in its place. Then, progressively, you can find that good habits develop which are as powerful as the old, and that these will keep you on the right track.

At the start of this chapter it was said that the most important two things are how you think about things and what you do about them. There are specific mental attitudes to address, but there are practical reasons underlying why it may be difficult to be confident about something. So now we turn to this, because focusing on solving difficulties and how you think at the same time can work wonders.

Fact-check (answers at the back)

1 Lack of confidence should be what?
a) Ignored ❏
b) Addressed positively ❏
c) Recognized as 'just one of those things' ❏
d) Addressed primarily in the past ❏

2 Change should be regarded as what?
a) Likely to exaggerate low confidence ❏
b) The final straw ❏
c) An opportunity ❏
d) To be avoided ❏

3 What is the value of optimism?
a) It has no relation to confidence ❏
b) It can be encouraged and used to combat low confidence ❏
c) It is an unchangeable personal characteristic ❏
d) It makes low confidence worse ❏

4 How should you view your previous success (and surely there is some)?
a) It does not mean anything will go well ❏
b) It means you are now due a failure ❏
c) As a basis for encouraging future success ❏
d) It has no relevance ❏

5 What is the prime route to boosting confidence?
a) You taking the initiative to positively affect it ❏
b) Doing nothing ❏
c) Therapy ❏
d) Waiting for an outside input ❏

6 When things go wrong, whose fault is it usually?
a) Yours ❏
b) Your boss's ❏
c) A mix of circumstances ❏
d) Gremlins ❏

7 When you do achieve something, what should you do?
a) Regard it as a fluke ❏
b) Think of it as a minor matter ❏
c) Not dwell on it at all ❏
d) Give yourself credit ❏

8 Low confidence is often prompted by problems, which should be what?
a) Addressed practically to seek a solution ❏
b) Ignored ❏
c) Regarded as insoluble ❏
d) Seen as unimportant ❏

CHAPTER 10

The nature of the workplace

The workplace is the stage on which you perform, as it were. It can be a daunting environment, but also a supportive one. It can sap your confidence, or see it stifled, but it can also boost it in a variety of ways. Ensuring that you survive and prosper, and that you are able to undertake confidently the various tasks you must perform and perform successfully, means understanding the nature of the workplace and how you can use the way it works to assist your endeavours.

In this chapter, the workplace is explored to seek opportunities for boosting confidence. Some are very much part of ongoing activities, some need more effort to set them up, but there is considerable support available here. As has already been emphasized, the first step is a positive outlook. In some ways, you may see the workplace as one cause of your having insufficient confidence. Of course, there are difficulties and some are outright hazards, but the net effect should be positive. There is a real opportunity to pile things on the positive side of the scales here, and in supermarket jargon 'every little helps'.

In the twenty-first century we must all be realistic about the modern workplace. As Richard F. Stiegele said: 'The business world is an extension of the kindergarten sand box – but with quicksand'. The workplace has changed radically in recent years; if one wants one word to describe it, then dynamic is as good as any. As the twenty-first century moves on, any individual is right to wonder how their career will progress, and whether they can make it give them what they want.

Many people, certainly those with several years' experience, may feel they remember 'better times', that is, times when there was more certainty about how a career would progress. Many organizations commonly once had defined career paths for people and, although progress varied somewhat, once on a specific path the direction in which you would be able to go was reasonably clear. In some industries this was particularly so. Banks make a good example, yet banks have changed too, more than many kinds of organization and, many would say, not for the better. Now, though this kind of prescribed career path does still exist, it is less common.

Some people may hanker for a return to those 'better days', but waiting for things to return to normal is simply not one of the options. There are currently few, if any, safe havens, and few, if any, organizations that seem likely to be so again in a situation where change is the norm. Organizations are always likely to be under pressure and the well-being of their employees, perhaps especially those whose lack of confidence does not help them shine, is often a lesser goal than sheer corporate survival.

TIP *Success in the workplace may have many influences, but the strongest is that success is based on the achievement of goals. And achieving goals may sometimes involve you in tasks that tax you and which you may feel little confidence in being able to do well. Furthermore, the workplace is increasingly competitive and if you do not have the confidence to forge ahead, then there will certainly be others who do.*

All sorts of factors contribute to there being a different workplace and work culture today than in the past:

- Organizations being under greater market and financial pressure
- Changes in the way businesses and organizations operate (think of the IT revolution or international pressures, for instance)
- Lower staff numbers and more pressure on individuals
- Reduced budgets and thus a reduced ability to fund personal development
- Changed terms of employment (think of how the pension schemes offered have changed in the last few years)
- More competition between employees to succeed
- Higher unemployment
- A general increase in both the amount and speed of change
- The greater likelihood of employers having to take sudden and negative action to protect themselves (such as making people redundant).

Despite all this, you no doubt want to thrive, prosper and get on; and ideally you probably want to enjoy your job while you do so. And remember, it is said that if success was easy, there would be no such thing as failure. So what is the moral? How can you ensure that you do well? The simple answer is that there is nothing you can do that will *guarantee* success (if there ever was). But there is a great deal you can do to make success more likely, ranging from learning new skills to surviving the office politics of a large organization.

Actively increasing the chances of doing well, by ensuring that your confidence is at a good level may be a crucial part of this. The concept of ensuring that your confidence levels are an *active* process is vital. For the most part, success does not come automatically to those who sit and wait, nor even to those who take advantage of opportunities as they occur, though this should be part of it. So too with confidence; brooding about your lack of it, or just worrying about whether or not you can cope with some task will not help. So let's see what there is about the workplace that can help.

Who's who and how they can help (or hinder)

People characterize the workplace. And, as has been said, the advice and encouragement of others can certainly boost your confidence. Essentially, the categories of people who matter here are:

- colleagues
- your line manager
- other managers.

Let's take these in turn.

Colleagues

Let's get the bad news out of the way first. Some people will never help you. Remember that the workplace is hectic (so they may not have time) and competitive (so they may not want to help you; at worst they see themselves as better off if you fail). This needs saying, yet actually because most people need help to some degree, and you are all thus in the same boat, collaboration and goodwill are often plentiful.

The key is in the fact that you are not alone and it may be that you can prompt individual initiatives by offering help. Maybe someone is struggling with something that you regard as entirely straightforward. Offer help, and perhaps even arrange it as a swap: 'You can get so close to these things you can't see the wood for the trees. If I check over that report for you, perhaps you could spend five minutes making some suggestions about the presentation I'm preparing.' Even if you are terrified of making the presentation, you don't need to say that (though, if you know the person well, you might), but just when you are convinced that your every planned word is useless it may be a boost to your confidence to have someone else critique it and find it mostly fine. If they can help improve aspects of it, then better still.

Relationships with colleagues may just sort of develop, but they can also usefully be guided so that they foster mutual support. Sometimes this mutual support may be practical. You might suggest a better way of starting a presentation, one that you find yourself using that makes you feel more confident. Alternatively, it may be simply a morale booster. For example, in the film *The Lady* (which tells the story of Aung San Suu Kyi and her husband), as Aung San Suu Kyi is sucked into taking a public stand, she must make a speech. Tens of thousands attend and, as she mounts the steps to the platform, she hesitates, pointing out to her husband that she has never spoken in public before. He directs her up the steps with a firm 'You'll be fine.' And of course she is, though I bet those three words were a powerful help.

Assistance of this sort, either just an encouraging word or sound advice, that makes something seem more possible and less worrying, works well. When it does, it is easily recognized, encouraged by both parties and becomes a useful routine. It is wise to regard such things as two-way, which is why a swap arrangement is good. You do not want to become known as a nuisance: someone always wanting help, help that others may feel should not be necessary.

Relationships with colleagues are sometimes seen simply as what circumstances dictate. A consideration of the possibilities, coupled with some action to create the right involvements, can see you in a much more supportive group and gaining in confidence as a result.

Your line manager

A manager is responsible for ensuring that members of their team perform satisfactorily. Part of that may be checking on progress, but it should also involve other things, primarily here motivating people so that they *want* to perform well and developing them so that they *can*.

A good relationship with a good manager is invaluable to your job satisfaction and level of confidence; I would go so far as to say that if you work for the 'boss from hell', working with the confidence you want may always be difficult, if not impossible. At worst you may resolve to move away from such a boss. That said, for most people, it is worth taking the initiative to create the kind of relationship with your boss that will be supportive and allow them to act to encourage you in a way that builds your confidence.

There needs to be a sound basis – a routine and a structure – if such a relationship is going to be constructive. This premise is easy to adopt, but then, unless your boss does all the work and creates exactly what you want, it demands two things of you:

1 **That you think the relationship through.** *You* need to take the initiative and think about what factors constitute a sound working arrangement. You can do worse than list them.
2 **That you make it happen.** Again, where necessary, take the initiative for creating and agreeing the appropriate basis, albeit step by step – and making it stick.

Any shortfall here will dilute your ability to succeed; if you cannot get precisely the arrangement you want first time (and this may well be the case), then you need to keep working at it.

Among the things that help this process are to:

- adopt a day-to-day routine, especially with regard to how you communicate and how and when you have meetings; this is an element of good time management (something else perhaps worth some study, it does not help your confidence if you are forever struggling to keep up)
- ensure regular communication (of all sorts, but especially meetings) and ensure you have sufficient time together to agree matters between you
- make sure that project timing is agreed, and particularly that checkpoints or progress meetings are scheduled in advance (by stage if not by date)
- agree also the nature and style of all the above: for example, what exactly is a progress meeting? How long is it likely to take? Should it be preceded by a written document of some sort and, if so, what level of detail is involved?
- make sure that such practice relates appropriately to tasks (that it is what is needed to get the job done) and to the people involved (so that both parties feel comfortable with it)
- address both long- and short-term issues. Think about what is needed day-to-day, right through to annual matters (like planning or regular job appraisal meetings).

It is important to relate all this to the nature of work and tasks. A progress meeting on an essentially routine matter may not take long or involve anything complicated; though it may still be vital to keep things on track. At the other end of the scale, a meeting that is designed to be creative – discussion that aims to identify new ideas or methods – will take longer and is also more likely to be squeezed out by more urgent matters. The routine should help make all things happen effectively.

Describing such a good working methodology is one thing, achieving it may well be another. Certainly it will not just happen (unless you have an exceptional manager), or will not happen consistently. So you need to be prepared to think it through, and see organizing how you work with your boss as something else on which you must be prepared to take the initiative in the following ways:

- **Ask:** Ask for the opportunity to discuss things, and have some ideas ready (with a less approachable manager start on just one issue, a project perhaps, as a way of creating good practice).
- **Suggest:** Put forward ideas, offer suggestions, and use what other people (chosen because they will be respected) do to exemplify your case. Discuss, negotiate, request a test (plead?) – but get something agreed, even if it is at first a starting point that you return to, and refine later to move nearer to the ideal.
- **Act:** Take the initiative and take action. In other words, just do it. For example, as a project starts, set out a timetable for scheduling the progress meetings and send it without comment, put (or through a secretary get put) the date in the diary, send an agenda ahead of the due date and appear ready for the meeting. Taking such action (assuming it is sensible and will be approved) makes sense; your boss may actually find it useful (maybe to the surprise of you both!) and not only react positively but also react well to similar things in future.
- **Match their style:** Finally, as you approach all this, bear in mind the kind of person they are. What will suit them? Aim high by all means, but, if ultimately some compromise is likely to be necessary, plan what you might do. For example,

attitude to detail is important here. Your manager may be a 'put it on one page' kind of person, or want every 'i' dotted and every 't' crossed. You cannot just ignore such characteristics; a well-matched case has the best chance both of being agreed – and of working.

TIP *Start as you mean to go on: suggest something practical, act to get it agreed and make it work so that your boss will want it to continue. Success breeds success, and confidence is fuelled by seeing the results.*

Much here can act to boost your confidence. For example, embarking on a project when you have arranged some checks and opportunities to discuss it along the way is very different from seeing the whole thing stretching in front of you and being uncertain about it. All occasions when you cross paths will present opportunities for you to seek information or simple encouragement. But remember that bosses want staff to be pretty self-sufficient. Saying 'I don't know what to do about X' and asking for help may not go down very well. Rather, make suggestions: 'I think the best way for me to do this is X' followed by checking to see whether they agree, asking for advice about one aspect of the approach, or both. Make no mistake, a good, ongoing working relationship with your boss can improve both how you work and how much confidence you have in what you do.

Other managers

Similarly, it is worth thinking about other people in the organization with whom it might be beneficial (because they could provide help, advice or encouragement) to have good and regular relations. Who is appropriate will depend on the position you have and the sort of organization for which you work, but many staff managers can be useful, for example, a training manager. Again, position what you do appropriately and so that you are not seen as inadequate but, rather, keen to learn, develop, get on and do a good job.

It can be useful here to make a list of all those you want to explore or maintain contact with, testing out who proves useful and keeping a simple record of contacts so that you establish a useful frequency (one that's not too much for others) and know when to make contact again.

One particular approach is useful here.

The role of the mentor

Encouragement breeds confidence and goes hand in hand with development. One source of it, beyond colleagues and your line manager, is a mentor. A mentor is someone who exercises a low-key and informal developmental role. Their role is to promote learning, but very much also to give encouragement and instil confidence. More than one person can be involved in the mentoring of a single individual. What they do is akin to some of the things a line manager should do, but a mentor is specifically *not* your line manager. Your mentor might be someone more senior, someone on the same level or from elsewhere in the organization. An effective mentor can be a powerful force in your development and success. So how do you get yourself a mentor?

In some organizations this is a regular part of ongoing development. You may be allocated one, or able to request one. Equally you may need to act to create a mentoring relationship for yourself (something that may demand some persuasion). You can suggest it to your manager, or direct to someone you think might undertake the role, and take the initiative.

What makes a good mentor? The person must:

- have authority (this might mean they are senior, or just that they are capable and confident)
- have suitable knowledge and experience, counselling skills and appropriate clout
- be willing to spend some time with you (their doing this with others may be a positive sign).

Finding that time may be a challenge. One way to minimize that problem is to organize your mentoring on a swap basis: someone agrees to help you and you line up your own manager (or you for that matter) to help them, or one of their people.

Then a series of informal meetings can result, together creating a thread of activity through the operational activity. These meetings need an agenda (albeit just an informal one) and, more importantly, they need to be constructive. If they are, then one thing will naturally lead to another and a variety of occasions can be utilized to maintain the dialogue. A meeting (followed by a brief encounter as people pass on the stairs) to discuss a project, with a promise to spend a moment on feedback (an email or two passing in different directions), may all contribute. What makes this process useful is the commitment and quality of the mentor. Where such relationships can be set up, and where they work well, they add a powerful dimension to the ongoing cycle of development, one that it is difficult to imagine being bettered in any other way, and which, by their very nature, boost confidence too.

Overall, what you learn from the ongoing interactions and communications you have with your line manager and others can be invaluable. It may leave some things to be dealt with in other ways, but it can be the best way to cope with many matters, and also to add useful reinforcement in areas of development that need a more formal approach. As both parties become familiar with the arrangement, and with each other, it can become highly productive. Having been lucky enough to have someone in a mentoring role myself for many years, I well know that often just a few minutes spent together can crack a problem, lead to a new initiative or simply send you back to work more confident of what you have to do.

Note: a mentor is usually taken to be someone senior to the person for whom they act as mentor. But a similar relationship is possible with colleagues (for example, other members of your team or department). There is no reason why you cannot forge a number of useful and reciprocal alliances, perhaps each designed to help in rather different ways or on different tasks and topics.

Mentoring is often an underrated methodology and is well worth investigating, experimenting with and using. The following section shows just how this can work and how useful it can be.

Mentoring in action

A mentor may act in various ways over time, but equally they may focus on a particular problem in the short term. Perhaps you could consider making another presentation. If you have to do one and dread it, then this may be an ideal topic for mentoring.

Once some help is arranged, and a promise to spend some time on it agreed, you can decide what to do and begin to set a timetable for it too (not least so that you always leave one encounter with the next defined, agreed and set in your respective diaries). Here you might start generally, the brief being that you need to know something about what makes a good presentation. In this regard you might:

● read up on the subject
● attend a course
● talk through the essentials with the mentor (perhaps, to save time, having read a book first)
● attend a presentation given by the mentor, with them meeting you afterwards, so that you could analyse it together and you could find out why different things were done the way they were.

Then you might link all this to your pending presentation:

1 Explain what it is to the mentor and discuss broadly how you will go about it.
2 Prepare and make notes.

3 Discuss the specifics of what you now plan to do and perhaps fine-tune it after some critique.
4 Rehearse, then make the presentation to your mentor (and perhaps others), a session followed by a critique and perhaps again by more fine-tuning.
5 Make the presentation (perhaps it could be videoed, or the mentor could sit in).

This is followed by a post-mortem. This discussion will shape how you prepare your next presentation.

Of course, you may not follow this progression slavishly and could do more or less, but I am certain you will find that your confidence builds at every stage. The process is practical, it links to real life and a real project. You experience the progress you are making as you go through, with feedback contributing to your abilities and your level of confidence.

Setting up such things correctly makes sense. It makes success both more likely and happen sooner than a more ad hoc approach, or one where you struggle to get through solo.

Avoid getting sucked into the less savoury aspects of office politics (which always exist in an organization of any size) or being seen as starting or passing on rumours. These things bring negativity to the workplace and will sap your confidence.

Workplace confidence boosters

- be well organized
- manage your time effectively
- focus on the results you are charged with producing
- avoid distractions
- don't procrastinate.

Summary

The workplace can seem hectic, confused and overpowering – an environment that crushes confidence rather than promotes it. And, unless considered and got to grips with, it is. On the other hand, if you think about your position, if you are clear about what is expected of you in your job, and consider what and who can help make the path you must take a little easier, then there is much you can do.

The trick is to tackle individual elements separately and on a considered basis, rather than allowing the whole to overwhelm you. Thus organizing a good relationship with your boss (and working on it on an ongoing basis), finding and benefiting from a mentor and seeing who else might be useful, all help.

It is difficult to summon up confidence when you are submerged in chaos. You need to be thinking straight and knowing that you are actively organizing everything around you, so that it helps rather than hinders.

Fact-check (answers at the back)

1 The workplace is dynamic and this should be regarded as what?
a) A passing phase ❏
b) Likely to continue ❏
c) Likely to continue and intensify ❏
d) Just an illusion ❏

2 Your manager is best regarded as what?
a) Someone to avoid ❏
b) A potential help in boosting confidence ❏
c) Part of the 'low-confidence problem' ❏
d) Irrelevant ❏

3 How should you deal with colleagues?
a) Avoid them if possible ❏
b) Cultivate them carefully in terms of relationships ❏
c) Deal with them on a task-by-task basis ❏
d) Be totally confident with them ❏

4 In working with your boss, what should you do?
a) Just do as you are told ❏
b) Avoid discussions ❏
c) Ask questions and take initiatives ❏
d) Avoid them as much as possible ❏

5 If a mentor offers informal support, what should you do?
a) Find and work with one if at all possible ❏
b) Regard this as 'not for me' ❏
c) Refuse any offer of such help ❏
d) Relate only to your immediate manager ❏

6 How should you behave in the workplace?
a) Concentrate on your job and ignore things around you ❏
b) Observe and analyse your workplace for anything that will help you ❏
c) See it solely as a hindrance to your confidence level ❏
d) Leave any thought about it for later ❏

7 When dealing with staff managers (e.g. a training manager), what should you do?
a) Keep your head down and minimize contact ❏
b) Deal only with the 'business of the moment' ❏
c) Look for and cultivate useful inputs for the future ❏
d) Avoid contact with those outside your immediate circle ❏

8 What is a good tactic to obtain feedback and assistance from colleagues?
a) Making collaboration a two-way process ❏
b) Becoming a real nuisance ❏
c) To drastically limit what you ask ❏
d) Forget it, it's not possible ❏

CHAPTER 11

Working at creating confidence

Three main routes to increased self-confidence include:

- the way you think about things
- the development of knowledge and skill
- addressing difficult matters in a practical, problem-solving way.

The latter, an area that links to the development of knowledge and skill, is the subject of this chapter.

If you are a sensible person (and why else would you be reading about this subject) you may say, 'okay I can sort problems', but you may still not be maximizing this approach. Joseph Jastrow once said: *Create a belief in a theory and the facts will create themselves.* This is so true of confidence. You become convinced that something is difficult just for some emotional overall reason (*I just can't do it*), and this belief allows you to avoid any analysis, and putting into effect any simple solution that might redress the balance, at least to some extent.

So let me encourage you to take a very practical view here.

Problem-solve your way to confidence

The best way of demonstrating the possibilities here is through an example. I have already mentioned making a presentation and now, because so many people have to make them in their work (and almost everyone has experience or can imagine how easily lack of confidence handicaps the ability to make a good one), we'll use this as an example. Of course, all sorts of things contribute to being able to make a good presentation, and preparation and a grasp of the 'tricks of the trade', as it were, both help. To focus on matters that potential speakers rate as a significant contributor to nerves, consider the common fears, which are of:

- butterflies in the stomach
- a dry mouth making it difficult to speak
- not knowing where to put your hands
- the reaction of the audience
- not having enough material
- not being able to get through the material in the time
- not knowing how loud to pitch your voice
- losing your place
- over – or under – running on time
- being asked questions you cannot answer
- drying up.

All pose real hazards, but the way to deal with them, the way to ensure your confidence level is not affected by them, is to take a practical view. It is worth noting here that such fears are very often exaggerated. For example, last in the list above is drying up. Often during presentation skills courses, where usually I am using video to record what participants do and prompting discussion about it, people will regularly criticize themselves about one perceived fault: *I dried up at one stage,* they say, *there was an awful great gap.* Yet during their talk often no one else noticed, and often, too, when the video is replayed they cannot even spot where it happened. A pause just seemed too long to them at the time.

TIP *The preceding perception is very common. You may have fears about doing all sorts of things, but in all likelihood you see them as worse problems than they are; indeed, knowing you do so may help – in fact this alone may make you think of something that you can change.*

Returning to the list, there are actions possible in response to all these points that actually sort out and remove the problems, or at the very least reduce them. For example:

- **Butterflies in the stomach:** this is a physical manifestation of any worries you may have. In their mild form they do no harm and fade as the adrenalin starts to flow when you get under way. Even so, a number of practical measures undoubtedly help reduce the feeling. Certainly, knowing a presentation is well prepared is a major help. Other things are seemingly small, perhaps obvious; they do work, however, and may work better when used together. They include:
  - a few deep breaths just before you start
  - no heavy food too soon before you start
  - no starvation diets, or the butterflies will be accompanied by rumbles
  - no alcohol (some would say very little) before the off.
- **Dry mouth:** again, this is a natural reaction, but one simply cured. Just take a sip of water before you start. And never be afraid of asking for, or organizing, a supply of water in front of you. Place it where you are least likely to spill it and you may, like me, prefer to avoid the fashionably fizzy waters supplied by many of the venues where speakers often find themselves, especially hotels and conference centres. I am sure it is nice for the audience and offered with good intentions, but it is inclined to make you burp if you are the speaker. The longer the duration of your talk, the more you will need to take the occasional sip. Talking makes you dry and air conditioning compounds the problem. Act accordingly, throughout your talk.
- **Somewhere to put your hands:** because somehow they can feel awkward. They seem like disproportionately large lumps

at the end of your arms. The trick here is to avoid obvious awkwardness: give your hands something to do – hold a pen perhaps – and then *forget* about them, though they should be involved in some gestures. Incidentally, it is best that a man should remember that while one hand in a pocket may look okay, both hands in pockets always appears slovenly.

Though there are similar points to be made right down the list of presentational fears set out earlier, this is no place for a complete rundown on making presentations.*
A fear analysed can be turned into a problem with a solution. However long a list of fears, it can usefully be viewed in this way. Doing so can produce a radical shift: first you are just reacting, perhaps blindly, to a fear; then you have worked out a solution to a problem that alleviates what you fear (either completely or partly). Not only does the tangible result – there being one less thing to worry about – help, there is psychological advantage too. Knowing you have sorted the problem, indeed knowing that the overall balance of positive and negative effects is now adjusted just a bit more in your favour, helps boost your confidence.
There is perhaps another level here, different from simply perceiving and solving a problem, and that is finding things that simply suit you and make you feel easier about something; what you might think of as personal comfort factors. Continuing the presentation example, I find I speak regularly from behind a standard-height table. Fine, one of reasonable width usually gives plenty of room for notes, slides, projector and more. But if I lay any notes I have flat on the table, then I cannot see them clearly if they are in standard-sized type. I wear spectacles and have found that if I lay a good-sized, hard briefcase on the table and put notes on that, just four to six inches higher, then I can focus at a glance and, from the perspective of the audience, do not appear to be looking down so much. It suits me, looks fine and is easy to arrange. Having this in mind, I can walk into an unfamiliar room carrying a briefcase and I *know* this will help

---

*I have written about this in *100 Great Presentation Ideas* (Marshall Cavendish) but these few examples make a good point.

me to be comfortable and so, too, will choosing a good-sized font. Such thinking and practice are proven and work well, and again such things shift the balance just a little more in your favour.

Consider one more factor on my list of presentation hazards: that of not knowing how loudly to speak. This may be a reasonable fear in a strange room, but you can test it. Ahead of the meeting, find someone to stand at the back and check how you come over, until you get the level right. In fact, a moment's thought shows that it is not really a very difficult problem. In other circumstances, if a single person came into the room from a door at the far end, you would probably speak to them naturally at just the right level. Try not to worry and just think of yourself as addressing the back row.

One further thought about this relates to an apocryphal story of a speaker checking and asking an audience 'Can you hear me at the back?' The reply comes back 'Yes ... but I'm prepared to change places with someone who can't.' Now, this may not be fall-about funny, but bringing a humorous thought to mind in any kind of stressful situation can help.

 Always try to turn a, maybe amorphous, fear into a specific problem. Problems can have solutions, and identifying and using those solutions can quell fears and boost confidence.

Overriding the uncomfortable

Everyone has some things they find difficult.

Take me: despite being, I like to think, knowledgeable about and practised in various areas of management and business, there are, I admit, some tasks where my approach falters. It is difficult to admit this (damn it, I have written a book about time management!) – but I have been known to procrastinate. When does this happen most often? On examination that is easy to say: it is when something is not just potentially difficult, but when it is a particular kind of difficult – when it is actually *uncomfortable.* This may be conscious: for example, there are things about my computer skills that mean action is delayed – I *know* that my skills have gaps and am conscious that it is easy to get into deep trouble, yet I still fear the solution and have little confidence in it proving straightforward. Everyone probably has things that prompt such thoughts, and which make delaying action more likely.

So, difficulty can translate into lack of confidence and thus inaction, and difficulty plus an uncomfortable awkwardness produces a worse effect. Consider an example that affects many of those who manage others.

When performance is inadequate

Imagine: one of your staff is performing under par. This might be anything from not hitting sales targets to more minor matters; the details are unimportant. One thing is clear – it demands action. The rewards are considerable, let us say, and easily recognized. Dealing with it will produce more sales, higher productivity – whatever, depending on the precise details. Yet ... with such things there can seem to be many reasons for delay. We think (or rather hope) that matters will get better. We wait for other things: the end of the month (bringing further figures or evidence) or a forthcoming appraisal (which we know means we cannot put it off later than that). More than anything, we blame other things. We are busy, we have greater priorities (really?) or, even less convincingly, we are sorting other problems – firefighting.

It may be an uncomfortable truth, but the truth is we do not *want* to deal with it. We may be unsure how to do so, and the resultant lack of confidence breeds procrastination. More likely we *do* know what to do, but know it will be awkward or embarrassing to do so; this is especially the case in some circumstances, for example where people managed may be senior or experienced. Addressing it will take us into what we might call the *discomfort zone,* and we would rather distance ourselves, busying ourselves elsewhere (with something we tell ourselves is more important!) and remain safely outside this zone of personal difficulty.

The facts of the matter are often clear, and can usually be dealt with if things are addressed directly. With the right approach and knowledge that the problem can be sorted, confidence rises and a good job can be done (even though there may still be some discomfort).

Poor performance is a good example. It is important, yet it is not complicated. Essentially only three options are possible:

1 Put up with the poor performance, and allow it to continue (which is surely something no manager would defend or recommend).
2 Address the problem determined to cure it, persuading or motivating someone to perform better; or training or developing him or her to do whatever it is better if poor performance is due to a shortfall in or lack of some skill or competence.
3 Conclude, perhaps after option two has failed, that they will never get better and fire them (or otherwise move them to other areas of responsibility).

Both options two and three may be awkward. It *is* embarrassing to tell someone their performance is unacceptable, and most people would find firing someone worse. So, confidence falters and action is delayed.

Recognizing reality

The situation described needs to be addressed head on. Any such situation is not a failing of logic, not a deficit of information or understanding, or anything else that mistakenly leads us away from the sensible and necessary course – *it is a personal decision: we put avoiding personal discomfort above sorting the problem and, very likely, delay makes the problem worse.*

Before you say *But I never make that kind of decision*, consider further. If this thinking is partly subconscious – we lack the confidence to do something rather than being unable to – then that means we push it into the back of our mind, refusing to really analyse what is occurring, or simply allowing other activity to create a blinding smokescreen. Now, thinking more constructively, which elements of your work are likely to run foul of this kind of avoidance technique? Here are some examples:

- **Raising a difficult issue at a meeting** – it gets put off rather than risking controversy or argument
- **Cold calling in selling** – many of us should do more, but it is not our favourite thing
- **Networking** sounds good: we all hope to meet people at that conference we attend, but then come out with one business card because we are *not quite sure how to approach people.* Worse, the card is from whoever sat next to us rather than someone selected for a good reason
- **Follow up** is when someone, a customer or colleague, has said *I'll think about it* – how many times do we make one perfunctory phone call to be told they are *in a meeting*, then leave it so long that the moment passes because we are not quite sure what to say next time
- **Chasing debtors** – we hate it, avoid it or do it half-heartedly and so cash flow suffers; yet we should all recognize that an order is not an order until the money is in the bank.

 TIP *A word about the last of these (or things like it). Next time you have to make such a phone call, don't sit at your desk – make the call standing up. It may sound odd, but do not reject this idea: I promise you will find it easier to be more assertive. Not only is it easier, but it also shows how mechanistic changes can improve confidence.*

Such things are, to an extent, routine. Others may be more personal, linking to a particular skill or activity. For instance:

- **Avoiding presentations,** even when they offer promotional opportunity, because *It's not really my thing*
- **Avoiding writing reports** seems often to be regarded similarly
- **Avoiding sitting on a committee** where you might make valuable contacts because meetings are in the evening and *It's not fair on the family*, though it is contributing to the meeting you fear.

You may well be able to extend the list in these categories (be honest, since only that makes the analysis useful).

Fill any information or skills gap, taking time to do so if necessary. This is usually time well spent. For example, if you fire someone without checking out the employment legislation first, you may make a small hole very deep (for more on this, see Chapter 14).

Identifying opportunities

So, what do we conclude from this? There is a significant opportunity here.

You need to resolve to *actively seek out uncomfortable situations*. You need to see the discomfort zone as an attractive place to go. It is somewhere where you can use analysis to raise your confidence, so that you can take action and influence results, and often you can do so quickly and easily. Indeed, having done so, you may well end up saying: *I just wish I had done that sooner.* Give yourself a pat on the back.

The following technique for overcoming this undesirable element of human nature is a simple, sure way to boost confidence and thus increase your effectiveness and enhance the results you achieve. Try it. This approach works – and as you discover that, your confidence in it will rise.

'Entering the discomfort zone': a programme for action

Programme difficult tasks into your list of 'things to do', giving actions their true priority, having worked out what you have to gain from achieving them (after all, you deserve some motivation if you are going to choose to be uncomfortable). Make this approach a habit and make *entering the discomfort zone* a catchphrase. This approach is the antidote to a lack of confidence that allows things to go by default. It needs some resolve, but surely you have that.

Summary

The moral here is simple: some things seem worse than they are, so assume that they are. Think about it (analytically) and you can identify the real problem, find a solution and be much more confident of taking action to surpass or remove the fear. Make this a habit and adopt a systematic approach:

1 Spot the areas needing attention and identify an analytical approach and what action to take.
2 Ask yourself why you are turning away from something and check specifically that it is not simply to avoid what will (apparently) cause some personal discomfort.
3 Check that action is possible: do you know what to do? Do you have the skills to do it?
4 Take the action and take note: when you solve a problem, give yourself some credit, learn from it for next time and watch your confidence build – *Good job!*

Fact-check (answers at the back)

1 If a task fills you with dread, what's the best thing to do?

a) Panic ❏

b) Blame ... anything ❏

c) Analyse the problem and seek a solution ❏

d) Hope someone else can assist ❏

2 Faced with a problem, what does low confidence make you most likely to do?

a) You will ignore it ❏

b) You will overrate it ❏

c) You will underestimate it ❏

d) You will not notice it ❏

3 If you sort a problem, what (other than the solution) do you gain?

a) Brownie points ❏

b) A psychological boost (*I sorted it!*) ❏

c) Nothing ❏

d) Things get worse ❏

4 If a problem is especially *uncomfortable*, how should you approach it?

a) Delay any action to avoid the discomfort ❏

b) Just sit and worry ❏

c) Do something – anything – instantly ❏

d) Make sure you address it promptly and in a considered fashion ❏

5 What can change your attitude and ability to tackle something instantly?

a) Holding your breath ❏

b) A physical change (such as standing to make a phone call) ❏

c) Nothing ❏

d) Putting it out of your mind ❏

6 How will avoiding an issue because of lack of confidence affect things?

a) The delay won't matter ❏

b) I'll feel better ❏

c) It will guarantee nothing changes ❏

d) Something will turn up ❏

7 What analogy is useful in envisaging how problem solving helps boost self-confidence?

a) A microscope ❏

b) A telescope ❏

c) A set of weighing scales ❏

d) A calculator ❏

8 In the presenting example, what best helped the fear of knowing what to do with your hands?

a) Wearing gloves ❏

b) Putting your hands in your pocket ❏

c) Giving them something useful to do ❏

d) Making exaggerated gestures ❏

CHAPTER 12

The contribution of appearance

There is an old saying that if you look like a doormat, then people will walk all over you. And lack of confidence can show. People who appear to be lacking in confidence look uncertain, they look worried, or worse. This apparent lack of confidence can create something of a continuing problem: people read a lack of confidence as a lack of competence. They treat people displaying it differently, and that in turn makes it more difficult for the person so treated to rise above the situation.

Thus how you come across to others is important, and so this chapter is about how personal appearance affects confidence and thus performance.

It was Oscar Wilde who said: 'Only fools do not judge by appearances.' He was right. The first thing to take on board here is that how you appear (and, as we will see, it is more than just your personal appearance) is important. It makes a difference. Look confident and you will feel confident. Look confident and other people will rate your competence more highly. As they say in the world of advertising 'perception is reality'.

It is not difficult to do, either; creating the right visible persona is thus a straightforward step to take. In terms of the balance mentioned earlier, it puts distinctly more weight on the plus side.

Making a judgement

Think of someone in your organization perhaps whom you do not know very much about. Ask yourself what you think about them. Are they busy? Competent? Confident? Approachable? Expert? Ambitious? Efficient? If they are a manager, what opinion do you think their staff has of them? You will find that if you draw conclusions from what evidence you have, many questions can apparently be asked and answered, and a reasonable picture builds up. You feel that you can judge something about them. Whether it is true or not is, of course, another matter. Your own visibility also gives out many signals, and will do so whether you think about it consciously or not. Here we review some of the ways in which you can give signals that paint the right kind of picture of you: as a confident and competent person. This will both be read by others and make you see yourself in a more positive way, to boost your confidence.

Looking the part

I once attended an evening talk at a professional institute and heard someone give a review of what are sometimes called 'beauty parades' or competitive pitches. The speaker made a number of interesting points including this simple advice: 'Look the part.' He gave a number of detailed examples, one of which was the advice for men to wear what he called 'big-boy shoes' (ones with shoelaces rather than slip-on style). Now this is going a bit far, perhaps, but the point is well made.

First impressions, which of course can only be made once, are largely visual and take in many such things from clean fingernails to someone's overall prevailing style.

Now dress is a difficult area on which to advise precisely. I am not promoting designer fashion or any specific style of dress. You have to be reasonably natural, but you want to be seen positively. You can be smart without spending a fortune. You must always be clean and tidy, and the details matter. The Americans, who have a jargon phrase for everything, talk about 'power dressing'. This is a concept that is too contrived for many; indeed there is a real likelihood that going too far in this way becomes self-defeating, and is just seen as pretentious.

It may be important in some jobs to meet the standards and style of those with whom the organization does business rather than internally. Once, having met with a major bank to discuss possible training work, a colleague of mine, one who took a pride in his appearance, was dismayed that a letter came back requesting the work to be done by someone *shorter in the hair and longer in the tooth!* An older and more traditional alternative was found and the work went well; that is the client's right. Internally, styles vary in different organizations and types of job, and certainly dress codes are less formal than they used to be. Any variable may influence things: summer and winter, a totally internal role or one meeting customers, and geographic location (for instance business suits may not be worn in a hot country).

 TIP *In terms of dress, the best advice is to be towards the smarter end of the range exhibited by colleagues around you. Feeling you have this right, that you fit in and fit well, will be a foundation to feeling confidence in your appearance.*

So, what specifically is certain? The following are often mentioned:

- Clean fingernails and tidy hair
- Smart (rather than over-fashionable) clothes
- Clean shoes.

And, though it is more difficult to judge, your appearance should reflect an appropriate spend; hence the comment in the tip above. It is worth noting that men and women have different styles to consider, with the greater choice facing the women, frankly making their choices more difficult. Whatever your style, whatever you opt for, think about it, relate what you do to the corporate culture and practice, and remember that your appearance says very much more about you than you might think. You *will* have an image; the only question is what precise image you will make it.

Improving your workspace

The same principle applies to your desk or workplace. It should be tidy, it should look well organized, you should be able to find things promptly, and certainly it should be uncluttered (not too many photos and probably no stuffed animals); and it should say to others: here works someone on top of the job, organized, competent and professional.

If your desk is an untidy muddle, if it looks as if a bomb hit it and you have difficulty finding things, then remember the old saying that a tidy desk means a tidy mind. You may sensibly not want a look that seems to flag inactivity (there is nothing wrong with looking busy) but do consider this advice.

Have a tidy up, create a look you feel is appropriate, and you will not only feel better about it and yourself, but the picture you paint of yourself to others will improve. This simple act alone can boost confidence and begin to change any inadequate image that may exist. There is an important link here: changing things so that your appearance is strengthened can also act to change your view of yourself and how confident you feel. More is necessary, but this can be a positive step in the right direction. That said, what else can have this sort of effect? The following can be useful.

Watching your body language

This has perhaps been over-inflated in the way it is written about. It is not really a science, but at the basic level there are things here to note because they do signal something and you will want to control this.

Take two examples: we all know how we feel if we are given a really limp handshake, or if someone fails totally to make eye contact with us. Both are to be avoided. It is easy, if you are feeling a lack of confidence, to find yourself evading eye contact, but knowing it is important surely helps. Make a point of meeting someone's eyes: they will judge you differently and as they do so you will feel better about yourself.

A conscious effort just to look more confident is worth some effort. Without it you become trapped in a downward spiral: your look says the wrong things about you and you are judged accordingly. This is especially important initially, on first meeting someone, at the start of a meeting, or the beginning of a conversation, interview or presentation. Remember that first impressions last and that you should start as you mean to go on. This is precisely the sort of area where making a good start is so important: you look someone straight in the eye, their respect for you increases, and you quickly see the benefit. Later, such things become habits that need little thought.

Taking an interest

In many companies, particularly large ones, there is considerable social interaction among staff. Just how much there is and how it works will vary, and is affected by such things as whether there is a social club and where the office is located: some city centre locations where people typically travel long distances to work may mean people live as much as a hundred miles apart and this will reduce social possibilities. It is easy, if you lack confidence, to avoid all of this, but that is almost certainly a mistake.

There will also be a culture within the organization relating to social activity. In some companies, senior people are involved in some of this and others are clearly expected to be. In others, it is seen as a lower-level activity and you may not want to get too involved, in case you are seen as essentially frivolous.

Another issue here is that, rightly or wrongly, people have a total image. Though interference in employees' private lives is not the style of many organizations, and would be resented by many staff, you may be expected to have certain interests. Some of these are perfectly reasonable. It is useful for executives, especially those who have contacts outside the firm, to be generally well informed in terms of current affairs, for example. If you are in a technical area, you may need to keep up to date on a broad range of scientific matters, simply to be able to relate well to others you work with. On the other hand, there are organizations where the style of the chief executive – evidenced by a passion for, say, golf, science fiction or undersea diving – is mirrored by aspiring staff around the office forever plunging into the sea or Arthur C. Clarke. Whether this last is useful or not is uncertain. I would like to think it is not, but there are organizations where this kind of fitting in is important. It is certainly worth a thought. You are unlikely to have to rearrange your whole life around such things, but some accommodation with such perception may be useful.

Taking steps to become socially comfortable within the workplace, and finding that you are, is a direct boost to both self-confidence and how you are seen. Avoiding contacts and events, not because those things are difficult but because you are embarrassed about a poor presentational ability, say, just makes things worse. Aim to move forward in parallel: tackle the specific problems and you will not have anything standing in the way of your fitting in.

Gender in the workplace

The gender of any individual inevitably has an effect on how they are seen. This is no place for a major debate on women in business; suffice it to say that they are still, in many cultures, not taken as seriously as men. Leaving the reasons on one side, what is the effect? Let me start with an illustration.

I used to have a young woman working with me who moved from a secretarial position to one of more executive responsibility, and then to a position where she joined a small management committee. Halfway through the first meeting she attended, someone delivered a tray of tea and coffee and left it on a side table. Discussion continued and, after a few minutes during which no one moved, she got up, poured and handed round the drinks.

After the meeting, she asked me how she had got on. She had done well, contributing some sound comments, but I remember asking, *'Why did you pour the tea?'* She did not hesitate, saying at once, *'Right, I won't do that again.'* Now I am not suggesting that every woman early in a management career is in danger of being typecast as the tea lady, or secretary/hostess, and it did not in fact matter who did the chore; the point is that perceptions stick. Sometimes women are in danger of being underrated and thus, rightly or wrongly, they have to think twice as hard as men about how they are seen. So in my view, her response was right (and her subsequent progress proved she made sure that she was very much seen in the right light). Of course, women can increasingly fight their corner, and I like the quotation, attributed to (a presumably confident) Charlotte Whitten: 'Whatever women do, they must do twice as well as men to be thought half as good.' Luckily, this is not difficult. Even so, this area may need some conscious thought.

 For everyone, there is merit in making sure all dealings around the organization are on the basis of jobs done, expertise and merit rather than gender (whichever gender is involved). This does not mean preventing the occasional normal social interaction and, in organizations the world over, some people will continue to have the confidence to say: How about dinner?

Do not drink to excess

This is common sense, but worth a word. A lack of confidence can lead in this direction: a stiff drink before you must make that dreaded presentation, say. In many organizations, a certain amount of socializing is not only pleasant but it is also part of the way the business works. On the other hand, someone being the worse for drink gives few, if any people, confidence in them and most, if not all, managers will always prefer to promote the office cat before promoting someone with even a hint of a drinking problem.

Learn to give and take

Beware: a lack of confidence can promote a selfish outlook and think of the effect a selfish attitude in others has on you. It is not the most endearing characteristic imaginable. Success and effectiveness are assisted by co-operation. Liaison with others has been mentioned elsewhere, and a selfish attitude to others hardly makes them co-operate in ways that will help you become more confident (that is a foregone conclusion).

When I first went into consulting, I worked with a group of people who were less selfish than any other I have encountered before or since. No one ever seemed too busy to help. You could walk into any office and get advice, information and support of all kinds – from just a word to a complete rundown on something (and if it could not be given at once, a time was set). Information was regarded as for sharing, not for exclusive hoarding, and the whole firm, far from grinding to a halt because time was taken in this way, seemed to thrive on the attitude. For a newcomer, it was a godsend. I made full use of the learning, accelerated experience and greater confidence it provided and, in due course, found myself part of the network spending time giving as well as receiving.

There is an self-interested side to this attitude. You never know in an organization how things will go and how things will turn out. The person whose head you bite off because they want a moment of your time when you are busy turns up a while later in a position of authority or influence, and with not the slightest intention of sharing anything with you. You cannot have too many allies; contact and collaboration are a prime source of increased confidence and being seen to be involved in this kind of way is a positive image factor.

Avoid being typecast

Every kind of business activity seems to run this risk. In my own business, it is very difficult to stop some clients seeing me exclusively as a consultant and others seeing me exclusively as a trainer or a writer (though I work at it!). Some companies have a similar problem in selling the range of what they make; they are known for one or two main items, and the others always seem to get left behind. There can be a similar situation with people and sometimes the effect can be negative.

For example, if a lack of confidence in the past has seen you hiding your light under a bushel, failing at some tasks and avoiding others, then there is a danger that, well, let's just say you are not the first name to jump into the boss's mind when some new and interesting project needs staffing. Image is part of the story; so too is your track record. There is a virtuous circle possible here. Look the part, and you will be taken more seriously. Being taken more seriously, perhaps being given new tasks you find you can excel at, changes your image still more, while fuelling your confidence level in the process. One good thing leads to another, and in terms of getting started, one small step forward can make sure the next one follows.

Create image opportunities

You may feel that your role within an organization is too low-key ever to contribute very much to what you might call your corporate profile. If so, then one option may be to add opportunities. This may not be for everyone, but you could surprise yourself by examining what you could do. The following is a dramatic example perhaps, but it makes an important point.

Once waiting to do a radio interview, I remember meeting another interviewee who was there to comment on some technical matter. We got chatting and I asked him who he was. He said that he worked for a large company and had made a point of becoming known as the company's expert on the particular technical issue in question. *Do you run the technical department?* I asked him. *No,* he said. *But I aim to.* Hearing what he was doing to establish himself as the technical 'guru', I was inclined to believe him.

This tale makes a good point: public relations is not only a valuable tool to promote the company, it has personal development potential as well. It is tightly linked with some of the communications skills reviewed in the next chapter. My fellow interviewee at the radio studio would not have been there unless he could talk fluently about his chosen topic; just being knowledgeable about it was not enough. What is more, if he performed well, then he stood a good chance of being asked back, while his boss, who was fearful of undertaking the task, stayed in the office.

Radio is perhaps a dramatic example to take, though by no means unattainable, but public relations activity incorporates many different possibilities. Given that you have or can create some expertise worthy of comment, and very many jobs have this possibility, start internally and review the possibilities. For instance:

- is there a company magazine or newsletter?
- are there groups or committees you can take part in or speak at?
- should you be seeking to write articles?
- can you speak at the local management institute or trade or professional body?

There may be many options, and this is very much an activity that creates its own momentum. If you lack confidence in meetings, perhaps you simply need more practice. Though it may be the last thing you believe you want, volunteering for a committee role may provide a useful low-key introduction, in which you can experiment and build confidence for those meetings that matter more to you.

One such thing can lead to another, with your confidence building along the way. For example, an article published in the company newsletter might be adapted to go in an external publication, a copy of that being sent to a professional body might prompt an invitation to speak, and at that meeting you might meet someone who ... but you get the point.

If such activity grows up naturally, and has a use for the organization as well as for you, then it should not create ripples (though others may well wish they had thought of it first) and it can become an ongoing part of how you signal to others that you are going places. Nothing succeeds like success, they say, and being seen to have achieved things is certainly potentially useful. There is a chain of events possible here where each step can build confidence, and the success achieved step by step does the same. Before you know it, what you thought of as a lacklustre image of someone unwilling or unable to say boo to a goose can have been transformed. See you in the studio!

Personal image is not a given. You create it, wittingly or not, and you can build it into something that influences others and influences you too, making you better able to take on more because you believe you have the wherewithal to do so.

Summary

Be aware: every aspect of how you appear plays a role in how you are seen. As the examples here have shown, the range of things contributing to the overall picture is considerable (from how you look, to the state of your desk, and your manner when conducting a meeting); so it is worth some thought and some care to get this right.

The right personal profile – consistently – is important in a career sense and that may benefit you long term, but it is also something that you can draw strength from, so that your confidence builds (and is seen to do so) as the cumulative effect of a number of individual manageable actions.

Know the kind of profile you want to have, in detail, and work at everything that helps to create, maintain and project it. Why not start with a review of how your work area looks?

Fact-check (answers at the back)

1 Does appearance matter?
a) Hardly at all ❏
b) No ❏
c) Yes, it conditions your professional persona ❏
d) It's the only thing that matters ❏

2 How much do people infer from appearance?
a) Just what it obviously shows ❏
b) Very little ❏
c) Nothing ❏
d) Far more than it actually shows ❏

3 What else contributes to your visual profile?
a) The appearance of your workspace (desk or office, etc.) ❏
b) Keeping a low profile ❏
c) Wearing dark glasses ❏
d) Only communicating by email ❏

4 What easily positively boosts first impressions?
a) Your choice of tie ❏
b) Direct eye contact ❏
c) Speaking extra loudly ❏
d) A crushing handshake ❏

5 How will a stiff drink affect your confidence?
a) Not at all ❏
b) Likely to make things worse ❏
c) One isn't enough ❏
d) Boost it dramatically ❏

6 When is appearance most important?
a) On special occasions ❏
b) On Tuesdays ❏
c) Throughout working hours ❏
d) When the boss is around ❏

7 What forms an inherent part of appearance?
a) Nothing else ❏
b) Your behaviour and manner ❏
c) The car you drive ❏
d) Your favourite colour ❏

8 How often should you review and fine-tune how you appear?
a) Once a year ❏
b) Every five years ❏
c) Every time you look in the mirror ❏
d) Regularly, but without wasting time on it ❏

CHAPTER 13

Communication to the rescue

Think about this: how quickly and easily could you tell someone who doesn't know how to tie a necktie? And no, you cannot demonstrate – words only. Are you confident you could do it? No? Well, perhaps many would agree, certainly it would be difficult without some thought.

We all communicate, much of the time, and the workplace is no exception. Often all goes well. Often we hardly think about it. It's easy enough to say, 'What time do you call this?' to the postman but asking for a salary increase, making a presentation to the Board or writing a report that will actually be read (and influence a decision towards the one you want made) can be another matter.

Well, leaving aside the postman, the answer may be not only that such things can be difficult, but also that when they are poorly executed, problems can appear not far behind. In most workplaces you do not have to eavesdrop for long to hear the immediate results of poor communication: *But I thought you said ... You should have said ... What!?* Similarly, failing to get your point across at a meeting or making a lacklustre presentation can change the course of subsequent events – to your detriment. Here we review communications, recognizing that some, for instance presentations, are almost inherently confidence sapping, and that even seemingly more routine matters can be made difficult by a lack of confidence.

The fact is that communication is often *not* easy; indeed, a host of factors combine to make it more difficult. And one such, without a doubt, is a simple lack of confidence. You ponder and pause – *How can I put this?* – or you rush into something, quickly getting tongue-tied – *Sorry, I suppose I mean sort of ...* Furthermore, such stumbling is highly likely to make you less confident: an awkward start deteriorating into self-talk that just says *I can't do this* and the avoidance of conversations that would in fact be helpful to you. Alternatively, if you assume all will be well, and give the matter no great thought or preparation, then of course the dangers increase. And, of course, any such stumbling risks you being taken less seriously by your peers and others; as the entertainer Tom Lehrer said, *I wish people who have trouble communicating would just shut up.*

Hello, I must be going

One notoriously difficult kind of communication is indicated by the idea of networking, which is the work equivalent of joining a cocktail party where you know no one and are trying to think of something to say. At work it may literally be networking, trying to forge contacts at a trade conference perhaps, or meeting any unknown group, attendees on an all-comers course, or just visiting a department or location of your own organization where you don't know anyone.

You want to feel fine, not flustered, so the way ahead is to have a firm idea of how to handle the situation. How do you go about this? First, remember that this is a common problem and many people present are probably also wondering what to say. It is best not to interrupt passionate conversation, but easier to start a conversation with someone alone or just starting some small talk. Use the mnemonic FINE. It is most straightforward to talk about:

- **F**amily
- **I**nterests
- **N**ews
- **E**mployment

And it is easiest to make a start with open questions – that is, those that cannot be answered with the words yes or no. The best start is with the likes of What, Where, How or Who and phrases like *Tell me about …*

Of course, it may still be difficult to steel yourself to take the initiative, but knowing you are on an easy topic and that most people like nothing better than to talk about themselves does make it easier. It may help to remember something like FINE, but so too does it to understand something about the psychology of communication.

Roman teacher and rhetorician, Marcus Fabius Quintilianus said:

> **'One should not aim at being possible to understand, but at being impossible to misunderstand.'**

Communication is, in fact, *inherently difficult.* However tongue-tied any lack of confidence may make you, understanding the difficulties, and what makes it work well, enables you to position what you do correctly, and this alone makes things easier. Let's consider why.

The difficulties of making communication effective

If communicating is going to flow easily and make things happen, everyone must make sure that people:

- hear what you say, and thus listen
- understand, and do so accurately
- agree, certainly with most of it
- take action in response (though the action may simply be to decide to take note).

Such action could be a whole range of things, from agreeing to spend more time on something, attend a meeting or follow specific instructions.

Consider the areas above in turn:

Ensuring that people hear/listen (or read)

Here, difficulties include the following:

- People cannot or will not concentrate for long periods of time: so this fact must be accommodated by the way we communicate. Long monologues are out, written communication should have plenty of breaks, headings and fresh starts (which is why the design of this book is as it is), and two-way conversation must be used to prevent people thinking they are pinned down and have to listen to something interminable.
- People pay less attention to those elements of a communication that appear to them unimportant: so creating the right emphasis, to ensure that key points are not missed, is a key responsibility of the communicator.

 Always remember that you have to work at making sure you are heard – you have to earn a hearing. That is just how things are (it is not that people are being perverse, they are being normal!)

Ensuring accurate understanding

Difficulties here include the following:

- People make assumptions based on their past experience: you must make sure you relate to just that. If you wrongly assume certain experience exists then your message will not make much sense (imagine trying to teach someone to drive if they had never sat in a car: *press your foot on the accelerator – what's that?*).
- Other people's jargon is often not understood: think very carefully about the amount you use, and with whom. Jargon is 'professional slang' and creates useful shorthand between people in the know, for example in one organization or one industry, but dilutes a message if used inappropriately. For instance, used in a way that assumes a greater familiarity

than actually exists, it will hinder understanding (and remember, people do not like to sound stupid and may well be reluctant to say *I don't understand,* something that can apply whatever the reason for a lack of understanding).

- Things heard but not seen are more easily misunderstood: thus anything that can be shown may be useful; so, too, is a message that 'paints a picture' in words.
- Assumptions are often drawn before a speaker finishes: the listener is, in fact, saying to themselves *I'm sure I can see where this is going* and their mind reduces its listening concentration, focusing instead on planning their own next comment. This, too, needs accommodating, and where a point is crucial, feedback can be sought to ensure that concentration has not faltered and the message really has got through.

Prompting action

Often this is an objective and one you must aim for, despite the following difficulties:

- It is difficult to change people's habits: recognizing this is the first step to achieving it; a stronger case may need to be made than would be necessary if this were not true. It also means that care must be taken to link past and future. For example, don't say *That was wrong and this is better* – but rather: *That was fine then, but this will be better in future* (and explaining how changed circumstances make this so). Any phraseology that casts doubt on someone's earlier decisions should be avoided wherever possible.
- There may be fear of taking action – *Will it work? What will people think? What will my colleagues think? What are the consequences of it not working out?* And this risk avoidance is a natural feeling: recognizing this and offering appropriate reassurance are vital.
- Many people are simply reluctant to make prompt decisions: they may need real help from you and it is a mistake to assume that laying out an irresistible case and just waiting for the commitment is all there is to it.

In addition, you need one more objective:

Stimulating feedback

The difficulties here are as follows:

- Some (all?) people, sometimes deliberately hide their reaction: some flushing out and reading between the lines may be necessary
- Appearances can be deceptive. For example, phrases such as *Trust me* are as often a warning sign as a comment to be welcomed – some care is necessary.

The net effect of all this is rather like trying to get a clear view through a fog. Communication goes to and fro, but between the parties involved is a filter; not all of the messages may get through, some may be blocked, and some may be warped or let through only with pieces missing. In part, the remedy to all this is simply watchfulness. If you appreciate the difficulties, you can adjust your communication style a little to compensate, and achieve better understanding as a result.

 TIP *If you know that every utterance you make is likely to be met with confusion, antagonism or just ignored, then it hardly acts to boost your confidence, but if you know the likely difficulties and know how to work to overcome them, then your confidence benefits.*

One moral is surely clear. Communication is likely to be better for some planning. This may only be a few seconds' thought – the old premise of engaging the brain before the mouth (or writing arm) – through to making some notes before you draft a memo or report, or even sitting down with a colleague for a while to thrash through the best way to approach something.

There are antidotes hinted at above to these inherent difficulties, but are there any principles that run parallel and provide mechanisms to balance the difficulty, and make matters easier? Indeed there are.

Aids to effective communication

Confident and successful communication comes largely from attention to detail. Just using one word instead of another can make a slight difference. Actually, just using one word instead of another can make a *significant* difference (as you see!). And there are plenty of other factors that contribute, but there are also certain overall factors that are of major influence, and which can be used to help your communications.

Four factors are key:

1. The 'What about me?' factor

Any message is more likely to be listened to and accepted if how it affects people is spelled out. Whatever the effect, in whatever way (and it may be ways) people want to know *what's in it for me?*, and also wonder *how will it hurt me?* People are interested in both the potential positive and negative effects. Tell someone that you have a new computerized reporting system and they may well think the worst. Certainly their reaction is unlikely to be simply *good for you*, it is more likely to be *sounds like that will be complicated*, or *bet that will have teething troubles or take up more time*. Tell them they are going to find it faster and easier to submit returns using the new system. Add that it is already drawing good reactions in another department. Spell out the message and what the effects on them will be together and in the right sequence, rather than leaving them wary or asking questions.

 Whatever you say, bear in mind that people view it from their own perspective; build in the answers to their fears and you avert their potential suspicion and make them more likely to want to take the message on board.

2. The 'That's logical' factor

The sequence and structure of communication is very important. For example, if people know what your proposition is, understand why it was chosen and believe it will work *for them*, then they will pay more attention. Conversely, if it is unclear or illogical then they worry about it, and this takes their mind off listening.

Information is remembered and used in an order – you only have to try saying your own telephone number as quickly backwards as you do forwards to demonstrate this – so your selection of a sensible order for communication will make sense to people, and again they will warm to the message. Using an appropriate sequence helps gain understanding and makes it easier for people to retain and use information; as with much of what is said here this is especially true for a technically orientated or complex message.

Telling people about this is called *signposting*: flagging in advance either the content or nature of what is coming next. One important form of this is describing a brief agenda for what follows.

Signposting is a very useful device. Say *Let me give you some details about what the reorganization is, when the changes will come into effect and how we will gain from it* and, provided that makes sense to your listener, they will *want* to hear what comes next. So tell them about the reorganization and then move on. It is almost impossible to overuse signposting. It can lead into a message, giving an overview, and also separately lead into subsections of that message. Sometimes it can be strengthened by explaining why the order has been chosen – *let's go through it chronologically – perhaps I could spell out ...* – within the phrase.

 Whatever you have to say, think about what you will say first, second, third and so on and make the order you choose an appropriate sequence for whoever you are communicating with. You will gain confidence from the certainty of having this worked out.

3. The 'I can relate to that' factor

Imagine a description: *It was a wonderful sunset.* What does it make you think of? Well, a sunset, you may say. But how do you do this? You recall sunsets you have seen in the past and what you imagine draws on that memory, conjuring up what is probably a composite vision based on many memories. Because it is reasonable to assume that you have seen a sunset, and enjoyed the experience, in the past, I can be fairly certain that a brief phrase will put what I want in your mind.

It is, in fact, almost impossible not to allow related things to come into your mind as you take in a message (try it now: *do not* think about a long, cool refreshing drink. See?) This fact about the way the human mind works must be allowed for and used to promote clear understanding.

On the other hand, if you were asked to call to mind, say, the house in which I live and yet I describe it to you not at all, then this is impossible – at least unless you have been there or discussed the matter with me previously. All you can do is guess, wildly perhaps – *all authors live in a garret* or *all authors are rich and live in mansions* – (and this is wrong on both counts!).

So, with this factor also inherent to communication, it is useful to try to judge carefully people's prior experience – or, indeed, to ask about it if you have not known them for long and you are unsure of their past experience. You may also refer to it with phrases linking what you are saying to the experience of the other person. For example, saying things like – *this is like – you will remember – do you know so and so? this is similar, but -* all designed to help the listener grasp what you are saying more easily and more accurately.

Beware of getting at cross-purposes because you think someone has a frame of reference for something which they do not; link to their experience and use it to reinforce a message in which you can have greater confidence.

4. The 'Again and again' factor
Repetition is a fundamental help to grasping a point.
Repetition is a fundamental help to ...

Sorry. It is true, but it does not imply just saying the same thing, in the same words, repeatedly. Repetition takes a number of forms:

- Things repeated in different ways (or at different stages of the same conversation)
- Points made in more than one manner: for example, being spoken and written down
- Using summaries or checklists to recap key points
- Reminders over a period of time (maybe varying the method: phone, email or meeting).

This can be overdone (perhaps as in the introduction to this point here), but it is also a genuinely valuable aid to getting the message across, especially when used with the other factors now mentioned. People really are more likely to retain what they take in more than once. Okay, enough repetition.

Positioning your communication

So far in this chapter, the principles outlined have been general; but they can be useful in any communication. However, exactly whom you communicate with is important. Consider staff, reporting to a manager, as a special category. If you want people to work willingly, happily and efficiently with you, one useful approach to any staff communication is to remember not to allow your communication style to become too *introspective*. If you want to influence them, then relate to them in a way that makes *them* the important ones. Although you speak *for* the organization, staff members do not appreciate an unrelieved catalogue of information that focuses predominantly on your side of things:

- The organization is ...
- We have to make sure ...
- I will be able to ...
- Our service in the technical field is ...
- My colleagues in research ...
- Our organization has ..., and so on.

Any such phrases can be turned round to focus on the people, thus:

- You will find this change gives you ... you will receive ... you can expect that ....

A slight mixture is, of course, necessary, but a predominantly introspective approach always seems somewhat relentless. And it is more difficult when phrasing things that way round for you to give a real sense of tailoring what you say to the individual: introspective statements sound very general. Using the words *you* or *yours* (or similar) at the start of a message usually works well, and once this start is made, it is difficult for you to make what you say sound introspective.

Considering the message

Almost always, the emotional fear that can stop you even trying to communicate (as with asking for a pay rise or sorting out a difficult relationship) is not rational. It is more likely that you do not know the best way of asking the boss for more money, rather than that you do and do so badly.

Again, the route to success is often just thinking about what the problem really is and searching for a remedy. Given the 'to and fro' immediacy of much communication, the trick is not to rush in, but to deliver only a considered message and, as it said on the cover of *The Hitchhikers' Guide to the Galaxy,* 'Don't panic!'. Too often, people rush into saying something instantly when there would be no harm at all in saying 'Let me think about that for a moment'. In the moment that follows, you may be surprised how much consideration your brain can bring to the matter.

Summary

Any difficulties with communication, and the lack of or negativity of response that results, quickly have you feeling inadequate. You should take comfort from the overriding truth that communication is *inherently* difficult (just listen for a while to any group or around an open-plan office). If you stumble because you do not really understand why this is so, and what can help make communications flow smoothly, then don't knock yourself out – just resolve to learn more about it.

The other truth flowing from the inherent difficulty of communicating is that doing it successfully needs some thought (remember the old saying about engaging the brain before the mouth) and some planning. Often, the difference between what falls on stony ground or actually causes upset is just a little thought and a few words differently selected.

Knowing that you understand communication in a way that will help you do it successfully will itself give you confidence.

Fact-check (answers at the back)

1 What is the main reason why communicating is difficult?

a) It presents inherent difficulties (that can be negated) ❏

b) I am inherently bad at it ❏

c) Actually, it's easy ❏

d) People don't like me ❏

2 What topics make networking conversations go best?

a) Religion ❏

b) Politics ❏

c) Death ❏

d) FINE: family, interests, news and employment ❏

3 Why is getting people to pay attention difficult?

a) They are not interested in me ❏

b) They are not interested in what I say ❏

c) Paying attention is inherently difficult (and can be combated) ❏

d) They are just perverse ❏

4 What will most readily boost confidence in communicating successfully?

a) A stiff drink ❏

b) Understanding (and using) the psychology of communication ❏

c) Not doing it ❏

d) Shouting ❏

5 Communicating is made easier by what?

a) Speaking off the top of your head ❏

b) Putting your message over at great speed ❏

c) Thinking (preparing first) – engaging the brain before the mouth ❏

d) Being extremely brief ❏

6 How can you make things clearer?

a) By signposting what is to come ❏

b) Through sign language ❏

c) By using lots of jargon ❏

d) By constant repetition ❏

7 What sort of logical sequence works best?

a) Alphabetical order ❏

b) Largest to smallest ❏

c) A sequence chosen to make sense to the other person ❏

d) Random ❏

8 Which word, used regularly, enhances good communication best?

a) Me ❏

b) You ❏

c) The organization ❏

d) Them ❏

9 Which statement is the truest?
a) Emails are quick and easy to use ❏
b) Emails are damaging to communication ❏
c) Emails should always be well considered ❏
d) Emails can use mainly standard phrases ❏

10 What's a good phrase to use to buy some thinking time?
a) Hold on, not so fast ❏
b) Let me think about this for a moment ❏
c) I must go to the bathroom ❏
d) Let's pause ❏

CHAPTER 14

A foundation of knowledge and skill

Whatever you must do, it has already been made very clear that a prime promoter of confidence is that you know you have the knowledge and skill to do it. This has been shown through example and is something surely that every reader can relate to from their own experience. For example, driving a car is certainly a complex skill, and if you can do this, I bet you went through a stage of virtual despair when you were convinced that you would never get all the actions you had to take co-ordinated together. And yet millions of people move past that stage and drive successfully – once they know what to do and have had sufficient practice.

Because an utter lack of confidence in doing something can be overcome and transformed into comfortable performance, and even relegated to habit you don't even think about (though please drive carefully!), you need to both assess your skills and take action to acquire the skills you need, and then keep up to date. This needs some thought and some initiative. Knowing how much it can improve your confidence must be an incentive.

The best confidence builders

It should now be clear that having a good understanding of something, then developing skill in doing it, are the best confidence builders of all. Getting and remaining in this position is an ongoing process: as Henry James said, *Experience is never limited, and it is never complete.* To pursue this thought, you need to assess how exactly your development should proceed. Doing this, and implementing a plan flowing from the analysis, can prove to be one significant, ongoing confidence-building exercise.

It is worth thinking this through in a systematic way and, of course, doing so honestly; deceiving yourself and ignoring gaps in your knowledge or skills will not help either performance or confidence. Remember that development can:

- improve your knowledge
- develop your skills
- change your attitudes.

With that in mind, consider the thinking involved as a ten-step process:

1 **Identify the requirements of your present job in terms of knowledge, skills and attitudes** – you need to be honest about this and think broadly about it (and it is clearly easier if you have a precise job description).
2 **Identify your own current level of such knowledge, skills and attitudes** – look at how well you are currently equipped to perform in the job.
3 **Identify any additional factors indicated as necessary in future because of likely or planned changes** – in today's dynamic business climate there are likely to be some of these.
4 **Consider and add any additional aspects that a long-term view demands** – this can look as far ahead as you wish, but realistically should concentrate on the short/medium term.
5 **Set priorities** – note what needs to be done (there may well be more than it is realistic to change very quickly) and then set clear priorities to help you make progress – in this context things linked to your greatest lack of confidence.

6 **Set clear objectives** – always be absolutely clear what you are trying to do and why.

7 **Consider the timing** – in other words, decide when any development might take place, and this in a busy life means one thing at a time, and perhaps at a slower pace than you would ideally like.

8 **Implement** – do whatever is necessary to complete the development involved. This could be very simple: you doing something that you can control. Or it could involve discussion and debate with others (e.g. your line manager) to get agreement about the need, and to committing the necessary time and money (for instance, to attend a course).

9 **Evaluate** – this is important. Many people forget to really think through how useful and relevant something, like attending a course, has been. A little review can ensure much better linking to your real job and make future tasks more manageable.

10 **Assess against the job/career factors** – as well as evaluating general usefulness of anything done, it is useful to match its effect on both current tasks and future career plans.

Then you are back to the beginning again. The process is a continuous cycle, something where regular review is necessary, if not month by month then certainly year by year. Next, you need to relate this to a plan and then think about the actions that are required to see it through.

Have a self-development plan

In today's dynamic world, development must be a continuous process. There will be new skills you need to acquire during your career and perennial skills to be kept up to date. If you are with an organization that has a sound development policy, the thinking needed here may well be prompted by what action is available for you. If not, or if what is done is (in your view and for your needs) inadequate, then you will need to initiate more. You need a plan. Not something cast in tablets of stone that stretches into the future and is unchangeable, but a rolling plan, something that sets out immediate actions or intentions clearly, and an outline for the longer term. The detail of this will have to change as events unfold, and you must adjust to changing circumstances and needs. To relate this to the example of presentation, to help with this and boost confidence too, you might:

- read a book about it
- request and arrange to go on a course
- arrange to do more (yes, for practice)
- work with a mentor to help your preparation and evaluate your progress.

Just knowing you have some of this arranged, and believing it can boost confidence (even ahead of the development activity taking place), will help.

When you have thought this sort of thing through and made some commitments, trust your judgement. There is a lovely line in the film *Loch Ness* when the monster-hunting scientist tells a little girl claiming to have seen the famous beast that he'll believe it if he sees it. No, she tells him, you can only see it if you believe. Trust your judgement – believe that what you have arranged *will* help and your confidence can get an immediate boost.

The options in terms of action are several:

- The organization may suggest something (e.g. attendance on a course).
- You may want to suggest something to them.
- You, or they, may want to amend or adapt an original suggestion.
- You may conclude that whatever the company does, you will do more to meet your own personal objectives, including working in your own time.

The permutations are, of course, many. The key thing is that you regularly devote a little time to considering what you feel would help (for example, the company will be more inclined to spend money on things that have a reasonably short-term impact for them, while you may want to look further ahead).

TIP *Keep your personal plan – which will have more formality if it is in writing – up to date. Checking it and updating it regularly should be a source of confidence as you remind yourself of what you have planned and fixed and how it will help.*

There is an important link here with any company job appraisal (or performance assessment) scheme, which you find yourself taking part in – many organizations have their own schemes. Some consist of just an informal annual meeting. Others are more formal and more regular. Such schemes, if they are good, are very much to be commended and, well handled, can be a catalyst to both development and raising confidence. After all, the focus of an appraisal should be on making things go well *in the future*. They offer an opportunity to link your personal plan with that of the organization for which you work. With the support and approval of your immediate boss, you will probably find you can do more that will benefit your current job (and the tasks it entails) and help yourself proceed more confidently into the future as well.

Although the details are beyond the brief here, it is worth emphasizing that appraisals should be a major source of information and confidence building. This should not be something you regard as being 'done to you'. Prepare for such meetings, know what you can get from them, and help your manager make them work. How to get the best from them may be worth some study.

Having a development plan really works. Creating and maintaining one should not be regarded as a chore. If you take a moment to keep your thoughts straight about this area, you will be able to action more of what you want, and better able also to take advantage of circumstances. Consider some of the following simple development options.

Read a business book regularly

As I make my living, in part, by writing, this may seem like a plug, but reading business books is certainly among the simplest forms of development and a good deal can be learned from them. It takes some time, but is also something that you can allocate to certain moments when perhaps time would otherwise be wasted. Such time includes travelling; and I know more than one salesman who always carries a business book to read in those sometimes long moments he regularly spends in his customers' reception areas.

The first rule is to make it a habit. Always have such a book 'on the go' (even if it takes you a while to get to the end) and keep watching for what is current in bookshops, by reading reviews in the press and getting yourself added to publishers' mailing lists.

The kind of book to concentrate on is one that links directly to your development need, like *How to write a report* or whatever. Your choice here may reflect immediate needs or something you wish to develop for the future. Remember, it may be useful to come at things in different ways. Constructive repetition will help you take in the message, so it is worth reading more than one title on certain topics. Other more general titles may be useful too, but informing yourself about something specific that you need to build up confidence about should be the priority.

This may seem a small point, but applied conscientiously its effect may be considerable. A book every quarter, for instance, is still quite an input of information over, say, five years of your career. Six a year is better still, and you can apply the same principle to a range of things, from technical journals to websites.

Attend a course

Courses, seminars, workshops – whatever word you use – can be very beneficial. Do not regard attending as a sign of weakness or be embarrassed about it. Remember that everyone attending a course is in the same boat and all want to know more about the topic. And in the long run, spending a couple of days on such an event is not too high a price to pay compared to what may be gained from them. Some employers will regularly give you the opportunity to attend both external courses or those set up and run only for their personnel. If not, you may want to prompt them. If you are making such suggestions, particularly to attend outside events, remember that you must put your case persuasively. Just ask to attend, even if some of the thoughts that come to their mind may be negative: *That's expensive* or *Once they have extended their skills a little more they will be likely to leave the organization.* So, tell them what *they* will get. Explain what more you will be able to do for them and for the organization; will you be more effective, more productive, and better able to save or make money? If so, explain how.

Choose carefully. If you make wild suggestions, something that clearly only benefits you in the long term, or ask to attend something every week, you are unlikely to get agreement. Make practical suggestions and get approval, and you perhaps create the right kind of precedent and habit. I remember once battling for three years for the budget and time to attend an annual conference in the United States. Once I had attended it and it proved useful, it rapidly moved to being a regular event. Certainly, the most important consideration is the course topic and content, but realistically there are other things to think about. Where is it being held, who is organizing it, speaking at it, and attending it?

One single new idea, or even one single existing idea (confirmed with sufficient weight to prompt you into action in some particular area), is all that is necessary to make this process worthwhile. At best, there is a great deal to be gained by it, with benefits going way beyond increased confidence. Under the next three headings, we investigate specific aspects of course attendance.

Getting the most from course attendance

It is said that you only get out of something what you put in. Certainly this is true of course attendance. First, once attendance is arranged, you should think through what you want to get from it. This will help you and the course tutor. I know my heart sinks if I ask people on seminars, which I conduct, why they are present and their only answer amounts to, *I was told to be here.* Never go to a seminar without a written note of your objectives and any specific questions you want to obtain comments on. Most trainers are happy to get a note of questions in advance, though in my experience this is rarely done. Such forethought gives you confidence, too, to ask something in front of a group; you will have thought it through and know it's a sensible point.

Thereafter, you need to think about how you will behave 'on the day'. If the programme is internal (in-company), you may know all the other participants and the whole tone of the event may be informal. If it is external, it can be a little more daunting to arrive in a room of participants knowing no one. Everyone is in the same situation, however, and the informal contacts and the comments and shared experience of your fellow participants may be an important part of your attendance (this is essentially similar to networking).

The checklist which follows sets out suggestions to course participants and makes, I think, some useful points about being open-minded and adopting an approach which is constructive. In view of the time and cost of attending such events, it is a great pity to walk away at the end with any key question still unanswered.

NOTES FOR DELEGATES

This manual contains all the basic details of this training programme. Further papers will be distributed progressively during the course, so that a complete record will be available by the last session.

This is *your* seminar, and represents a chance to say what you think – so please do say it. Everyone can learn from the comments of others and the discussion they prompt.

● Exchange of experience is as valuable as the formal lectures – but you need to *listen carefully* and try to understand other points of view if this is to work.
● Do support your views with facts in discussion, use examples and stick to the point.

- Keep questions and comments succinct – do not monopolize the proceedings, but let others have a say, so that various viewpoints can be discussed.
- Make points in context as they arise. Remember that participation is an attitude of mind. It includes listening as well as speaking, but also certainly includes constructive disagreement where appropriate.
- Make notes as the meeting progresses. There is notepaper provided in this binder. Formal notes will provide an aide-memoire of the content and coverage, so any additional notes should primarily link to your job and to action on your return to work. Even a few action points noted per session can act as a catalyst and help ensure that action follows attendance.

A meeting with colleagues, staff or your manager on your return to normal working can be valuable. It acts as a bridge between ideas discussed here and action in the workplace, and can make change more likely.

It will help everyone present if you wear your name badge, respect the timetable, and keep mobile telephones and pagers switched off during the sessions.

This is an opportunity to step back from day-to-day operations and consider issues that can help make your job more effective. Be sceptical of your own operation, challenge ideas, remain open-minded throughout, and actively seek new thinking that can help you to prompt change and improve performance.

Note: here also you may find listed any necessary 'house rules', the observance of which can improve the course experience for everyone attending.

It is important to adopt the right approach. Time at such an event goes by all too quickly, and it is easy to leave and then wish you had had the courage to ask something else. Try not to worry about what people will think. Sometimes you may feel others are all ahead of you in understanding. Usually they are not. A question postponed, because it seemed obvious and likely to make you appear stupid, actually (once asked) can prove to be a common question, which can lead into a very useful discussion for all.

Maximize course attendance benefits

The most important thing about any course you may attend is what happens after it is finished. Courses may be interesting, they may even be fun, but what really matters at the end of the day is the action that they prompt. So even more important than the notes you make before attending is the action plan you make afterwards.

For the most benefit, such a plan has to start at once. It is inevitable for most people that, if you are away for even a couple of days at a short course, you are going to have more in the in-tray afterwards than if you had not attended. The likelihood is that you will get involved in catching up with work and everything you learned on the course will be put on one side and forgotten. Yet the moment to start any action resulting from the course is the following day. Nothing later will do.

So, whatever else you do, take ten minutes on the day after attendance to list – in writing – the areas of action you noted during the programme. At least get them on your 'to do' list, whether they are things to think about, to review further or to take action; whether they represent things you can implement solo or things you will need support or permission for and must raise at the next appropriate meeting. If you do this much, with a systematic approach and an eye on the priorities, something is more likely to happen. If you miss this stage, the danger is not that you will do less but that you will do nothing.

 Early action is easier too, because you will be more confident of something while it is fresh in your mind. Putting things off (perhaps through lack of confidence) just makes something more likely to be difficult.

So, follow up your notes; do not just have good intentions, but make firm action plans. Consider also:

- Review and keep safe any course notes that were useful.
- Have a debriefing session with your boss, the training manager or whoever sent you. If they are convinced it was useful, then future requests may be that much easier to make and get agreed.

When you do this is worth considering. There cannot be much implemented action to report immediately, but your recall of the detail will be greater. Later on, you can review what you have done more realistically.

Thus two meetings may be worthwhile. If your company asks you to complete an assessment form about the course attended, always do so thoroughly and on time. They are useful to the process of deciding what training is used in the future. Not doing this may be seen as indicating you have no interest in training.

Just attending a developmental event is nearly always useful. If it is a well-chosen and practical one then it may be very useful; and if you go into the process with the right attitude and take the right action before, during and after the event, you will maximize the benefit that comes from it.

Continue learning – at a distance

Change, including technological change, affects almost everything in our lives, including education and training. What is called 'distance learning' is now widely available in many forms. This is a rather imprecise term that covers a range of rather different things, but the principle in all cases is similar – that of receiving some kind of formal training (including education resulting in a qualification) by working alone, linked to, but not actually attending, the establishment providing the tuition. These days this will often involve working online via the Internet.

The options are many and varied, and allow you to study part time while continuing to work full time and develop your career on the job front. You can undertake anything from an MBA to a short course covering some individual skill area. The form of the course will include conventional study, with things to read, but may also involve a series of other methodologies: videos, exercises, programmed learning and, in the best formats, the ability to complete projects and papers that are sent away and then receive individual critique and comment to help you through the whole exercise. Some courses do involve some group activity. Weekend sessions are sometimes used to fit this aspect in, without making it impossible for those working full time to attend.

The area is worthy of some investigation for anyone wishing to extend their learning. However, because of the profusion of material that has become available, there is, among excellent material and schemes, some that is frankly not so good. A good deal of work is involved in any lengthy distance learning course, so it is worth selecting what you do carefully, and there are also considerable differences in costs.

Having some continuing activity of this sort provides an ongoing confidence booster as you progressively work your way through something and benefit from so doing.

Take on new things

Make a point of taking on new things. Low confidence may steer you away from doing so, but experience and the range of your competence are both things that must be kept moving, like sharks which must keep swimming or sink. There is a temptation in many jobs to stick with the areas of work that you feel are 'safe', by which I mean where you do not have to stretch and where you are sure of what you can do. This is almost always a mistake. Allowing that if you spread your learning too wide you may end up with some expertise across too broad a front rather than a real strength in particular areas, an ongoing objective to broaden your range of skills, expertise and experience is likely to be helpful to you in the long run. The result will be a more confident and competent you.

Monitor how this goes, record what you do and succeed at something new. It can provide additional job satisfaction and your confidence will grow as you make your new skill a habit – I did that okay, so now why not this?

You never know what the future holds and, at the risk of my sounding very old, it is an easy mistake when young to rule out possibilities on the grounds that they are too difficult or challenging. I know from my own experience that skills which have helped me more recently in my career formed no part of my expertise early on; indeed, some were things I feared. With hindsight, I do not think I always predicted what would be useful in this sort of way. So, next time something new is on offer, something that will stretch your powers and even where the outcome is somewhat more certain, think very carefully before you allow yourself to say *I can't*, decide to avoid it or say *No*. You could be taking on something that will kick-start your abilities and your confidence.

Confidence and competence

A prime cause of low confidence is a lack of understanding or ability. Usually both can be acquired and knowing that you have the necessary competencies is a solid foundation to achieving what you want. Of course, even things you are familiar with may worry you to some extent. Boosting confidence may not remove fears, but it will reduce them and allow you to focus on the positive. For example, for all my experience with training and making presentations, standing up in front of a new group always has a daunting quality. A good start helps disperse it; so, too, does knowing that what you are doing is well prepared and deploys the techniques that make such a thing work well.

Summary

Development will not just happen. Take the initiative, base what you do on sound analysis and make it make a difference to your work, your confidence and even your career. In doing so, I believe that you will find the whole exercise confidence building in a number of ways. It is good to have:

- assessed your skills portfolio and know the state of play
- a plan of development activity on the go and in the diary
- plans to keep you up to date and help you tackle new things
- actually done and completed activities scheduled (albeit step by step)
- experience of having undertaken development of some sort that manifestly makes you able to tackle something with more confidence and do it better.

Every stage here can build confidence.

Whatever you must do, you will do it better, more easily and more confidently with a firm foundation of knowledge and skill. Recognize this fact, address the issue and your confidence will surely rise.

Fact-check (answers at the back)

1 What gives you confidence for many a task?

a) Knowing how to go about it ❑
b) Knowing little about it ❑
c) Guessing what might work ❑
d) Giving up before you begin ❑

2 What is the timescale for development?

a) Six months ahead ❑
b) An annual cycle ❑
c) A life-long process ❑
d) A moment now and then ❑

3 Significant useful formal development is possible on what?

a) Holiday ❑
b) A training course ❑
c) A train journey ❑
d) Wednesdays ❑

4 Added confidence is built through what?

a) Putting something off ❑
b) Practice ❑
c) Ignoring skill development ❑
d) Astrological prediction ❑

5 Progress is often best made in what way?

a) Stepping unprepared into the deep end ❑
b) Making a mountain out of a molehill ❑
c) By taking one step at a time ❑
d) Proceeding without thought ❑

6 How best do you maximize development time?

a) Just drop everything and do it ❑
b) Plan carefully and make use of flexible low-time methods (like reading a book) ❑
c) Accept that you just can't ❑
d) Alter your watch ❑

7 What's one thing that helps you get the best from a course?

a) Linking content and coverage to your needs ❑
b) Keeping quiet throughout ❑
c) Asking no questions ❑
d) Ignoring other participants ❑

8 What attitude to new things helps build confidence?

a) They are to be avoided ❑
b) They are opportunities ❑
c) I should stick to what I know ❑
d) They should be ignored ❑

Postscript

So where are we? Looking back over the seven chapters, we have examined the business of confidence in various ways and there is only a single conclusion to be reached. Whatever level of self-confidence you have comes from you.

You make it happen.

That said, there are a variety of (largely practical) things that help you do this. Various factors can act to strengthen both the level of confidence you have and also the level it appears to be to others. To end, I believe an old traditional story strikes the right note:

In medieval times, a baker in the King's household found himself condemned to ten years' imprisonment for some small misdemeanour, burning a cake perhaps. Languishing in his cell, he thought about his plight and he sent a message to the King promising that, if he were released, he would work day and night in the Royal stables and, within a year, he would teach the King's favourite horse to talk.

This amused the King, and he ordered the servant to be released to work in the Royal stables. The servant's friends were at once pleased to see him released, yet frightened for him too; after all, horses do not talk, however much training they get. 'What will you do?' they all asked. 'So much can happen in a year,' he replied. 'I may die, the King may die, or – who knows – the horse may talk!'

Who knows indeed; I'm sure he had no confidence in teaching the horse to talk, but he clearly saw it as a step forward (after all, he was no longer in a cell). I for one hope that by the time the year was up he had thought of another ruse to take him forward. The tale makes a good point – well, several good points – that link to our theme:

- Thought, analysis and planning (and perhaps creativity too) tend to lead to success, making a change to your level of confidence and your ability to achieve what you want.
- Confidence goes closely together with persistence; making sure it is positive needs working at.

Progress may sometimes be made only in steps. Just like the baker in the story above, there may not be a magic formula or something instantly applied that bestows instant change and thus instant confidence. But there may well be a series of steps, each of which takes you forward a little, and in so doing, makes whatever you are contemplating more able to be done, done well and without agonies of doubt.

Of course, for most of us there are some things that are beyond us, and perhaps always will be; I remain utterly without confidence that I will ever juggle with flaming torches. But there are many things that are within our capabilities to do and do well, but for which we need confidence. A good level of confidence is usually the result of consideration and action. It can make things possible, it can make things easier, and it can lift you from just coping into achieving excellence.

The process starts, as we have seen, with consideration. That consideration, and the results of it, become a habit which at best can boost confidence, in turn enhance performance, and, quite possibly, transform your life.

7 × 7

1 Seven key ideas

- Believe you can influence your level of confidence, and work practically at doing so.
- Take time to analyse your current behaviour and habits.
- Be aware of the power of habit: beware of retreating into bad habits and work actively to develop new good ones.
- Tackle negative factors individually and find practical solutions to help you move towards greater confidence.
- Identify areas where you lack skill and fill the gaps so that you don't have a shortfall that saps your confidence (and effectiveness).
- Cultivate an appropriate personal profile – having assessed what that should be.
- Take a systematic approach to working on any problem of confidence, and you *can* and *will* see improvement.

2 Seven of the best resources

- http://www.ted.com – The TED talks have become well known as effective idea spreaders, and it is a joy to see people having the confidence to give a talk in this context. The content is interesting and the range of examples of how it is done is something to take on board.
- http://www.wikihow.com – Though the information on broadly based sites needs careful assessment, this is a good example of one that addresses the issue of confidence.
- http://www.mindtools.com – If you want to develop specific skills to provide a firm foundation to confidence, a site such as this (focused on business skills) may be useful.
- If you want to come at things from a scientific viewpoint, there are many books about the mind aimed at the layperson; one such is *A mind for business* by Andy Gibson (Pearson, 2015). It is possible that understanding more about how the mind works may help you take a more analytical approach.

- http://www.mumsnet.com – A site such as this (providing advice, support and problem solving for mothers) may be useful if difficulties outside the workplace, in this example coping as a working parent, affect your situation.
- http://www.nhs.uk – A good site for medical information such as this one may be useful if a shortfall in confidence links to health issues such as the effects of stress.
- Remember that, as this text has made clear, your best resource is you. If you put phrases into Google about confidence you will locate a plethora of sites, all promising to make you confident overnight (and, in many cases, charging you for the privilege). Such sites should be treated with great care; there is no magic formula.

3 Seven things to avoid

- Letting negatives overpower you when you can take action to remove or minimize them.
- Believing that low confidence is unchangeable when it's not.
- Failing to recognize that there are usually practical solutions to seemingly intractable problems.
- Using an ad hoc approach: changing things needs a systematic approach.
- Becoming isolated: other people may be part of the solution.
- Not recognizing improvements: give yourself credit and build on successes, even modest ones.
- Thinking over-emotionally about difficulties rather than seeking practical solutions.

4 Seven inspiring people

- Dr Walter Doyle Staples, author of *Think like a Winner* (Heinemann Asia, 1991), on the value of positive thinking.
- J. K. Rowling, of Harry Potter fame: writing in cafes while an unemployed single mother, she was turned down many

times by publishers but persevered and eventually achieved success.

- Paul McKenna: the well-known hypnotist has a track record of helping solve a range of problems, including support to quit smoking; his book *Instant Confidence* (Bantam Press, 2006) offers techniques for building confidence.
- Dale Carnegie: his iconic book from 1936, *How to Win Friends and Influence People,* remains in print (Vermilion, 2006) and may be useful if only to show that lacking confidence is not a new issue.
- Anyone who has the confidence to give a TED talk designed to spread good ideas makes an inspiring example (see above).
- Any of the many how-to authors (including, dare I say, myself) who sets out information showing that apparently difficult tasks can be done if gone about in the right way (e.g. the notoriously seemingly difficult area of presenting).
- Above all, your own mentor, formal or otherwise: recruit such a person from friends, family, colleagues or work bosses, anyone who is able to give some serious help and inspiration to your endeavours.

5 Seven great quotes

- 'Courage is very important. Like a muscle, it is strengthened by use.' Ruth Gordon
- 'Every day, in every way, I am getting better and better.' Emile Coue
- 'The more I practise, the more luck I have.' Arnold Palmer
- 'Success doesn't come to you, you go to it.' Marva Collins
- 'It's amazing what ordinary people can do if they set out without preconceived notions.' Charles F. Kettering
- 'If you think you can, you can. And if you think you can't, you're right.' Mary Kay Ash
- 'If you want to do something, you find a way. If you don't want to do anything, you find an excuse.' Arab proverb

6 Seven things to do today

- Make a note of any problems with confidence you encountered during the day.
- Do the same for successes, even modest ones.
- Review them at the end of the day and link them to a plan.
- Create a note of what you must focus on curing or making still more effective.
- Put some priorities on your list, bearing in mind that you have to work on things individually.
- Make a link to something you have to do tomorrow that might cause you problems in terms of confidence.
- Believe that you are making a difference.

7 Seven trends for tomorrow

- The workplace will become more competitive.
- Pressure on time and resources will increase.
- The temptation to panic rather than work at building confidence systematically will be ever present.
- Sometimes you will feel you are going backwards rather than forwards; that's life.
- As you progress in your job, you will accrue more tasks that demand a level of confidence.
- Colleagues will experience increased pressure too and may volunteer less help; their support must be sought.
- Worked at systematically, your level of confidence *will* improve. You can make it happen.

PART 3
Your Assertiveness Masterclass

Introduction

Much has been spoken about the assertive communication style, not all of it complimentary! Many people confuse it with being aggressive, bamboozling others into submission and getting what *you* want, despite what *they* want. However, assertive communication is not domineering; it's just a means of saying what you mean, meaning what you say and allowing others to do the same.

Taking the decision to adopt *assertive* behaviour will mark the beginning of a new way of life: a way of life where you make your own decisions and choices without feeling guilty, and where *you* are in control, not those around you.

By working through some simple steps, and by testing the techniques out in a 'safe' environment, you will soon become confident in your new-found powers of assertion. You will be able to command the respect of others, achieve your personal and professional goals and raise your self-esteem.

The steps to assertive behaviour are:

- Understand the different styles of communication and the effect they have
- Identify your own style(s) of communication
- Know your own worth *and* the worth of others
- Be clear about your goals
- Be prepared to learn from your successes *and* failures
- Be flexible, and don't expect too much
- Learn to listen.

CHAPTER 15

Preparing the foundations

In this chapter we will prepare the foundations for developing assertive behaviour and learn the different styles of communication: passive, passive/aggressive, aggressive and assertive.

This is the beginning of a long journey but it will be one that you'll not regret as it puts you in the driving seat of your own life. This is the point – it is you who drives your life, not others, nor circumstances. You may make mistakes from time to time but, as your assertiveness skills advance, you'll develop the understanding and the resources to pick yourself up, brush yourself down, and start all over again!

There are two main tasks here. The first is to identify your own style of communication:

- passive
- passive/aggressive
- aggressive
- assertive.

Your second task is to know your worth:

- understand yourself
- accept yourself for the way you are
- decide to change – *if you want to*
- give yourself permission to succeed – *and fail.*

Communication styles

In order to understand ourselves, and why we don't behave assertively, we must first examine our current **pattern of behaviour**. We will not dwell on our failures; we will merely use them for information – and for our motivation to change.

Note your behavioural pattern in both your personal and professional life. It is these behaviours that determine the way people respond to you and it is these behaviours that determine the outcome of all your communication.

If you have difficulty identifying these patterns in yourself, ask a friend to help – but remember, they are doing you a favour so try not to get defensive.

For instance: are you very aggressive, uncompromising, fixed in your views, intolerant or impatient? Are you sarcastic, manipulative, dismissive, arrogant or superior? Are you acquiescent, apologetic, deferring, self-effacing or inferior?

It is interesting to note that most people who want to develop assertive behaviour fit into the last category – that of 'victim'.

What's your message?

People always treat you the way you 'ask' to be treated. Understanding what you are 'asking for' is half the battle. You may think you are using assertive language but the way in which you convey your message and the demeanour you adopt when you do so can counteract any intention to be assertive and can undermine your success in doing so. Try 'sitting on your own shoulder' and observing yourself in action. What are you doing? What are people's reactions to you? Are you getting your message across unambiguously? By observing yourself carefully, and honestly, you can identify the changes you'd like to make and make the changes that *will* make a difference.

Try not to feel hopeless at this point: from now on, everything is a positive step.

 TIP ··· *Remember, all it takes to change is a decision.*

Most people's behaviour patterns will demonstrate some characteristics from each of the four categories – **passive, passive/aggressive, aggressive** and **assertive** – depending on the circumstances of the communication. However, one category will most likely dominate your style. Read through the descriptions below and see which one holds true for you most of the time.

Passive

Passive behaviour is usually associated with the 'loser': one who is always backing down, giving in and being submissive. Apologies are rife in this mode of communication, as are reluctant agreements and negative statements about oneself. Passive behaviour conveys the message 'You're OK, I'm not OK.'

Passive/aggressive

Passive/aggressive behaviour is usually associated with the 'saboteur'. It is by no means overt, but the aggressive motivation is obvious nonetheless. The distinguishing features of this mode of communication are sarcastic comments, comments with double meanings and non-verbal signals such as mockingly gazing heavenwards. The underlying message is 'I'm not OK, you're not OK.'

Aggressive

Aggressive behaviour takes no account of the rights of others. Although this person may be perceived to be a 'go-getter' or one of life's 'winners', they are usually feared and their style encourages deceitful behaviour from others who would rather not face up to their wrath. The message conveyed by this person is 'I'm OK, you're not OK.'

Assertive

Assertive communication does not diminish or 'put down' another human being, it does not trespass on any human rights and it does not shy away from important issues. Rather, it encourages satisfactory communication where everyone's needs are met in the best way. The identifying characteristic of assertive behaviour is the use of 'I' statements. This indicates that the person communicating is taking responsibility for the message that is being conveyed. For example, 'I am not happy with this decision, I would like to discuss it further.' This form of communication is based on respect for oneself and others. It is driven by the belief that 'I'm OK, you're OK.' There are no losers.

A word of caution. Assertive behaviour does not necessarily mean that you get your way all the time. It does mean that the chances of getting to the best solution, with everyone's self-esteem intact, are significantly enhanced.

What's your communication style?

If you are unsure of your dominant style of communicating behaviour, work through the following simple questionnaire. Do not worry if your responses fall into all the different categories; identify with the strongest trend. The mix of responses will help you focus on the specific areas in your style that you may wish to change.

Broadly speaking, if most of your responses fall into the 'Sometimes' category, you may tend to be aggressive or passive/aggressive. If they fall into the 'Never' category, you are certainly passive. If you find that your responses are predominantly in the 'Often' column, you are well on the way to being assertive.

Communication style questionnaire

	Sometimes	Often	Never
1 I feel that I represent myself well in all communications and am respectful of others.	☐	☐	☐
2 My ideas are considered valuable and are often adopted.	☐	☐	☐
3 I am able to say no without feeling guilty.	☐	☐	☐
4 I am able to make complaints without losing my temper.	☐	☐	☐
5 I am able to give feedback to another without causing offence.	☐	☐	☐
6 I can communicate effectively in a group, allowing each member to be heard.	☐	☐	☐
7 I am able to ask for help.	☐	☐	☐
8 I am able to meet my own and others' needs.	☐	☐	☐
9 I can control my temper.	☐	☐	☐
10 People find that I am good at talking through ideas and problems.	☐	☐	☐
11 I am free from disabling stress.	☐	☐	☐
12 I am comfortable with who I am.	☐	☐	☐

Know your worth

We all have basic human rights:

- the right to choose
- the right to 'be'
- the right to be respected
- the right to make mistakes
- the right to say 'no'
- the right to ask for what we want
- the right to ask for what we need.

Understand your fears

It is often our fears that prevent us from developing assertive behaviour. What are yours? For example, they might be: 'I will lose my friends', 'I will make a fool of myself', 'No one will like me any more' or 'I will become irritating'.

Our fears are usually much larger than reality. Face them; they have a habit of shrinking.

Accept yourself for the way you are

It is very easy to put yourself down. We are our own worst critics. In the main, we are:

- **what** we are supposed to be
- **where** we are supposed to be
- **doing** what we are supposed to be doing.

Release all your disappointments and guilty feelings – forgive yourself. Everything that you have done and experienced has brought you to this point of change. *Everything is to play for.*

Decide to change – if you want to

In making the decision to change your behaviour, you may find it helpful to project forward in time and imagine how it would look, and feel, if you were in control of your communication. Compare this to how you feel now.

The power of 'imaging' or 'visualizing' cannot be over-stressed. It is a very useful tool for achieving your objectives, whatever they are.

By 'bringing to mind' or 'picturing in your mind's eye' your desired state, you are actually putting images into your subconscious that, ultimately, determine your behaviour. Your subconscious mind can work only in images; it does not understand timescales or conditions. Imagine yourself as you would like to be and your subconscious will work tirelessly to make this a reality. It cannot fail. Keep reinforcing the images time after time, using positive affirmations if this helps, and the old patterns will soon be obliterated and replaced with the new ones that you have chosen.

Old habits die hard, but they do die, with persistence and determination.

If you continue to behave as you have always behaved, people will continue to treat you as they have always treated you.

Give yourself permission to succeed – and fail

You are embarking on a journey of transformation.

Sometimes you will succeed on your terms; sometimes you will fail. Try to regard these occurrences with dispassion. They are merely learning experiences. It will not always be easy but it will be rewarding.

By now you should have identified your dominant style of communication and decided whether or not you are completely happy to continue in this vein.

If not, you may have come up with a conditional 'maybe' in response to the desire to change. This is good enough. It will drive your awareness and allow you to choose how to respond in different situations. There may be times when you want to submit, for instance. And there may be times when you feel the need to dominate. Being assertive is about the choice to communicate in the way you feel is most appropriate at the time. Being free to flex your communication style at will is part of being assertive.

If you decide to make changes in the way you communicate and in the way you are perceived by your colleagues, then proceed with enthusiasm; there is much you can gain from the following chapters.

Summary

To recap, the different communication styles are broadly divided into the following categories:

- passive
- assertive
- passive/aggressive
- aggressive.

These may sound pejorative descriptors but they do convey the underlying motivations of the person using this form of communication.

They are loosely associated with the following characteristics:

- victim
- achiever
- manipulator
- dictator.

Think about how these terms resonate with you. If you have a strong reaction to one or other of them, it may be worth exploring why this is so. Is it something you find distasteful because you feel it is a 'bit close to the truth'?! Try to objectify the way you analyse your own style and try to prevent yourself from judging or criticizing yourself.

Fact-check (answers at the back)

Think about the following questions and use them to build self-awareness and challenge yourself.

1. My dominant style of communication is...
   a) Aggressive ❏
   b) Passive/aggressive ❏
   c) Passive ❏
   d) Assertive ❏

2. I am able to be assertive...
   a) At will ❏
   b) Sometimes ❏
   c) Occasionally ❏
   d) Never ❏

3. I can flex between communication styles...
   a) When I feel it's appropriate ❏
   b) With preparation and effort ❏
   c) When I want to get something for myself ❏
   d) I can't change my style at all ❏

4. I think the assertive style of communication is...
   a) Dominating and imposing ❏
   b) Manipulative ❏
   c) Highly effective ❏
   d) For wimps! ❏

5. I believe one of the advantages of assertiveness is...
   a) You can always get what you want ❏
   b) You can establish good rapport ❏
   c) You can make others feel like losers ❏
   d) There are no advantages! ❏

6. When I need to make a customer complaint, I...
   a) Apologize profusely for being a nuisance ❏
   b) Get angry so that I can fire my complaint boldly ❏
   c) Establish the context, the concern and discuss a solution ❏
   d) Leave with the product I'm complaining about! ❏

7. When someone comes to me and asks me for advice, I...
   a) Give it freely and tell them what to do ❏
   b) End up taking on their battle ❏
   c) Encourage them to think about how they're going to deal with the situation ❏
   d) Avoid getting involved in the first place! ❏

8. There are situations when assertive behaviour is definitely not called for!
   a) This statement is true ❏
   b) Assertiveness is always called for ❏
   c) Communication styles are driven by external situations ❏
   d) Communication styles are not dependent upon situations ❏

9. I believe that my personality drives my communication style and...
a) I'm stuck with the communication style that matches my personality ❏
b) I'm an 'introvert' and can never be assertive! ❏
c) I can learn different communication styles regardless of my personality ❏
d) I have to change my personality before I can change my communication style ❏

10. If I could develop more assertiveness, I would benefit by...
a) Getting people to do as they're told by me! ❏
b) Being in charge of my own life ❏
c) Making sure I was in situations that call for assertiveness ❏
d) There would be no benefit to me ❏

CHAPTER 16

Creating winning scenarios

Creating winning scenarios is the foundation stone for being assertive and being in charge of your own life. This does not mean that you always get your own way, but it does mean that you will be satisfied that you have represented yourself assertively and can live happily (or acceptingly!) with the outcome.

This chapter's agenda is to bring you that little bit closer to being in control of your own life – asserting yourself in the way you choose. In order to achieve this, we will look at:

- 'winning' language
- positive affirmations
- creative visualization
- building self-esteem.

Those who are adept at turning on assertive behaviour are also quite able to observe their actions, talk themselves through their learning and test the effect of new behaviours. Self-knowledge is the key to taking control of our lives.

Observing, questioning and asking for feedback are vital if we are to succeed.

'Winning' language

'Winning' language is the language of assertive behaviour. It speaks more than mere words to those you communicate with and tells them that you are in control.

Those who recognize this quality in you will nonetheless be hard pressed to say exactly what it is that you are doing to give them this impression. Actually, it is a subtle combination of body language, mental attitude and verbal language.

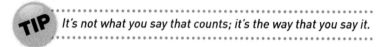

TIP *It's not what you say that counts; it's the way that you say it.*

The 'winning' qualities of an assertive communicator are:

- the use of 'I' statements
- direct, clear language
- an ability to demonstrate understanding and to empathize ('active listening skills')
- an ability to build rapport and maintain relationships
- good posture, voice and eye contact
- confidence in what they say – no self-effacing comments or profuse apologies!

Direct, clear language

Language can be a very inadequate and clumsy tool for communication. It can also be beautifully simple and, combined with reinforcing messages through the various physical channels of communication (body language), it can be extremely effective and evocative.

Here are some simple rules to help you practise assertive, 'winning', language:

- **Set the scene** by describing – very briefly – what you are referring to: 'When you called a meeting last Friday, I...'
- **Simplicity, clarity and brevity** are key to assertive communication. Do not ramble; you will lose the attention of your audience. Make your point quickly.

- **Take responsibility** for what you are saying. This is done by using the first person. Here are two examples, one negative and one positive: 'I am unhappy about the way this project is proceeding'; 'I'm delighted with the outcome of this meeting.'
- **Use repetition** if you feel that your message isn't getting across, but restructure your statement the second time.
- **Use silence appropriately** – it can say more than words. Don't be afraid of it; try it out.

Active listening skills

Active listening ranks highly in the league table of communication skills. It enables you to empathize with your audience and build successful relationships. Stated simply, active listening is listening with curiosity; or listening as if you've never heard the other person speak before. When you do this, you will be able to meter your own communication more precisely because you will have homed in on what others are saying without making premature judgements, assumptions or jumping to conclusions.

Good listeners do several things. They...

- **paraphrase** – briefly summarize what has just been said
- **ask 'open' questions** to elicit good information – 'how?' and 'what?' ('why?' can sound whiney or inquisitorial)
- **show an interest** – maintain good eye contact and prompt more communication by nodding from time to time, using encouraging words like 'Yes', 'Ah-ha' and 'Mmm'.
- **give feedback** – reflect back what they believe is being said.

Building rapport and maintaining relationships

Everybody needs to feel liked and valued. Others are likely to be generous in their dealings with you if you manage to develop a healthy rapport. It is a good investment *if done genuinely and generously.* If you do this as a manipulative technique, your motivation will almost certainly be exposed.

Developing good rapport is based on taking an interest in the other party, understanding and remembering what they have said and remembering to acknowledge significant events or achievements.

Body language also plays a part in developing rapport (more of this in Chapter 20).

It sometimes helps to write down others' activities as well as your own if you are forgetful. However, you will soon find that if you manage to develop active listening skills, you will start to remember things more reliably. This is because you will have been concentrating on what the other person has been saying, and you will have heard yourself summarize the main points.

Hearing yourself say something really does help you to remember. Talking to yourself is not a sign of madness; it is a valuable aide-memoire.

Good posture, voice and eye contact

It is somewhat galling to note that only about 7 per cent of what you say (the words you use) contributes towards the message you are trying to convey.

Much more of the message – 38 per cent – is carried in your voice. This includes tone, pitch, speed and the quality of your voice.

The remainder, some 55 per cent, is conveyed by your body – mostly the eyes. This is why communicating on the telephone or via email can be so misleading. Messages through these media have a tendency to take on a life of their own. Meaning can become distorted when the visual channel of communication is removed. Without the visual cues, it is sometimes difficult to interpret messages accurately and misunderstandings can occur. If read without the visible signals that accompany humour, for instance, messages can sound aggressive or sarcastic. It is important, therefore, to remember this and forestall any likely misinterpretation by signposting or symbolizing humorous remarks.

Good posture and an upright walk look good and convey confidence. Slouching or shuffling along gives completely the opposite impression. Try walking towards yourself in front of a mirror or catch a glimpse of yourself in a shop window. Notice the difference when you try to improve the way you move.

Assertive body language will be covered more fully in Chapter 20. There are several simple rules to consider for the time being:

- **Stand or sit proud** – taking up as little space as possible conveys lack of confidence or weakness
- **Gesture appropriately** – gestures can help to convey a message when used sensibly. Try not to overdo it, however; a lot of extravagant gesturing can be very distracting
- **Don't fidget** – this will make you appear nervous, as no doubt you are if you are fidgeting!

The use and quality of your voice will affect the other person's perception of what you are saying.

A high-pitched, whiney voice, for example, conveys a 'victim' message: 'I'm really rather weak and pathetic and I'm throwing myself on your mercy!' This style of voice can also sound spoilt and petulant.

By contrast, a loud, deep voice delivering words like machine-gun fire sounds incredibly aggressive.

Notice your own style of vocalization. Would you like to change it?

The optimum style – if there really is such a thing – is a calm pace, pitched mid-range with good intonation and clearly enunciated words. It's not always appropriate, of course, but it does for most eventualities.

To communicate assertively, you must maintain good *eye* contact. Aim to maintain almost constant eye contact while you are listening to another person. It is not so easy, indeed it can be actively disconcerting, to maintain constant eye contact while you are talking, so strike a comfortable balance between looking into and away from the other's eyes.

Your eyes will help in the expression of your message and they will no doubt be on the move much of the time. However you decided to use them, return your glance regularly to the other person's eyes throughout the delivery of your message to pick up how they are feeling about what you are saying.

It is worth noting that, if your body language is out of phase with your words, any hidden agenda will immediately become apparent – if not precisely what it is, at least the fact that you have one!

Confidence in what you say

Confidence is fine if you have it, but most unassertive people are sadly lacking in this department. However, here are some useful tips that you can learn to incorporate in your repertoire very easily.

- **Say what you mean and mean what you say** – be succinct and to the point.
- **Never apologize** – unless you sincerely mean it, then do it only once. (Notice how politicians and business leaders almost never apologize. Are we really convinced that they never make mistakes?)
- **Don't claim to be a fool to compensate for feeling a fool.** We often do this to prompt a contradiction. One of the dangers of this strategy is that you will be believed!

Positive affirmations

Used in the right way, positive affirmations can be enormously helpful. They are designed to retrain the brain to think about ourselves differently.

If we have a poor self-opinion (usually as a result of a series of childhood experiences), then as soon as we suffer a loss of confidence, we will return to these experiences and the feelings they engendered. It will take repeated effort to overcome this tendency and to replace it with something more positive.

For some people, positive affirmations can be very helpful in this process.

Positive affirmations are constant repetitions of a belief we wish to install in our brains to replace the less healthy beliefs we have grown up with.

Positive affirmations must be constantly repeated: if you think how long you have lived with your own negativity, just think how often you will have to repeat a desired belief before it will outweigh, and triumph over, the negative belief that is so firmly lodged in your brain.

How to reprogram your brain

Every time we have a thought, an electrical impulse sets off along a particular route through the brain. After this same thought has been through the mind many times, a physical path becomes etched in the brain. This will deepen with every thinking of the thought. If this happens to be a negative or undermining thought, it will colour what you believe about yourself and project to others. A new path must be created, therefore, that is even deeper, and easier, for the thought to follow – the path of least resistance. This can be achieved through positive affirmations.

Say your positive affirmations every day, like a mantra, and eventually you will find that you have reprogrammed your brain and installed a healthier belief.

There are several rules for designing positive affirmations.

- They must be in the present – 'I am...'
- They must *not* be conditional – 'When I... then I will...'
- They must *not* be undermined – hidden message: 'Who am I trying to fool with all this stuff anyway?!'
- They must be about *you*; nobody else.
- They must be spoken out loud – in private if you wish, but it is important to *hear* yourself say them.

Examples of good affirmations are:

- 'I can handle it.'
- 'I am professionally competent.'
- 'I am a valuable and capable member of the team.'

Creative visualization

Creative visualization is an extremely powerful technique for 'seeing' and 'fixing' your far-distant goals in your mind's eye and for planning and rehearsing the execution of the tasks that lead to the achievement of your goals.

As we have already said, the subconscious mind works in images, and when these are clear, it will work tirelessly to turn these images into reality.

What you need for effective creative visualization is a starting point, and an end point. That is to say, you need to understand your current situation completely and notice how far away you are from reaching your goal.

This is not a negative exercise; it is an unemotional and non-judgemental appraisal to enable you to take realistic, positive action and to measure your progress.

Picture your goal

Once you have isolated and fully understood your current situation, you must then form a very clear image of your goal and 'see', 'feel' or 'sense' it. Imagine it from a detached point of view, as if you were watching a film of yourself. Imagine it every way you can until you have a precise picture. Do not dismantle this picture; hold it clearly in your mind. Return to it regularly so that it becomes reinforced, time and again.

Set some time aside for this visualization so that you can build its strength over time. Do not try to hurry the achievement of your goal. Your subconscious will take the strain between your current situation and your desired state and will work to transform the first image into the second.

This method of achieving what you desire is infallible when done diligently. Indeed, you will probably have some personal experience of a time when you did this instinctively; when you desired something so badly, and so clearly, that you managed to bring it to reality.

Try it with big desires and small, but make sure that they are yours and no one else's. You will not be able to use this technique to manipulate others to do what you want!

Seven steps to creative visualization

In summary, here are the basic steps to effective creative visualization – a method that assertive people adopt without even thinking about it:

1 Notice your current situation and your distance from the goal.
2 Develop a clear image of your goal.
3 Breathe it, feel it, smell it, examine it from all angles.
4 Plan and execute your first and second steps only.
5 Do something else and leave your subconscious to work on the next stage undisturbed. Do not interfere, and do not undermine your images. The next steps will come to you in their own time.
6 Return to reinforce the image of your goal and observe your current position regularly – but not too often; the process needs time to work undisturbed.
7 Finally, trust the process; it will work.

Planning and rehearsing the tasks that have to be performed before reaching your goal are like 'mini' creative visualizations. Each step can be treated in the same way as those listed above for a major goal. Never plan more than two steps ahead, however, as the path your subconscious mind leads you down may be different from the one you expect. Follow it though: it will probably be more creative and more effective than your conscious mind.

If you have no clear idea of the tasks, don't worry; they will pop into your mind when the moment is right.

When you have executed the tasks in your mind's eye, you will find that the ease with which you perform them in reality will be truly remarkable.

TIP *Once you have a clear idea of your goal, everything you do and every decision you make will bring you closer to this goal.*

Building self-esteem

Self-esteem, as opposed to ego, is very difficult to recapture once it is lost. Self-esteem is a measure of how you value yourself, and it is built up from your first breath – or, as in many cases, it is destroyed by damaging experiences or relationships. It is one of the most helpful personal qualities that you can possess because from it stems the belief that you are worthy and able to succeed.

Sometimes people try to camouflage their low self-esteem by portraying excessive confidence. This is just 'noise' used to drown out their feelings of vulnerability and inadequacy. Don't be fooled or intimidated by this. Recognize it as a human solution to intolerable emotional discomfort. In this way, the threat of what appears to be a very confident person will disappear and you will be able to meet them on an equal footing.

Using some of the techniques described above can help to build self-esteem and confidence, but there is no substitute for knowing yourself and knowing the areas in which you are most likely to excel. There is nothing so powerful as a series of successes to lead you towards the establishment of a healthy self-esteem, so plan for them.

Here are some thoughts for you to consider when trying to raise the level of your self-esteem:

- **Let go of being responsible for those around you** – take responsibility for your own choices and feelings.
- **Don't take yourself too seriously** – once you lose your sense of humour, you have lost control.
- **Let go of your 'mad' self-perceptions** – in your rational mind you will know what these are.
- **Know yourself** – understand what is blocking your progress, usually fear of failure, or guilt that you are not good enough.
- **Nurture yourself** – give yourself treats.

Summary

This chapter offered some tips and techniques to enable you to be assertive and to be seen to be in charge of your own thinking and actions. Don't diminish the importance of these tools. If you practise them often, they will become second nature to you and you will soon reap the rewards of your efforts.

Soon your colleagues will notice that you are more decisive, effective and confident. This is excellent news for those who are managing or leading a team.

Remember the following. Project a positive image by:
- adopting 'winning language'
- using body language to reinforce your messages
- developing a positive mental attitude
- listening actively
- building rapport through empathy.

All this will lead to a healthy self-esteem.

Please note, there is no danger of losing your personality by doing these exercises. Your personal style will continue to distinguish you among your colleagues – even if they too are successful at being assertive. Indeed, you will feel freer to express your individuality as you become more comfortable with your powers of assertion.

Fact-check (answers at the back)

Think about the following questions and use them to build self-awareness and challenge yourself.

1. Winning language is the hallmark of assertive communication. When I use winning language, I should...
   a) Use lots of 'I' statements ❏
   b) Tell people of all my successes ❏
   c) Ensure I come out on top ❏
   d) Find ways to undermine others' efforts ❏

2. Active listening is a powerful tool for communication. When I listen actively I should...
   a) Look down and stay quiet ❏
   b) Get involved and anticipate what's about to be said ❏
   c) Ask open questions and remain curious about the answers ❏
   d) Remain actively involved in my own tasks or thoughts while listening to the other person speak ❏

3. I know I have built good rapport when...
   a) I have succeeded in getting my message across ❏
   b) The person I am talking to leaves with lots of tasks ❏
   c) I have convinced the other person of my point of view ❏
   d) I have learned something new about the person I'm communicating with and have shown empathy ❏

4. Good body language involves...
   a) Lots of gestures to underline the message I'm delivering ❏
   b) Sitting on the edge of my seat to show enthusiasm and interest ❏
   c) Gazing into the other person's eyes for the duration of the conversation ❏
   d) Alignment between the physical and the verbal message ❏

5. I use the technique of creative visualization when...
   a) I want to convince others of my good idea ❏
   b) I'm bored in a meeting and need entertainment ❏
   c) I want to define my own goals ❏
   d) I'm designing my PowerPoint presentations ❏

6. I use positive affirmations when...
   a) I want to reward someone for their good performance ❏
   b) I'm trying to convince myself that I have confidence ❏
   c) I'm wanting to transform the negative beliefs I hold about myself ❏
   d) I want to get my own way, no matter what else is going on ❏

7. Positive affirmations...
a) Work whether I believe in them or not ❏
b) Work when I put them far enough in the future to give them time to come true ❏
c) Work when I speak of them as if they are true now ❏
d) Don't really work – they're just a gimmick! ❏

8. Being assertive demands that I...
a) Take full responsibility for my decisions ❏
b) Get my own way ❏
c) Am never aggressive or passive ❏
d) Can be relied upon to fight others' battles ❏

9. Assertive people are...
a) Extraverted ❏
b) Loud and gregarious ❏
c) Bullies ❏
d) People with a healthy self-esteem ❏

10. The ability to be assertive is dependent upon...
a) My personality ❏
b) My levels of confidence ❏
c) A desire to dominate ❏
d) A belief in myself ❏

CHAPTER 17

Dealing with the 'negative'

We are constantly challenged by the stresses and strains of life. Finding strategies to manage these in a balanced way may well be the key to feeling happy, healthy and in control. Not only are these stresses and strains to do with the mechanics of living, but also they are to do with the people and situations we encounter. This could be anything from an overcrowded train of tired commuters on a hot day to a curmudgeonly shopkeeper who won't listen to our complaint. It is hard to recover from getting off on the 'wrong foot' but, with awareness and determination, it is possible to turn these events around and protect ourselves from getting swept up in other people's negativity.

In this chapter you will learn some techniques for negotiating your way through this most difficult of territories. To do this, we are going to look at:

- handling anger – yours and others'
- resolving conflict
- giving and receiving critical feedback
- saying no
- handling rejection and failure.

Handling anger – yours and others'

Most of us have an innate fear of anger. This may be a throwback to our childhood years when we felt powerless and vulnerable, or to our more primitive state when we perceived the threat of marauders or predators. When we encounter anger, therefore, our bodies tend to react by preparing us for 'fight or flight' – rapid heartbeat, rapid breathing, an increased supply of blood to the muscles – all as a result of the release of adrenalin into the bloodstream. This is the natural defence mechanism that 'kicks in' when we are threatened, and, at the right time, it is a life-saver. Sometimes, the same set of physiological responses results in a 'freeze' response when we stay stock-still, full of nervous tension, in the hope that the danger will disappear without it noticing us.

In most modern situations, however (on the road or at work, for example), these reactions are inappropriate and unhelpful, and it would benefit us if we learned to override them by reducing our fear and increasing self-understanding and self-control.

What is anger?

Anger is just energy. It will be directed by an angry person indiscriminately at objects or at people. It is like a heat-seeking missile looking for a target and it needs to be deflected, damped or avoided.

The thing to remember when *you* are on the receiving end of someone's anger is that it is not you that has precipitated the anger, but some action or stance that you have taken which has struck an unhappy chord with them. You are still an acceptable human being with rights. The anger you are fielding has risen as a result of the other person's conditioning – sometimes unreasonable conditioning. The same is true of your own anger, of course.

One method for dealing with another's anger – in all but pathological cases – is to remove your personal investment from the situation. View it dispassionately and observe its nature while letting it burn itself out. Don't fuel it.

Try to identify the source of the anger by listening carefully to what is being said – or SHOUTED. You may find that the angry person feels criticized, unimportant, thwarted, hurt – any number of emotions. This will give you a clue as to how to proceed.

If you are still struggling, ask questions to clarify your understanding but try not to be patronizing.

If you are in a public place and you feel embarrassed, just remember that you are the one in control at the moment and that it is the other party that is drawing attention to themselves – and they will, of course; we are a sensation-seeking society.

Once the heat has died down, communicate your understanding of the situation from the other's point of view and negotiate a way forward or a resolution.

If you feel that it is important to douse the anger rapidly, a useful technique to adopt is to match the energy being expended. This is done by making a loud proclamation such as 'I UNDERSTAND WHY YOU ARE SO UPSET and I would feel exactly the same if I were you, but...' As you proceed with your comment, you can drop the pitch of your voice and start to take control.

As an observer, you can often hear when the heat is rising in a situation because voices tend to increase in volume and pitch and words are delivered like bullets.

Try not to be tempted to use 'reason'. The purpose of reasoning is to get the other to agree that their behaviour is unreasonable, and nobody wants to do that when they are at fever pitch. This will obviously build resentment. Reasoning can be a passive/aggressive stance as it attempts to lure the other into a submissive position.

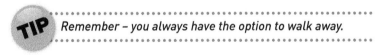

TIP *Remember – you always have the option to walk away.*

When you feel angry yourself, try the distancing technique. (Deep breathing or counting to ten helps some people.) You can observe your own behaviour quite dispassionately with practice. The observations you make of yourself will contribute enormously to your self-knowledge if you can do it honestly. You will reap untold rewards in your ability to communicate assertively if you can develop the presence of mind to lower your energetic response to a situation and ask yourself 'Are things going to be resolved if I get angry?' If the answer is no, try calming yourself and think of something else.

Here is a checklist for helping you to cope with anger:

- Distance yourself – don't take others' anger personally.
- Understand the cause of the anger by listening and observing carefully.
- Say little or nothing until the anger has died down.
- Respect yourself and the other party; you still both have rights.
- Once a certain degree of tranquillity has been achieved, demonstrate understanding by acknowledging the other's viewpoint – not the same thing as agreeing with it (don't use reason).
- Negotiate a way forward.
- If all else fails, walk away. This is another way of respecting yourself.

Resolving conflict

For the purposes of clarity, conflict is separated from anger, although one can sometimes lead to the other.

Conflict can be invisible, insidious and elusive, particularly with those of the *passive/aggressive* persuasion. It can lead to an impasse, a block which is extremely difficult to move. We have seen many such conflicts in the industrial quarter with unresolved disputes leading to the destruction of organizations or an entire industry.

Conflict can also be clear, reasonable and helpful. Used positively, it can sharpen the mind, increase understanding and lead towards a very satisfying and creative solution.

Many of the techniques for dealing with conflict are similar to those used for dealing with anger. The issues may be more complex because the two opposing positions are often well thought out and rehearsed in advance. The goals of the two parties may at first appear totally different and incompatible. This is rarely the case in reality, however.

Here is a checklist for resolving conflict:

- Establish the desired outcome and priorities for both parties.
- Acknowledge and appreciate the other's position.

- Discuss the points of mutual agreement to establish rapport.
- Compromise on issues that are not central to the desired outcome.
- Identify and clarify those points that are left unresolved.
- Delve for deeper understanding by questioning thoroughly and listening carefully.
- Negotiate a resolution or agree a plan for the next step.

Giving and receiving critical feedback

This is always difficult territory. We usually give critical feedback badly because we are not very good at receiving it.

Giving critical feedback

Giving early critical feedback prevents a bad situation developing into dreadful one.

Here is a guide to giving feedback which may be helpful:

- Be considerate and, above all, be private.
- Don't 'pussyfoot' around – have confidence in what you want to say.
- Take responsibility for the feedback; don't do it because you have been cajoled into doing so and don't base it on rumour or hearsay.
- Make sure that the feedback is based on the behaviour you would like to see changed, not on the personality of the individual.
- Use positive body language (see Chapter 20).

Critical feedback may be given on the back of what is called a 'positive stroke'. For instance: 'I liked the way you handled that call and it might portray better customer service if you used their name.' This is often called the 'feedback sandwich' and, because it is so well known, people often wait for the 'kick' after they've received praise. Try to be sensitive to the individual you're giving feedback to and avoid being formulaic.

Receiving critical feedback

None of us enjoys receiving critical feedback. Indeed, most of us are looking for a confirmation that we are liked and accepted the way we are. However, if we put our vulnerabilities behind us for a moment, it really can be very helpful to hear how others perceive our behaviour or our work. We are then in a better position to make the desired adjustments – if we feel that they are valid.

Sometimes we may feel that the feedback is unfair. If this is the case, try to retain your dignity, state your disagreement and move on. Try not to argue for yourself; you will not convince anybody and you will hand your power straight to the person giving the feedback.

Here is a quick checklist for receiving critical feedback:

- Attend carefully to what is being said.
- Judge for yourself if it is valid; if not, disregard it and move on.
- Do not argue; you will only draw attention to your vulnerabilities.

If you are unfortunate enough to be criticized in public, a dignified reaction will elicit a disproportionate amount of respect from observers while the standing of the person giving the feedback will be severely diminished.

Saying no

We are rewarded with masses of praise when we acquiesce to another's request. This is not surprising as, in doing so, we have taken responsibility for somebody else's task or burden. By comparison, the emotional reward for saying no is somewhat barren.

We are often made to feel guilty and mean when we say no. This is a form of manipulation, a last-ditch attempt to make us change our mind and co-operate after all.

Dealing with this requires a particular kind of resilience. It helps if you really do believe that it is perfectly acceptable to make choices according to your own set of priorities, values and beliefs. This does not mean to say that you need always say no just to prove that you are in control of your own decisions. What it does mean is that you *can* say no.

Here is a list of useful tips that you can use when wishing to say no:

- Really mean it – if you don't, it will probably show and the person making the request will probe and prise until you change your mind. You do not have to give reasons for saying no.
- If you want to think about your response, say 'I will get back to you,' or 'I need some time to think about this.' This is your right – who is doing whom the favour?
- Don't milk the apology, wring your hands anxiously or overplay the excuses.
- You may be able to offer a compromise solution.

Handling rejection and failure

It is very difficult to separate rejection and failure because they are so intrinsically linked. They can bring despair and dejection, a feeling of foolishness, of being unworthy and so many other negative emotions.

Accepting that this is the case for so many of us, the healthy thing to do is to learn from these emotions, work with them and view them from a more positive perspective. This may sound trite and unhelpful, but with a bit of determination your perceived failures and consequent feelings of rejection will disappear into humorous anecdotes: 'Did I tell you about the time when I asked the Chairman if he was authorized to be in the building?!'

Try not to confuse your self-worth with one fleeting, albeit negative, experience. To be too harsh on yourself is unhelpful and, at a time like this, you need all the forgiveness and understanding you can get – even if it has to come from you.

One useful tactic you may like to employ to avoid the feeling of total defeat is to make a series of contingency plans. In thinking through possible, probable or even improbable scenarios that are likely to tarnish your reputation, you can spend some useful time preparing coping strategies. In this way, you can redeem yourself rapidly and divert the destructive feelings of rejection and failure into a more positive arena.

Don't dwell for too long on the negative; you may find you have creatively visualized something you would rather not come true.

These tips may be helpful as part of your survival package:

- Try not to link your own worth to negative experiences.
- Never be short of alternatives – develop contingency plans.
- Know that the significance of negative experiences changes with time.
- Try to distil some learning from the experience – it will protect you next time.
- Be kind to yourself.

The whole gamut of negative experiences and emotions are uncomfortable at best but, having conquered your fear and having successfully dealt with a few difficult situations, you will soon re-educate your reflex reactions to co-operate with the way you would rather be.

Developing a balanced view on these matters will make you much stronger because you won't be trying to avoid issues; instead, you will be making choices and following them through confidently.

You are not invincible, so try not to get over-zealous in your enthusiasm to tackle negativity. There definitely are situations that are best avoided because there can be no victor in their resolution. Anger that turns to physical violence is an irrational act and therefore cannot be approached in a rational way. In these circumstances, self-preservation is the key and, if your body prepares you for flight – do it!

Summary

In summary, what we have been dealing with is 'negative energy'. When this is understood, fear can evaporate, and this energy can be transformed into a positive outcome for everyone. Negative energy is frightening and difficult because it 'pings' us back into a vulnerable position and gives rise to fears of survival. These primitive responses are hard-wired into our brains and still operate, whether the trigger is imaginary or real.

Being able to identify with another human being caught in the grip of fury may enable us to empathize with their plight, and in so doing enable us to behave generously.

It is worth noting that behaving assertively, as you would be if you managed to control an angry exchange without destruction to either party's, or your own, esteem, is not always the 'right' solution. Being passive may be the best response if, for instance, you're being mugged. Or dominating aggressively might suit an emergency situation, where people need direction from someone in charge.

Being assertive means that you can make choices about how and what you communicate. It puts you in the driving seat of your own relationships and allows you to remain robust and confident – yet not insensitive. You can achieve this 'healthy self-esteem' if you're prepared to be conscious and make some disciplined changes to your behaviours.

Fact-check (answers at the back)

Think about the following questions and use them to develop your skills in managing negative energy.

1. When someone is angry, it's best to...
   a) Reason with them ❏
   b) Shout back with equal ferocity ❏
   c) Submit to their power and escape at the earliest opportunity ❏
   d) Stand firm and try to understand what's going on for them ❏

2. When someone is angry with me, I should...
   a) Freeze and submit to their request ❏
   b) Fight and endeavour to win the battle ❏
   c) Flee from the situation in the hope that they'll calm down ❏
   d) Sum up the situation and respond in a way that will lead to a win/win ❏

3. Here is a checklist for resolving conflict. Which is the *incorrect* item on the list?
   a) Acknowledge and appreciate the other's position ❏
   b) Compromise or relinquish issues that are not central to the desired outcome ❏
   c) Seek deeper understanding by questioning and listening thoroughly ❏
   d) Ensure that you retain the 'upper hand' by withholding your trump card ❏

4. When you wish to give critical feedback, how should you back up your comments?
   a) Canvas others' opinions and add these to your feedback ❏
   b) Remind people of their ingrained and persistent personality faults ❏
   c) Wait until the situation becomes intolerable and then launch your arsenal ❏
   d) Base it on your observations only and focus it on the person's behaviour ❏

5. When you say no, what should you be aiming to feel?
   a) Guilty ❏
   b) That you're being unreasonable ❏
   c) That people will dislike you ❏
   d) Fine saying no ❏

6. When you go into a situation that you feel may be 'negative', how should you prepare yourself?
   a) Just go in and hope for the best ❏
   b) Go in guns blazing to ensure that no one gets the better of you ❏
   c) Think about the tensions and tell yourself that they are not personal ❏
   d) Try to keep as quiet as possible in the hope that no one notices you ❏

278

7. When you receive challenging or negative feedback, how should you respond?
a) Tell the person who's giving you feedback to mind their own business ❏
b) Thank the person and tell them you'll think about what they've said ❏
c) Argue your case. No one is going to criticize you and get away with it! ❏
d) Say sorry and that you'll not do it again ❏

8. When handling someone's anger, it is best to...
a) Shout at them to calm them down ❏
b) Reason with them and get them to see they're wrong ❏
c) Appraise the situation and see if you can discover what's causing the problem ❏
d) Leave them to it until their anger burns out ❏

9. When you feel rejected, you should...
a) Blame yourself for being 'wrong' ❏
b) Tell yourself the other person doesn't know what they're doing ❏
c) Try to retain your self-esteem and recognize this is not to do with 'you' ❏
d) Tell them you don't want to be included anyway! ❏

10. Active listening can be done while...
a) Texting friends ❏
b) Emailing work colleagues ❏
c) Being curious about the other person's situation ❏
d) Interrupting enthusiastically to build the conversation ❏

CHAPTER 18

Creating a positive impression

There are many possibilities for making the best of yourself and creating a positive first impression. In this chapter we will be examining some of the techniques that can be adopted to achieve this. They include:

- creating a positive first impression
- developing assertive interviewing skills
- building confidence.

In order to create a good first impression, you will need to manage the perceptions of others. These will be formed through the persona you project – which may, of course, be light years from the one you revert to in private.

It is worth remembering that when people form a perception of us they act as if this is the truth. Once formed, this 'truth' is seldom revisited and reviewed. Rather, it is taken on board as fact and the 'impression-holder' orientates their behaviour towards us accordingly. If we have inadvertently created an unhelpful or misleading first impression, this can give us a long-term problem as people are often reluctant to discuss their initial thoughts about us.

If we attempt to 'manipulate' the perceptions people have of us, it may be hard to sustain – and we may feel alien to ourselves as we are not being authentic. We will now explore this phenomenon further.

Creating a positive first impression

The first opportunity we have to create a good impression is at an initial meeting or during an interview for a job.

It is undoubtedly true that human beings are judgemental. We generally look for similarities in those we are meeting for the first time because this reinforces us as individuals and gives us common ground to explore. We are less tolerant of those who take diametrically opposed views to our own or who live by a different set of values.

When meeting someone for the first time, you can be absolutely sure that they have this lightning ability, as you do, to sum you up in something under ten seconds and be utterly convinced that their powers of perception are completely accurate! You have only these very few seconds, therefore, to create the impression of your choice.

Very often our first impressions are proven wrong in the long run. However, it does take a huge amount of time and effort to dismantle a first impression and substitute it for a more accurate one.

Let us now examine the many factors that go in to creating a first impression:

- appearance
- size, mobility and national origin
- handshake
- gait, body language
- voice, accent, speech pattern, speech impediment, tone, etc.

Judgements will be made on a combination of some or all of the above factors before we start saying anything of consequence.

We will look at these factors one by one.

Appearance

In order to decide how to make your impact, you must first determine what impression you wish to create. An obvious point, perhaps, but often neglected.

Here are some factors to consider when planning your impact at a job interview:

- the culture of the target organization
- the nature of the job
- the note you wish to strike with your clothes:
  - a large amount of bright **colour** can be overpowering
  - **style** can be appropriate/conventional/unconventional
  - **accessories** – shoes, ties, scarves, hairstyle, hair colour, jewellery, bags, belts and briefcases all contribute to the overall impression.

If you decide to create the image of a non-conformist – beware. Although this gives you greater freedom and enormous scope for painting a very individualistic picture, it is a high-risk strategy, especially in a conventional environment. The question to ask yourself is: How seriously do I want this job?

Size, mobility and national origin

There is very little most of us can do about our size, degree of mobility or origin. Unfortunately, it is undeniable that these factors strongly influence a first impression, so be aware of them and quickly remove any concern that the interviewer may have.

If you think that you may encounter some form of prejudice, be proud and be direct. This is very disarming and will soon put the issue (if any) into the background, leaving you with the upper hand. It will also create a relaxed atmosphere for further discussion. This is an essential step to take if there is any possibility that the interviewer will perceive a physical barrier to your suitability for the job, so deal with likely issues honestly and without apology, then move on.

Here are some examples that illustrate how an interviewee can remove prejudice at the outset:

- 'Although you can see I am very large, I would like to reassure you that this does not hinder my performance.'
- 'I would like you to know that my physical restrictions have enabled me to develop other skills to an extremely high level.'

Handshake

Within a split second of meeting someone for the first time, we are there, proffering our hand as the best etiquette has taught us. There are many varieties of handshake, some desperately disconcerting, others businesslike and almost unremarkable. The conclusions we draw from a handshake are out of all proportion to its significance. However, getting it wrong puts a large obstacle in the way of creating a good impression.

We have all experienced the limp handshake... the 'tip of fingers' handshake... the ferocious 'bone-breaker'... the sweaty handshake... and the 'won't let go' handshake...

The model way to shake someone's hand is to:

● offer an open hand, your palm facing towards theirs
● look the other party in the eye and smile
● take a firm hold of their hand and shake it up and down once or twice (no more)
● release.

Gait, body positioning

Body language will be dealt with in much greater detail in Chapter 20, but as we are on the subject of first impressions, it is necessary to touch on the matter here.

How you enter a room, move towards a greeting, walk or sit, all go towards forming an early impression.

Assertive behaviour can also be demonstrated non-verbally in the following three ways:

1 moving assertively (including the handshake)
2 sitting assertively
3 use of the voice (yes, it is considered to be a non-verbal mode of communication).

Moving assertively: when preparing to enter a room, knock firmly on the door and wait for a response. Once you have been asked to 'come in', open the door fully, step in and close the door behind you. Walk confidently into the room towards the greeting, hand at the ready.

Don't be timid. If you tap lightly on the door, no one will hear and you won't be asked to 'come in'. Then you will probably be anxious and uncertain – you have sabotaged yourself.

If you creep round the door, hug the wall and shuffle hesitantly towards the greeting, you will appear insipid and lacking in confidence. This is typical passive behaviour. However, if you stride in, throw your briefcase down and sit without being invited to do so, it will not appear confident, as you might hope, but aggressive.

Sitting assertively: sit straight and tend to lean slightly forward. This gives the impression of meeting someone part way on their territory and looks interested and enthusiastic.

If you slouch or lean back on your shoulder blades with your bottom pivoting on the edge of the chair, you will appear uninterested and disrespectful.

Contrarily, if you sit huddled and small with your toes pointing together and your hands gripped firmly between your knees, you will look childlike and helpless.

Voice: there are many dimensions to your voice, most of which are difficult to control, such as a national or regional accent, a speech impediment or the quality of your vocal cords.

Some of the vocal properties that you can control are the clarity of your speech, the pitch, the tone and the speed of delivery.

The words that you use, the grammatical patterns you favour when constructing your sentences, and the way you reinforce what you are saying with your hands all have a direct bearing on how you will be perceived, albeit unconsciously. More of this later.

Creating a positive first impression – invisibly

Our first contact with a person may be through email, by letter or on the telephone.

Because these modes of communication are stripped of the normally abundant visible information such as appearance, style, movement and, in the case of the written word, voice, it becomes all the more important to make the most of what is left. 'Remote' modes of communication are still filled with opportunities for creating a good first impression.

We will look at the potential of three forms of 'remote' communication.

Email

Email is quite an informal mode of communication with a tradition for grammatical shortcuts and abbreviations. However, most people now offer their email address and invite contact electronically. If you use this channel of communication to create a first impression, ensure that you do so through a high-quality message. Use the attachment facility to carry properly formatted documents that can be printed by the recipient.

Letter

There are significant advantages to making your first impression by letter. When initial contact is made through the written word, you have the luxury of time to plan the impression you wish to create.

Listed below are some useful tips on how to create a good impression by letter:

- Ensure that the quality of the paper and the appearance of the writing are excellent: no spelling mistakes, daubs of correction fluid, colloquialisms or bad grammar.
- Handwritten letters are fine if you possess a 'good hand' that is attractive and legible. Many bad characteristics are associated with poor handwriting. Word-processed letters look very professional, so do use this method if you can.
- Make sure that what you have to say is succinct and to the point. Any information that you give in addition to what is necessary should be carefully chosen.

The telephone

When communicating by telephone, you have the benefit of being invisible so you can get really comfortable with yourself and what you plan to say.

Here are some helpful tips on making a good first impression using the telephone:

- Do not use a mobile.
- Smile when your call is answered; this can be heard in your voice.
- Use a pleasant greeting and state your name and purpose clearly.
- Plan what you are going to say (writing down key words will ensure you cover all the essential points).
- If you are trying to get your thoughts together, pace about if it helps and use gestures.
- If you are interrupted during your call, explain what has happened so that your distraction does not appear rude or offhand.
- Summarize and confirm all agreements verbally so that you can be sure you have understood accurately.
- Establish who will initiate the next contact; if you are anxious, it is as well to take the responsibility for this yourself.
- It is often useful to follow up a telephone conversation with a letter of confirmation.
- If you seem to be listening for a long time, acknowledge what is being said by using terms like 'Ah-ha', 'Mmm' and 'Yes'. Long silences can sound as if you are no longer there or have stopped paying attention.
- If you find you need to be assertive, stand up while talking on the telephone; it really does help to convey a feeling of strength.

Assertive interviewing skills

Many specialist books have been written on the subject of 'the interview'. However, this chapter would not be complete without some reference to 'the interview' and how you can manage this assertively.

During a professionally conducted interview, the interviewer should talk for 5–10 per cent of the time only. Ideally, therefore, you will have the remainder of the time to give as much relevant information about yourself as possible.

Your curriculum vitae will have conveyed all the professional, technical and experiential information necessary to determine your suitability for the post. The interview is primarily geared towards finding out whether you will fit in to the culture of the organization and work effectively with the rest of the team.

You will be prompted to give information about yourself through 'open questions'. Listen out for these because they provide you with the opportunity to show yourself in a good light. Examples of open questions are:

- 'What made you decide to...?'
- 'How would you tackle...?'
- 'Explain more about how you...'

They are 'open' because you determine the content and limits of the answer; there are no bounds to them. They give you masses of scope to talk about your approach and your achievements.

'Closed' questions, for comparison, are those such as:

- 'How long did you work for...?'
- 'How many staff were you responsible for at...?'
- 'When did you pass your driving test?'

These questions prompt short, defined responses and, as a consequence, the interviewer has to work extremely hard to extract sufficient information from you to reach a decision.

If you happen to be at an interview where the interviewer asks you 'closed' questions, take the initiative and open them up yourself, saying something like:

- 'Yes, I enjoyed being an apprentice because it gave me an opportunity to...'
- 'I worked for Hobson's Choice for ten years and thoroughly enjoyed it because it developed my ability to...'

Remember, undertake some basic research on the organization and the nature of its business before you attend an interview. Interviewers often ask 'What do you know about this organization?' You can impress easily with a knowledgeable response to this question.

Summary

To close this chapter, let us look at what creating a positive image is all about – *confidence*.

By adopting some of the techniques and attitudes given to you, you will soon begin to trust that you are capable of forming and maintaining an image that pleases you. Initially, one small success is all you can ask of yourself. Having this safely behind you will be the beginning of building confidence. Start with something you find relatively easy, and move on to greater things from there.

Good habits, firmly established, are soon drawn into the subconscious where they form the bedrock of your behaviour. When you have progressed this far, you will find that your confidence level has increased significantly and you will be able to draw upon it quite naturally. Once you reach this stage, all your positive experiences will go towards reinforcing this new-found quality in yourself. You will have established a virtuous cycle! Confidence and a healthy self-esteem are priceless assets and, if you are not fortunate enough to possess them naturally, they are well worth working for.

A positive mental attitude is key. Many managers have learned this from the experience of athletes who develop their minds as well as their bodies. Belief in yourself, coupled with professional expertise, will ensure your success.

Fact-check (answers at the back)

Think about the following questions and use them to develop your skills in creating a positive impression.

1. What do you need to do to create a positive first impression?
   a) Tell people what you want them to believe of you ❏
   b) Behave authentically, taking account of the context and situation ❏
   c) Act out the person you want to be seen as ❏
   d) Adopt a 'what you see is what you get' approach and leave it to chance ❏

2. Which one of the options below is *incorrect* as a way of making a first impression?
   a) Considering my appearance – appropriate dress and grooming ❏
   b) Building rapport and being congruent with the situation ❏
   c) Demonstrating authenticity and confidence in myself ❏
   d) Acting as if I was the person I want to be ❏

3. Handshakes are very important in creating a first impression. How should you shake someone's hand?
   a) Offer little resistance so that they can determine the strength of the handshake ❏
   b) I dislike shaking hands so try to avoid it ❏

   c) Take the 'firm' approach so that they know you're confident in yourself ❏
   d) My hands are sweaty so I try to minimize contact ❏

4. When entering a room for the first time, perhaps to meet a prospective employer, how can you command the space?
   a) I knock and enter without being invited to show my confidence ❏
   b) I comment on the (good, bad, indifferent) weather immediately to show I'm friendly ❏
   c) I respond confidently to the requests made of me to sit, speak and ask questions ❏
   d) I stand quietly and wait for instructions before I make a move ❏

5. Which one of the statements below is likely to create a *poor* impression when there are no visible channels of communication?
   a) I make sure my written communications are grammatically correct and high quality ❏
   b) I smile on the telephone, knowing that this will be conveyed in my voice ❏
   c) I use texting because it's quick and easy ❏
   d) I make sure my CV is succinct and points towards my capabilities and achievements ❏

6. Interviews that use open questions are designed to check the 'chemistry' between you and your prospective employers. Which statement *incorrectly* defines open questions?
a) They are designed to get you to talk more about yourself ❏
b) They begin with 'Who?', 'What?', 'Where?', 'When?' and 'How?' ❏
c) They are traps that encourage you to say things you don't want to! ❏
d) They are exploratory and encourage you to expand upon your points ❏

7. If you feel that you may possess a barrier to being considered for a new job, how would you diminish it to equal your chances?
a) I'd hope that the interviewer hadn't noticed and say nothing ❏
b) If they mentioned it, I'd deny it was a problem ❏
c) I'd be candid about the perceived barrier and explain why it would not be an obstacle to my suitability ❏
d) I'd point out that it was politically incorrect or illegal to focus on this issue ❏

8. Which statement is incorrect in describing how to communicate assertive behaviour non-verbally?
a) Through posture and well-defined movement ❏
b) By taking every opportunity to stand up and create a physical hierarchy in my favour ❏
c) By sitting slightly forward in the chair to convey engagement ❏
d) By speaking clearly and fluently ❏

9. If you were being interviewed and the interviewer was not asking you the questions you'd like to answer, how would you deal with it?
a) I'd give them a list of questions I'd like them to ask me ❏
b) I'd give feedback to the interviewer that they're not giving me the opportunity to sell myself properly ❏
c) I'd ask if I could outline a project that illustrates my suitability for the role ❏
d) I'd feel disappointed and wish they'd been better at their job! ❏

10. Which statement could endanger my growth in confidence?
a) I could be positive about my capabilities and achievements ❏
b) I could try not taking things too personally ❏
c) I could try envisaging my future successes ❏
d) I could over-act to convey that I really was confident ❏

CHAPTER 19

Being assertive in public

In the previous chapter we looked at ways of creating a positive impression in one-to-one situations: at a job interview, on the telephone and through the written word.

Now we are going to look at how to develop this transient first impression into a durable professional image. You may like to think of this as your 'brand' image. This will be an amalgam of the characteristics, traits and behaviours that you show to the outside world. If you are to transmit your 'brand' effectively, you will need to be consistent in the way your portray yourself. If you try out new things too often, it will fragment your brand and undermine the progress you've made and the reputation you've established.

To assist you, we will concentrate on your ability to communicate assertively in public, among work colleagues and customers. As you grow in professional stature, you will increasingly find yourself in situations where many pairs of eyes will be watching you. You will be visible to a wider audience.

Much of the assertive behaviour about to be described will be applicable to more than one arena. Here we will focus on three of the most frequently met situations in which your ability to communicate assertively will reap great rewards:

- meetings
- negotiations
- presentations.

Meetings

Meetings are often dominated by the most aggressive members of the group. In these circumstances, passive attendees can feel completely overtaken by events because they feel unable to interject and make their points. Passive types will often revert to passive/aggressive behaviour on such occasions – deafeningly 'loud' body language and more than a few sighs – or they will become silent and resign themselves to the decisions made without their input.

A good chairperson will ensure that the meeting is properly orchestrated and that everyone is given the opportunity to contribute. Often, however, this leadership is sadly lacking and meetings either take on the air of a battlefield or wander off the point and waste a lot of time.

For the purposes of illustrating how to handle meetings assertively, we will look at the worst scenario: that of a disorganized gathering dominated by one or two aggressive types. We will pepper this image with a few passive and passive/aggressive characters who are nursing 'hidden agendas'.

After a few words on how to prepare for a meeting, we will pull the above scenario apart and look at each component individually:

- assertive versus aggressive
- assertive versus passive/aggressive
- assertive versus passive
- assertive versus hidden agenda.

Preparing for a meeting

Before attending a meeting, make sure that you have a copy of the agenda and that you fully understand why the meeting has been called.

Take with you all the supporting information you are likely to need. If you are not clear why a particular item has been included on the agenda, ask beforehand.

Make sure you know where the meeting is being held and get there on time. You will lose credibility if you turn up late, confused or poorly prepared, and it will then be much harder to make an assertive and constructive contribution.

Assertive versus aggressive

Let's start by dealing with the aggressive component of the meeting. Aggressive behaviour often works in the short term. It intimidates and controls those who fear it, and many do. However, it is not worth adopting aggressive behaviour as a long-term strategy. Eventually colleagues will get angry.

The demonstrable lack of regard and respect that the aggressive person exhibits will eventually lead to unco-operative and undermining responses. Once commitment has been lost, there is no way forward for the aggressor.

The use of assertive behaviour in these circumstances can, however, draw the aggressor towards a healthier realm of communication. Here's how.

When faced with aggressive behaviour, be calm, breathe deeply and know that others at the meeting will be gunning for you. One word of caution, however: assertive behaviour is about taking responsibility for yourself, not for others; so don't speak for the group, speak for yourself. Use 'I' language.

You may have to field anger, criticism and insults before you can start influencing the communication. Remember, though, that aggressive behaviour is weak behaviour. Be confident; you can handle it.

Here is a checklist for dealing with aggressive behaviour:

- Be calm; listen carefully.
- Take a deep breath and look for an opportunity to speak. If you need to interrupt, try to catch the speaker's eye and indicate your wish to contribute. If the speaker is hell-bent on avoiding eye contact, call their name politely and state your intention to contribute.
- Match the volume of your interruption to the volume of the speaker's voice.
- Once you have successfully entered the dialogue, acknowledge what has just been said, then lead off with a statement such as 'I understand the point you are making, but I feel we could achieve more by...'
- If you are dismissed, repeat your comment in a different way. Repeat yourself assertively until you have been heard.

- Once you have the floor you may find you need to halt a 'return play' interruption. In this case, raise your hand to signal 'stop'. Using the person's name increases the power of your gesture.
- Summarize and confirm your understanding of a point or agreement before moving on.
- If you have not succeeded in making your point, register the fact. For example: 'I know that you are keen to cover a lot of ground in this meeting, but I still feel...'
- Maintain dignity even if you are frustrated, and reassert yourself on a later occasion. Persistence really does win out in the end and you will become more effective each time you attempt assertive behaviour.

Assertive versus passive/aggressive

Passive/aggressive behaviour is 'reluctant victim' behaviour. It attempts to be manipulative. A person may be angry with themselves for giving away their power so they do it with bad grace. This type of behaviour causes bad atmospheres, resentment, embarrassment and confusion. Often, one thing is said but the message is completely different. For instance:

Manager: 'Our best customer has just placed an urgent order; would you mind processing it immediately?'

Sales assistant (sarcastically): 'No, that's fine. I have all the time in the world!'

Passive/aggressive behaviour is thinly disguised. In a meeting it may exhibit itself through overt body language – rolling the eyes heavenward, exaggerated shifting in the chair, or impatient tapping with a pen.

Here are some ideas for dealing with passive/aggressive behaviour:

- Expose the 'hidden' message, whether verbal or non-verbal. For example: 'I see that you are feeling negatively about this. Would you mind discussing your objection openly?'
- Ask for their thoughts on the topic of obvious dispute.
- Listen actively and respond.

The passive/aggressive person has several options when their behaviour is exposed. They can rise to the challenge and redeem themselves; deny sending the message in the first place, claiming that you are paranoid; or get defensive. The first option is obviously the best strategy; the latter two will without fail diminish their standing in others' eyes.

Assertive versus passive

Passive behaviour attempts to engender feelings of sympathy in others. It is as manipulative as passive/aggressive behaviour but it pretends to be virtuous. Passive people have very little self-respect, they do not stand up for themselves and tend to get 'put upon' because they are frightened to say no and be rejected.

A distinguishing characteristic of a passive person is the use of silence. This can sometimes go on for a very long time and usually covers up a running dialogue in their mind which is 'victim' based ('Why are you picking on me?' or 'I wish you would shut up and leave me out of this!').

Dealing with passive behaviour

Dealing with a passive person is not dissimilar to handling someone who is passive/aggressive. First, expose their abdication: 'I am not clear where you stand on this issue; would you tell me what your feelings are?' (Note the use of the 'I' statement and the 'open' question, 'what?')

Match silence with silence. It takes an extremely passive person to remain mute in the teeth of a silent and expectant gaze, especially if everyone at the meeting is engaged in the same tactic. Once they start to talk, use your active listening skills to encourage the flow.

However, if you lose patience with their silence, repeat your comment or try a different approach if you think this will help. If you get to a point of exasperation, inform the passive person that you will have to deduce their feelings if they are not prepared to share them and that you will have to proceed according to your deductions. Invite them to support you in your course of action.

Assertive versus hidden agenda

You will inevitably come across people who play their cards very close to their chest, especially in organizations where internal politics are prominent. In these cultures, people are always on the defensive, protecting themselves from exploitation or disadvantage. Sometimes this fear is imaginary, sometimes it is real, but, whatever the cause, you will need common techniques to deal with it.

Identifying hidden agendas

You will probably be able to identify the 'political animals' among your colleagues because their behaviour will appear inconsistent. They will apparently change their opinion or approach without reason, leaving a trail of confusion and uncertainty behind them. Once this erratic style has caught your attention, look at the interplay of circumstances and try to identify the likely political, and usually personal, gain that is being sought. You may then be close to the real motivation of that person.

Significant coincidences that benefit one individual do not usually occur without some help. Look for coincidences, therefore, and identify the beneficiaries. Coupled with hindsight, the hidden agenda may suddenly be revealed to you and past, previously confusing behaviours will fall into context. This knowledge is useful; it is power. Do not try to tackle the individual. Hidden agendas, by their very nature, can always be denied and you will end up looking paranoid or foolish.

It is probably worth testing your theory by predicting the likely reaction of your colleagues in certain circumstances. If, when these circumstances occur, your prediction proves correct, the hidden agenda is likely to be what you suspected. If not, think again; maybe you *are* paranoid!

Planning your approach

Having understood a colleague's private motivation, you will have a clear picture of where you fit into the pattern of things. This will enable you to plan your own approach. This could be one of avoidance, of course, if you choose not to get caught up in the politics of the organization; or it may be a strategic option – the choice, as always, is yours.

Hidden agendas: checklist

Here is a checklist for identifying a hidden agenda:

- Examine coincidences that benefit one person, or a specific group of people.
- Look out for inconsistent behaviour – this may take the form of an unlikely relationship, non-verbal messages or a sudden and inexplicable abdication of responsibility.
- Put your observations into context using hindsight; this may help you identify the 'hidden agenda' specifically.
- Test your theory as innocuously and as anonymously as possible.
- It is probably best to keep your own counsel; you may be able to do more to your advantage in this way.
- If you are going to tackle someone on their private agenda, be absolutely sure of your ground and that you can handle it in the most assertive way possible.
- Look for a motivation – if you are suddenly flavour of the month with someone who is known to be ambitious, ask yourself why.
- Be vigilant – it would be naive to think that hidden agendas are not being worked out somewhere within your organization.

Negotiations

There are some very simple rules for conducting yourself effectively – and assertively – in negotiations.

Negotiations can fall into several categories. First, there are those taking place in the working environment with one other person such as your boss, a colleague or a member of your staff. Moving up in scale, the meeting room often witnesses negotiations among several colleagues whose views reside in different camps. Then there are those conducted between two opposing parties. When these two parties cannot agree, they may resort to the services of an arbitrator or mediator.

Whatever the situation, whether it is simple problem solving or a full-scale meeting between managers and a trade union, the basic rules for successful negotiating are the same. More often than not, it is merely a question of scale.

Negotiating in practice

Here are the basic steps for negotiating successfully:

- Know exactly what you wish to achieve and be absolutely clear on the level of your, and your opponent's, authority.
- Be assertive and use positive body language.
- Make sure that you understand the other's viewpoint.
- Convey your own viewpoint clearly and state your desired outcome.
- Look for areas of common ground to reinforce mutual interests and to develop a commitment to a satisfactory resolution.
- Listen actively and demonstrate understanding throughout the discussion.
- Never bluff, fudge, manipulate or lie.
- Never offer something you cannot deliver.
- If you are feeling pressured, ask for a recess.
- Communicate your proposals clearly and concisely and establish those of the other party.
- Summarize the areas of difference and explore the extent of these; identify the issues where compromise is possible.
- Having distilled out the main area of contention, discuss any concessions that you are both prepared to make.
- Summarize, agree and confirm in writing

Presentations

Presentations strike fear into the hearts of many managers, whatever their seniority. They are one of the most visible and exposed professional platforms and can leave your image enhanced, intact or in tatters.

Usually you will have advance warning of the requirement to make a presentation and will also, therefore, have time to prepare and practise for the occasion.

The two most important points are: *prepare* and *practise*.

Those who are 'naturals' at making presentations are the exception rather than the rule. Most good presenters are only good because they have invested time in preparation and practice. Everyone can do it if they try – and everyone can enjoy the experience.

There is nothing more satisfying than the glow of success when you step down from the platform having made an excellent presentation. It really is worth investing the time and energy to get it right.

Of course, much has been written on presentation skills, and clearly justice cannot be done to the subject in a few short paragraphs. However, here are a few pointers to help you add this mode of communication to the assertiveness toolkit that you are assembling:

Preparation and practice

- Make sure that you understand the purpose of the presentation.
- Have a clear impression of your audience, their level and their expectations; this will enable you to pitch your presentation correctly.
- Prepare your talk:
  - **beginning** – tell them what you are going to say
  - **middle** – say it
  - **end** – tell them what you have said.
- Most people will retain only about three points.
- Prepare visual aids:
  - **overhead projector slides** – these should be bold, clear and never more than a paragraph long
  - **handouts** – these can contain more detailed information along with copies of your slides. They should be of top quality
  - **35mm slides** – not always an advantage as you have to make your presentation in a darkened room.
  - **PowerPoint** has raised the standard of presentations and the level of expectation of audiences everywhere. Sound and animation features are available, but make sure they add to your message. Also, be comfortable with the technology, especially if you are projecting your presentation from your laptop on to a screen. If you plug in too early, your audience will be able to watch as you search your directory and open up your presentation.

- Prepare a set of cards with keyword prompts, facts or difficult names on them to help you if you are nervous.
- Practise – in front of a mirror, colleagues, friends and family. Make sure that you get the timing right and get your audience to fire awkward questions at you.

Making the presentation

- Wear clean, comfortable and unobtrusive clothes. If you don't, your audience will pay more attention to your attire than to what you have to say.
- Arrive in plenty of time; familiarize yourself with the equipment and check your slides are in the right order.
- Make sure that you have a glass of water handy in case your mouth dries up.
- If you are using torch pointers, telescopic pointers or infrared remote controls – practise (watch out for shake).
- Relax, by whatever means suits you.
- Tell your audience what you expect from them in terms of interruptions, discussion or questions; you may prefer to take these as you go along, or leave them to the end.
- Enjoy your talk but remain vigilant: it is too easy to be drawn into letting your guard down and saying something contentious. If you cannot answer a question, be honest about it and tell the questioner that you will find out and get back to them.
- Try to avoid jokes until you are a skilled presenter.
- Don't talk down to your audience but, equally, don't assume they understand the technicalities of your subject.
- Pause from time to time. This is a performance, and pauses are useful for dramatic effect – and to collect your thoughts.
- Of course, use assertive language and body posture.

Summary

By now you should have started to gather together some useful tools for developing your assertiveness skills. You may have had a chance to practise some of these techniques and found that they really do work. These early successes should increase your confidence and fire your enthusiasm to learn more, take control and have the courage to set your own goals.

It may be worth checking your progress to see where you are with your assertiveness aspirations and what there is still left to do. You could, for example, ask for feedback from one or two of your trusted friends or colleagues.

It is very easy to slip back if something doesn't go according to plan, so find some support to shore you up in these moments.

You might like to write down your experiences and your learning. It will ensure that everything stays conscious, which is where you need it if you are going to take command of your own communication skills.

Fact-check (answers at the back)

Think about the following questions and use them to develop your skills in creating a public image.

1. Which statement is *incorrect* in respect of how you should build your brand?
   a) I build my brand in group or departmental meetings ❑
   b) I build my brand with clients, customers and suppliers ❑
   c) I build my brand among my colleagues who have similar expertise to me ❑
   d) I don't build my brand, it builds itself ❑

2. When you run meetings, which statement would suggest that you do so unassertively?
   a) I keep things to time ❑
   b) I leave with clear action points allocated to the appropriate members of the team ❑
   c) I tap into the creativity and problem-solving capability of the team ❑
   d) I always end up with all the action points! ❑

3. When you've completed a negotiation, what outcome would suggest that you did so assertively?
   a) I conceded too much ❑
   b) I was not heard or understood ❑
   c) I reached a satisfactory win/win solution ❑
   d) I do not know or understand the other party's position and goals ❑

4. Which statement about passive/aggressive behaviour is *false*?
   a) People agree (unconvincingly) and then take no action – or sabotage the outcome ❑
   b) Often, the body language is 'loud' in its message that the person wants to be anywhere but at the meeting ❑
   c) Passive/aggressive behaviour uses sarcasm ❑
   d) Passive/aggressive behaviour is a contradiction in terms and doesn't exist ❑

5. Which is the *wrong* step to take when you are preparing for a meeting?
   a) Make sure everyone knows where the meeting is, what time it's being held and how long it will last ❑
   b) Ensure that an agenda has been circulated and forewarn of any preparation that needs to be done ❑
   c) Arrange for minutes to be taken, circulated and agreed afterwards ❑
   d) Meetings are best when they are called spontaneously to address an emergent issue ❑

6. What is the effect of aggressive behaviour in a meeting? Identify the *false* statement.
a) It derails the purpose of the meeting ❏
b) It adds a drop of excitement to the proceedings and encourages everyone to contribute ❏
c) It may be effective in the short term ❏
d) People may be fearful of the aggressor and fail to contribute ❏

7. When confronting aggressive behaviour, what should you *not* do?
a) Be calm and listen carefully ❏
b) Acknowledge what is being said and offer your own view ❏
c) Argue with the aggressive person and try to convince them they're wrong ❏
d) If your comment is dismissed, come back again in a different way ❏

8. Which strategy is a passive/ aggressive person *unlikely* to use to avoid taking responsibility?
a) They may tell you that you're paranoid ❏
b) They may deny that you read their signals correctly ❏
c) They may feign agreement and sabotage your plan later on ❏
d) They may apologize, tell you that you've read them correctly and take on a different stance ❏

9. In the event of suspecting someone has a hidden agenda, what should you do?
a) Accuse them of trying to 'get one over on you' ❏
b) Mention that you've noticed them trying to win favour with senior people ❏
c) Set up a 'trap' to see if they fall into it ❏
d) Give them feedback on your feelings and ask if they would clarify their motivations ❏

10. What good practice should you adopt as you step into the world of making presentations?
a) Telling 'good' jokes to get the audience laughing and 'on your side' ❏
b) Saying how nervous you are because you hate giving presentations ❏
c) Being technical to demonstrate how much you know ❏
d) Doing rehearsals to get you used to your voice and the timing of your presentation ❏

CHAPTER 20

Body language

The notion of 'body language' has drawn much attention and intrigue. It is tempting to think that words are the most important factor in communicating messages but, as we have seen, words form only a small proportion of the messages that are exchanged. You have only to think of a mime artist who has perfected the art of communication using the body to recognize the truth of this. Also, think of those people who are very still when they communicate. It is sometimes hard to 'read' them clearly and it may lead to misinterpretations or misunderstandings.

Now we will look at the forms of body language that have the most impact on others. This is by no means an exhaustive study of the subject, but it will maximize the effect you can create when you communicate assertively.

We will cover the following areas:

- assertive body language
- the use of gestures
- developing rapport
- the use of verbal language
- interpreting body language.

Your body really can speak louder than words.

Assertive body language

Because your body conveys such a large proportion of what you are communicating, it is worth concentrating on this area for a short time and considering what it is we convey with our bodies and how we can be sabotaged by them.

It is a useful exercise to 'body-watch' – but try to be discreet. You will notice that when two people are engrossed in riveting conversation, they are completely unaware of their bodies. (Unless the conversation is skirting around sex, of course; in which case we are *very* aware of our bodies!) We use our bodies at the unconscious level to emphasize points or to transmit secondary messages.

Assertive behaviour is distinguished by the continuity between the verbal and the non-verbal. In other words, your body reflects precisely what you are saying when you are in 'assertive mode' – it is congruent with the intention behind your message.

Because of the restricted time and space available here for this topic, we will address only the most potent aspects of body language:

- personal space
- stance
- senses.

Personal space

We all carry around an egg-shaped exclusion zone which varies in size in direct proportion to our circumstances, purpose and level of comfort. As a point of interest, you can usually measure the size of someone's 'egg' by the length of their focal attention.

On an underground train, this is almost zero (people often look glazed or they focus on reading matter); at work, it can extend to include one person or a small gathering of people; at a large presentation, it can reach to the extremities of an entire hall.

Varying the size of the 'egg' is an instinctive part of our behaviour. However, it can be very useful to understand the nature of this 'personal space' so that it can be used to good effect.

Learning point I. *If we do not include people in our personal space, it is almost impossible to influence them.*

Notice how you 'shut down' when someone you dislike comes too close, or someone you're not sure about comes too close too soon. I'm sure that we have all experienced backing away from someone as they repeatedly trespass on our personal territory until the next step takes us through the window or into a cupboard.

Remember, too, a time when you were part of a large audience, and the presenter or entertainer made you feel as if you were the only person in the room. This was because they extended their personal space to include you.

Notice how you use your own space, and how you act differently with family, colleagues and those in authority. As an exercise, practise drawing your space in until its boundaries meet your body. Then try filling a room with your presence by expanding your space. You can do this by changing your focal point and placing your attention on the walls. Accompany this with a visualization of yourself as an extraordinarily confident and influential person.

Learning point II: *The more space you use, the more impact you will have.*

Tall people tend to have a natural advantage because they occupy a large amount of space. Yet they are often shy and withdrawn. This can show in their posture, which may be round-shouldered, or in their gait, which may be 'in-toed'.

Short people, who may not enjoy the same natural impact, can make up for their lack of size by expanding the horizons of their space and adopting a good assertive style. Indeed, a large number of short people are considered to be taller than they are because of this ability, and they have become extremely successful in the process. Unfortunately, their communication style sometimes overcompensates for their lack of physical stature and can become overly aggressive.

There are ways of sitting and standing that look 'big' and carry impact. By adopting some of the following techniques, short people can actually 'grow' in others' perceptions.

Here are some techniques for creating presence:

- **Assertive standing:** stand straight and 'think' tall. Try not to twine your legs around each other or stand with your weight upon one leg. Nothing destroys the image like crumpling on to the floor because you have overbalanced!
- When you wish to **communicate powerfully,** again, stand straight, feet planted firmly on the floor, body centred, hands at your side. If it is hard to push you over physically, it will be hard to push you around verbally.
- **Assertive sitting:** convey confidence by using as much space as possible while sitting. Sit with your body on the diagonal, bottom well back in the chair and lean slightly forward. Sit 'small' and you will be perceived as small.

Stance

Your posture will convey a huge impression, so it is important to get it right.

Everyone will notice someone who stands upright and walks well. This is a good habit to cultivate. It portrays confidence and authority.

Tall people are notorious for stooping and they always say it is because they can't get through the doors. However, it is an enviable gift to be tall; many would give their eyeteeth for height – so, if you are tall, duck only when necessary. Stoop when you are young and you will have no choice but to stoop when you are old.

Short people can walk tall, too. In fact, people of under five foot three can look six foot tall if they have good posture. We often confuse confidence for size, so you can make the most of this misconception by cultivating your own personal stature.

Senses

Taking the liberty to touch someone in the working context conveys superiority. A boss can pat his or her staff on the back, but they probably wouldn't appreciate it if their staff reciprocated. A pat on the back is an authoritative action. When it remains unchallenged, a hierarchy is established.

A good way of putting things back on an even footing is to look for an immediate opportunity to touch them back in a different manner. You might say, 'Excuse me', as you pick a hair off their jacket, or 'You've brushed up against some dust', as you sweep their chest, arm or shoulder briskly with the back of your hand.

The use of gestures

Gestures can either reinforce your communication or they can draw attention away from what you are saying. They should be used prudently, therefore, to maximize their effect.

Gestures include everything from 'windmill' arms (sit on your hands if this is you) to almost imperceptible movements of the face, head, torso or arms – they rarely involve the use of the legs.

The most common gestures are made with hands alone and they serve to emphasize what is being said by the mouth.

The type of gesture you choose to use can indicate something about your personality. If you 'prod the air' more than artistically necessary, you will appear aggressive. Open gestures, arms out away from the body, can indicate an open and warm personality. Be too energetic and untidy with your movements and you will come across as shambolic and disorganized. This is especially true if the style of your dress also tends to be untidy or too casual.

Assertive gestures tend towards the moderate ground. Timing and relevance are crucial. They should flow smoothly and mirror as closely as possible what is being said.

Developing rapport

Empathizing with another does not depend solely on the words you use. Much of the rapport is carried in your body language.

If you watch two people talking enthusiastically and unselfconsciously, you will probably notice that their bodies take on virtually the same demeanour. For example, both may have crossed their legs, put an elbow on the table and their chin in the palm of their hands. If they are drinking, you will often find that the drinks diminish at exactly the same rate. They will have *matched* and *mirrored* each other's behaviour. If you do this consciously, but subtly, you will find that your ability to build rapport will have improved greatly.

Should you find yourself in an unpleasant or fraught conversation and you wish to alleviate the tension, it is possible to do this also by matching and mirroring the other's body language. Having matched and held their body position for some time, you can start moving your own body towards a more relaxed position. You will soon find that they start mirroring you and the tension will fade. It is impossible to remain aggressive when you are physically relaxed.

Beware: if you are not sufficiently subtle in your mirroring and matching skills, it will look as if you are mimicking the other's behaviour. If this is the impression you create, it will be very difficult to make amends.

Couple this technique with good eye contact, active listening skills, affirming head nods, 'Ah-has', 'Mmms' and so on, and you will be able to build rapport with the best of them.

Being able to empathize with someone involves understanding their feelings by getting beneath the surface. This can often be achieved by being able to relate what they are saying to a similar experience of your own. If you are at sea, however, with no common understanding, the mirroring and matching technique can be used to engender the same feelings in you that are being experienced by the other person. If the other person has lost confidence, for instance, and takes on the foetal position, try it out for yourself and see what emotions it brings up. You will probably gain a better understanding of their feelings and be able to empathize more effectively.

The use of verbal language

The words we choose and the way we construct sentences can assist us in the process of building rapport.

To illustrate this, think of the way we talk to children. We are constantly reflecting back to them the words they use themselves. It has to be said that sometimes we diminish their intellects, but nonetheless the principle is the same. Listen out for the kind of words used by the person with whom you are trying to build rapport and reflect this style of language back to them.

A manager often uses a distinctive language that is related to the function or specialism of his or her role. Finance, information technology, manufacturing, design and development all have their own language. If you use this language back to these specialists, they will feel comfortable with your style. Use a different language, and they will feel alienated.

Here are some examples of language compatibility:

- A **financier's** language includes words like: balance, bottom line, assets, investments, credit, etc.
- Some of the following words would be used by an **information technologist**: logical, image, capacity, network, hardware, upgrade, etc.

The same sentence can be constructed differently for each audience:

- To the **financier**: 'On *balance*, I feel it would be to our *credit*...'
- To the **information technologist**: 'It would seem the most *logical* approach to *upgrade* our *image* by...'

And to a **visionary designer** whose language may include words like see, impact, style, colour, create, proportion, impression, etc., say 'I can *see* that we could *create* the best *impression* by...'

Interpreting body language

BEWARE: this is not an exact science.

When watching someone for the tell-tale signs of a hidden message, don't engage only your brain; engage your senses, too. People often think that they are privy to the inner secrets of another person, but you have to be bordering on the telepathic to know, really.

However, here are a few guidelines to interpreting body language:

- **Be aware of the environment** in which you are making your observation. If it is cold, your subject may have a tense jaw or their arms may be folded tightly across their bodies. In these circumstances, they *may not* be either nervous or aggressive – but then again, *they may*.
- **Watch for 'leakage'.** One example of leakage is someone who is controlling their nerves extremely well, but subconsciously lets them escape through toes curling and uncurling at the end of their shoes; muscles clenching and unclenching round their jaw, grinding teeth, rattling change in their pocket and quivering knees. As resourceful human beings, we have many such outlets.
- Mostly, look for **discontinuity** and **coincidence.** If someone is pledging their unequivocal support but shaking their head as they do so – watch your back. If someone says 'I never lie' at the same time as moving their pointing finger from side to side – withhold belief in them for a while and watch them closely. This can be a gesture of denial. If someone says, 'I am not interested in scoring points with the boss' and yet is coincidentally around the boss at the most politically charged moments, watch you don't get sideswiped.
- **Watch people's eyes** – it sounds obvious to say that people look where their interest lies, but sometimes, during an unguarded moment, it is interesting to note exactly where this is – or who it is.
- Sometimes it is easier to **identify 'anti' body language** – people tend to be very clear when they dislike someone. You can see it in their eyes and in the way they orientate their bodies away from the object of their distaste. This is the opposite of mirroring. Sometimes their complete and habitual removal from the scene gives the game away.

When people like each other, they get into close proximity – into that personal body space that is circumscribed by 'the egg'. They may touch, they often have good and prolonged eye contact, and they smile, reinforce and reflect each other's behaviour. Sometimes you are aware of 'chemistry', when there are no identifiable body signals. It is interesting to observe this behaviour and speculate on what it is that causes this effect.

Summary

We have briefly looked at a very powerful aid to communication – and the interpretation of communication. We have learned that the body will not lie for you. If there is any incongruence between your message and your intention, it will find its way to the surface through 'leakage'. This makes your (and others') motivation visible, much more visible than you probably realized.

Your body, including your eyes and voice – not words – carries about 90 per cent of any message you are trying to convey. Because the proportion is so large, this aspect of communication has powerful potential. If you use your non-verbal knowledge skilfully, you will find that your level of control increases significantly. Beware, however, that you don't treat this aspect of communication as if it were a definitive code. You need to remember to put in it into context so that any risk of misinterpretation is minimized. Also, be aware that you may be looking for confirmation of a story or fantasy you hold about someone. This will result in you force-fitting the outcome of your analysis into a premeditated conclusion, which will 'muddy the water' of your communications.

However, you should now be more aware and be able to body-watch from a more informed position.

Enjoy body-watching!

Fact-check (answers at the back)

Think about the following questions and use them to develop your body language.

1. Body language is a powerful channel for communication. Which of the following statements is true?
   a) Communicating without the visual channel (without seeing the communicator's body) can be more revealing ❏
   b) By definition, gestures are distracting and misleading ❏
   c) Most of the message is conveyed by the words used ❏
   d) Tone, pitch and volume of the voice are considered to be part of body language ❏

2. When someone in the work context pats you on the back to establish their seniority, what can you do to redress the balance?
   a) Shrug their hand away and tell them you don't appreciate their touch ❏
   b) Pat them back immediately in like manner ❏
   c) Find an opportunity to make physical contact in a different, but appropriate way ❏
   d) Stand on a chair to make them feel small! ❏

3. What are gestures useful for achieving?
   a) Drawing attention to yourself ❏
   b) Maximizing the drama of your message ❏
   c) Emphasizing what you are saying ❏
   d) Distracting people from what you're actually saying! ❏

4. Empathizing with another is very helpful in building rapport. What can you do to establish an initial connection with someone?
   a) Tell them what you think they should feel ❏
   b) Mirror and match their body language ❏
   c) Share your story with them, assuming that your experience will match theirs ❏
   d) Say: 'I know how you feel!' ❏

5. Most people use their own distinctive language in their communications. If you want to establish rapport, what can you do to make a connection with them?
   a) Use your own distinctive language to draw their attention to your message ❏
   b) Reflect back language similar to their own ❏
   c) Say you don't understand what they're saying and ask them to speak in English ❏
   d) Get out a dictionary and make a play of looking up their words ❏

6. Body language can be used to assist in the interpretation of someone's message. What is the secret of body language?
   a) It is an exact science and the code is well known ❏
   b) It points towards what's going on under the surface ❏
   c) It enables you to cover up what you're really saying ❏
   d) It enables you to tell when someone's lying! ❏

7. In terms of body language, what is leakage?
a) The secretion of unpleasant bodily fluids ❏
b) The release of stress in repetitive small movements ❏
c) Spitting and spluttering during speech ❏
d) Excusing oneself repeatedly to go to the bathroom ❏

8. What techniques can you use on the telephone to convey the signals that your body would send if you were face to face?
a) Make exaggerated gestures to compensate for not being in front of each other ❏
b) Signpost what's going on for you – 'I was quiet because I was distracted momentarily.' ❏
c) Talk more loudly ❏
d) Make use of your invisibility to sit with your feet on the desk ❏

9. What do you notice when two people are locked in great conversation?
a) They both talk at the same time ❏
b) They mirror and match each other ❏
c) They each agree with everything the other person says ❏
d) They finish each other's sentences ❏

10. Tall people have an advantage because...
a) People are frightened of them ❏
b) They take up lots of space and have natural impact ❏
c) They can see over everyone's heads ❏
d) They can walk faster than anyone else ❏

CHAPTER 21

Personal power

We have almost come full circle now, so to close this Part's learning, we will discuss personal power – how to win it, how to hold on to it and how to succeed with it.

In the sense that we're using it, personal power is correlated with confidence and goal clarity. It's about believing in what you want and going out to get it. For those who are not naturally blessed with personal power, it is a quality that is worth striving for, and it does take some striving to acquire it. However, with consciousness and dedication, this prize can be won and used to enhance our lives and successes.

The interesting thing about personal power is that you don't have to be born particularly advantaged to have it. It is not dependent upon your looks, size, intelligence, wealth or talents. Some of these may help; but the good news is, anyone can acquire personal power.

Most, or all, of the following qualities are found in powerful people:

- clarity of vision
- well-defined values and beliefs
- confidence
- powerful communication
- an ability to build relationships.

Power remains only with those who respect it. There may be a short-term gain for those who win power through confidence tricks, but it is inevitable that their fall from power will be in direct proportion to the 'con'.

Let's take each element of personal power and examine it separately.

Clarity of vision

It is essential to create a framework upon which you can hang your power. It is only when you know where you are going and are 100-per-cent committed to getting there that you can plan the way forward to your success. It doesn't matter which path you take, or whether you change the route from time to time, as long as you keep your eye on the goal.

Identifying the goal in the first place does require vision. Once you have this, and this is usually acquired through self-knowledge, the rest will fall into place.

If you have difficulty establishing your primary goal, start with a series of smaller ones. These will soon form a pattern that will lead you towards an understanding of what you wish to achieve. Ask yourself where you would like to be in 10, 20 or 50 years' time. Is maintaining your present course and direction sufficient to give you long-term satisfaction? Don't be concerned if your goal is extraordinarily ambitious. All those who have succeeded started out with 'impossible dreams'. Equally, don't be ashamed if your goal is not particularly ambitious. This means that you are meeting your own needs extremely well and puts you way ahead of the game.

Visionaries take the following steps to create a framework upon which they can build their successes. They...

- identify personal goals
- see their goals clearly and imagine what it is like to have reached them
- make a commitment to achieve them by a certain time
- act as if their goals have already been achieved.

If you don't put a time limit on the attainment of your goals, your mind will always think of them as being in the future. Acting as if you have already reached your goals will help to bring them into the present.

Test out these steps for yourself. Start small to gain confidence in the process.

Well-defined values and beliefs

Know what you value and believe. This is really much more difficult than it appears because values and beliefs may change over time, especially if your circumstances change dramatically for one reason or another. Dig deep, though; these underpin all your behaviours.

In the process of getting to know your values and beliefs you will have to ask yourself certain questions. For example, what price are you prepared to pay for your success...

- **personally?** – intimate relationships (partner, family, friends)
- **ethically?** – what you feel is right or wrong; what you need to do to feel good about yourself
- **professionally?** – career progression, promotion
- **politically?** – being in the right place at the right time.

If you ask a successful person the question 'What price are you prepared to pay for your success?', they will often have a clear, well-thought-out answer that is right for them. They are absolutely comfortable living within the framework of their values and beliefs. Any conflict – and conflict will develop from time to time as the balance of their life changes – will be addressed in the light of this value set.

Confidence

Here, we get back to the basics of **successful assertiveness.** Respect and honour yourself. You are as worthy as the next person.

Self-worth is the precursor to building confidence. If you believe in yourself, others will, too.

True confidence enables you to handle any situation well. Even in situations that you have not met before, you will be able to draw on your experience and extrapolate from your past behaviour to meet the needs of the moment.

A sudden lack of confidence can petrify and paralyse the mind and all coping mechanisms disappear. This rapid evacuation of all that you have learned will undermine your attempts at building confidence and put you back to square one again. So be kind to yourself; know that these things happen to everybody and that you are still a worthy individual. Forgive what you perceive to be your mistakes and move on.

The more you practise assertive behaviour, the less often sudden losses in confidence will happen. As with your goals (gaining confidence may be one of them, of course), try believing that you have already succeeded and act that way. It will soon become a reality.

Powerful communication

Powerful people are often extremely good communicators. Their communication skills are characterized by typical assertive behaviour.

Having a vision is not enough. The only way a vision becomes a reality is through motivating others to play their part, and the only way to motivate is to communicate. Only in very rare cases are visions actualized in a vacuum; usually they are dependent upon someone, or many people, co-operating in some way.

Not many of us are natural orators but we can learn from those who are. Here are a few qualities that you can learn to develop in yourself:

- **vision** (remember Martin Luther King's 'I have a dream...' speech)
- **belief** – in your purpose, your own ability and the ability of your team
- **acute observation** (listening, watching, sensing)
- ability to develop **empathy**
- ability to judge the **mood of the moment** and respond appropriately (flexibility/intuition)
- a sense of **timing** and **theatre**.

Powerful communicators regard their public appearances as theatrical performances. They create an impact, build tension, move their audience and leave them on a 'high'.

An ability to build relationships

It is often difficult to build and maintain relationships at the best of times, but it is especially difficult when driven by the work environment. Nonetheless, this ability is crucial if you wish to rise to the top.

There is no magic formula for developing good relationships and they can be stamped with a variety of styles – friendly, nurturing, respectful, mysterious, controlling, aggressive and so on. Try to identify your own style and check out the impression you create with colleagues.

Professional relationships can be troublesome because they have to be developed with people who are imposed upon us, not chosen by us. Indeed, we might actively avoid some of our colleagues when out of the work environment. Building good relationships therefore demands patience, determination and the ability to step back and see things from a different perspective.

Most people do not try to be bad or difficult. If this is the behaviour that they exhibit, it usually indicates that they hold a belief that is being challenged. If you encounter this behaviour as a manager, you may need to spend some time delving below the surface to understand the problem. Beware, however; you cannot merely go through the motions, and you may learn some unpalatable truths about yourself in the process.

Much can be done to maintain relationships remotely (by telephone, letter, email, etc.) but first you have to know and understand the people who work around you. This is done usefully at times when the pressure is off or at times when you socialize together. There is a fine line to tread between being too involved and too remote. You will have to determine the best balance for yourself, but remember that power holders are often characterized by a certain amount of mystique.

Summary

In this chapter we have briefly touched upon the dominant features of personal power. You may want to seek feedback on how you come across. Sometimes we make the mistake of believing that others hold the same belief about us as we do about ourselves – either positively or negatively. We may think that they don't see our lack of personal power because we spend time hiding it. Or we may think that they interpret our over-domineering style as powerful. It is worth getting feedback from a trusted source so that you know where your starting point is. It may be painful (or it may not!) but having clarity in terms of how you are seen is really valuable.

Fact-check (answers at the back)

Think about the following questions and use them to develop your personal power.

1. What is personal power?
a) It is 'Popeye' physical strength ❑
b) It is the confidence to know what you want and know what you need to do to get it ❑
c) It is the ability to dominate situations ❑
d) It is the ability to delegate ❑

2. What do people with personal power possess? Identify the odd one out!
a) Clarity of vision ❑
b) Values and beliefs ❑
c) A position high up in the hierarchy of an organization ❑
d) Ability to build rapport ❑

3. We are goal-oriented beings. What is your goal for the future?
a) 1–5 years from now ❑
b) 5–10 years from now ❑
c) Lifetime goal ❑
d) I don't have a goal ❑

4. Which of these statements about goals is true?
a) Goals get in the way of spontaneity ❑
b) Goals are pointless because they always change with circumstances ❑
c) Goals help us make relevant decisions and take appropriate action ❑
d) Goals are always out of reach ❑

5. How easy do you find it to articulate your vision?
a) I carry a clear vision for myself and can describe it easily ❑
b) I have a vision but it changes so regularly that I don't bother to talk about it ❑
c) People tend to laugh at my vision when I talk about it, thinking it's too fanciful ❑
d) Because I can't control events, I don't have a vision ❑

6. If your relationship building style were assertive, what should it look like?
a) Friendly yet firm ❑
b) Political and manipulative ❑
c) Wilful and commanding ❑
d) Easily biddable ❑

7. If you are engaged in a 'challenging' relationship, what assumption may help you get it back on track again?
a) They may feel misunderstood and unfairly judged ❑
b) They may be disruptive and difficult ❑
c) They may hold a grudge against you for no good reason ❑
d) They may be trying to make you look bad ❑

8. What feedback have you had about your personal power quotient?
   a) I'm often told I'm too aggressive ❑
   b) I don't receive feedback – and I don't ask for it! ❑
   c) I seem to enjoy healthy, co-operative and productive relationships and people tell me they enjoy working with me ❑
   d) People say that I'll never get anywhere being as quiet as a mouse! ❑

9. If you had to deal with a conflict in your team, how would you do so assertively?
   a) I'd tell the opposing parties to get a life and sort it out! ❑
   b) I'd encourage each party to listen to each other's point of view and find some common ground ❑
   c) I'd try to resolve the issue for them ❑
   d) I wouldn't get involved at all. It's not my business ❑

10. How satisfied are you with your assertiveness skills?
    a) I am assertive in my dealings with others and feel comfortable with this ❑
    b) I am assertive sometimes but need to practise more in 'difficult' situations ❑
    c) I am not particularly assertive but would like to be ❑
    d) I get hyped up and tend to dominate situations ❑

7 × 7

1 Seven key ideas

- Assertiveness is a choice. It's not something that you have to do all the time!
- Assertive communication is a win/win style of communication. It allows both parties to feel heard and acknowledged.
- Being assertive is contingent upon you knowing what you want to communicate and communicating it consistently.
- Finding and flexing an assertive communication style is the beginning of self-understanding.
- Sometimes being passive, or being aggressive, is assertive (inasmuch as you are choosing to communicate in the most effective way for a particular situation).
- Listening is a major part of being assertive. Indeed, the balance of listening to speaking should be, at the very least, 2:1 – if not 5:1!
- Assertive communication also allows you to raise your children and manage your pets effectively.

2 Seven best resources

- http://www.mindtools.com/pages/article/Assertiveness.htm – Assertiveness: Working WITH People, Not Against Them (Management Training and Leadership Training, Online)
- http://www.wikihow.com/Be-Assertive – How to Be Assertive
- *Assertiveness Pocketbook* by Max A. Eggert – full of good advice on how to overcome self-defeating beliefs, and deal with common problem areas
- *Brilliant Assertiveness: What the most assertive people know, do and say* by Dannie Lu Carr – practical and accessible, *Brilliant Assertiveness* examines what it means to be assertive and contains exercises and case studies to help you establish your assertiveness skills.

- iTunes app: *Confidence Booster: Self-Esteem and Assertiveness Training* by Sean Gohara – a walk-through guide on boosting self-esteem and assertiveness utilizing powerful techniques to take you through a full 'internal transformation'
- *How to Say 'No': Politely but firmly take back control of your time and your life* by Claire Shannon – if you find yourself trying to please everyone but, in doing so, fail to please yourself, this is for you!
- *Emotional Intelligence: 21 ultimate tips for gaining control over your emotions and becoming a boss of your thoughts and behaviour* by Joseph Sanchez

3 Seven things to avoid

- Try not to confuse aggression (you win, they lose) with assertiveness (you win, they win). Assertiveness does not always mean that you get your own way!
- Don't try to be assertive ALL the time! It can become a tyranny if you beat yourself up every time assertiveness eludes you – and you can become a 'communication tyrant' to others!
- Try not to expect everyone to have the same communication style as you. By listening and asking questions, you can help others express themselves more effectively.
- Beware of responding to emails emotionally and instinctively. Put them to one side while you think about what you want to say and how you're going to say it.
- Don't try to assert yourself at every opportunity. Sometimes, it's best to take yourself off duty and let things go. Ask yourself, 'Will my intervention make a positive difference?'
- Try not to criticize or judge others' approach to their communication. Remember what it was like when you were not consistently assertive and be generous to those who are trying!

- Expecting yourself to get it 'right' all the time. With the best will in the world, you're likely to find yourself falling back into your old habits from time to time. Just review what happened and try again!

4 Seven inspiring people

- Paloma Faith – a songwriter, singer and all-round performer. Paloma is distinctively herself, with no compromises. Yet she engages empathically with her art and those that surround her. A marvellous role model of international standing.
- HRH Prince Harry – another uncompromisingly authentic human being with a big heart for doing important work and having a great time. He is lovely to his grandmother, too!
- Angela Merkel, Chancellor of Germany – conducts herself with great authority, consistency and genuineness in a tough political context as a minority representative of women.
- Dame Judi Dench – a brilliant and acclaimed actress who brings her personality fully to her audiences. She has endured serious personal loss yet acts as an exemplar of dignity, courage... and humour.
- Malala Yousafzai – a fabulously brave young Pakistani woman who defied the Taliban, after being shot, by advocating education for girls. At age 17, she became the youngest ever recipient of a Nobel Prize.
- David Beckham – formerly a footballer with Manchester United, he played for a number of clubs in Europe and America while also being the captain of the England team. He has been a Goodwill Ambassador for UNICEF since his early football career. A good father and a good role model.
- Sir David Attenborough – primarily known as a naturalist and broadcaster, he has travelled to the most remote parts of the world to bring unique images of animals and descriptions of their lives to television audiences. The enduring image of him being the plaything of two baby gorillas in Rwanda is perhaps defining!

5 Seven great quotes

- 'The difference between successful people and really successful people is that really successful people say no to almost everything.' Warren Buffett
- 'It's never too late to be what you might have been.' George Eliot
- 'If liberty means anything at all, it means the right to tell people what they don't want to hear.' George Orwell
- 'Get up, stand up / Stand up for your rights. / Get up, stand up, / Don't give up the fight.' Bob Marley
- 'Your playing small does not serve the world. There is nothing enlightened about shrinking so that other people won't feel insecure around you. We are all meant to shine.' Marianne Williamson.
- 'Be yourself; everyone else is already taken.' Oscar Wilde
- 'You may not control all the events that happen to you, but you can decide not to be reduced by them.' Maya Angelou

6 Seven things to do today

- Decide how you want to communicate and give yourself some early targets to achieve to get you going.
- Listen to yourself in communication with others and see whether you can identify your dominant communication style.
- Identify a role model, observe them in dialogue and see what they do that you could also do – authentically.
- Pick up a few sentences that allow you to open a 'difficult' conversation assertively.
- Read through your written communications and try to view them from the other person's perspective. Try to imagine the impression that they'll get from them.
- Tackle a difficult conversation that you've been putting off for a while.
- Ask a trusted friend to hear you rehearse some 'openers' or anticipated responses and give you feedback. Once you've heard yourself saying things differently (and to your satisfaction), you'll begin to find your new style more easily accessible and familiar.

7 Seven trends for tomorrow

- With the increase of social media in all aspects of life (including the professional), think about how your communication style is conveyed in the 'sound bites' you choose. Without much context, meaning can easily be distorted.
- People tend to be accessible, online, all the time. This creates a willingness in them to interrupt face-to-face communication in order to respond to a ring or a bleep – or a theme tune! 'Instantaneousness' is the biggest disturbance in the communication field and can lead less assertive people to feel unimportant and uninteresting.
- Virtual working patterns are both a blessing and a curse for the unassertive communicator. They are a blessing inasmuch as there is often more time available to plan responses to questions or prompts. They are a curse inasmuch as messages are devoid of the physical clues and cues that allow appropriate responses to be given and it is easy to misunderstand and miscommunicate messages.
- The increase in multigenerational working environments means that different styles of communication are called for and different meanings are projected on to different communication styles. It seems that we must be multi-skilled and multi-talented in order to 'hold true to ourselves'.
- Globalization brings with it the need to communicate across multi-variant cultures and social divides. Being assertive in one cultural context may be received as aggressive in another. It is important to take some time to understand the social mores of those with whom you are communicating.
- Virtual, yet face-to-face, meeting options are increasing in popularity due to the cost benefit. This type of meeting requires a particular type of etiquette to compensate for the physical distance and atmospheric difference. To avoid confusion or mixed messages, communicators must be participative and their communication clear and unambiguous.

- A 'counter-trend' may emerge that addresses the issue of privacy and confidentiality. To avoid old photographs and 'sensitive' conversations from getting into the hands of those with few reasons to respect their provenance, people may go back to hushed conversations and contact prints!

PART 4
Your Managing Stress At Work Masterclass

Introduction

It has been said 'employees join great organizations but leave because of bad managers' and from my own experience I can testify to the truth of the statement.

A number of factors, such as recognition, variety of work, achievement and prospects for promotion play an important role in job satisfaction and help good managers retain their staff. However, stress can be one of the most significant reasons for employees leaving or if not in a position to leave, at least wishing they could.

Some see stress as a problem for the individual or even a sign of some defect in character. Yet most forward-thinking managers and organizations see the effective management of stress as an essential part of their business practice, benefiting both employees and the business or organization.

Arguably anyone who comes into contact with another person needs to manage stress. Whether in the workplace, socially or at home, human interaction can create pressures, conflict and stress. Even when free from the influence of others we can often generate our own stress through our own desire to succeed or through innate fears and concerns.

Ultimately how you handle stress personally and as a manager will vary depending on a number of factors: types of people, the organization, inherent pressures of a job and specific economic factors. This Part of the book aims to provide you with information that you can use in assessing what is appropriate for you, your team and organization.

CHAPTER 22

What is stress?

We have all heard people saying they are stressed – you may even have said it yourself. Perhaps you have had a lot on at work or too much to think about or maybe others are making unreasonable demands on your time. In this chapter you will learn that the response to stress is hard-wired into our biology and has played an important role in the survival of the human race. We will look at how the modern world can confuse or trigger our natural response to danger and understand that what we call stress today isn't always bad, isn't the same for everyone and that stress can exist even if there are no visible signs of it.

We will also look at how to assess stress in the workplace, and consider the causes of stress that can be generated by organizations, other circumstances in our lives and even by our own outlook and expectations. Finally, we will examine some of the impacts stress can have on both individuals and organizations and in turn demonstrate the real value of the effective management of stress.

What is stress?

If you ask a group of individuals what they mean by stress, you will find some people talk about the causes of stress, giving responses such as 'too much work', or 'too much pressure', while others will respond citing the effects of stress, with responses such as 'feeling tired or depressed'. For clarity, throughout this Part we will refer to the causes of stress as **stressors** and the effects as the **response.**

The stress response

Stress is a commonly used word but one that means different things to different people and lacks a single coherent definition. At a basic level stress relates to the biological response of our body to certain situations.

Throughout prehistory people faced life and death situations on a daily basis with strong competition for survival. Since the earliest days of the human race, an inbuilt stress response has proved an effective means of protection in situations of extreme danger.

So from a biological perspective, stress is the natural physical reaction to events that make an individual feel threatened in some way. Sometimes the threat is real, such as coming face to face with a predator, or sometimes the threat is imagined – e.g. the wind moving the bushes may cause you to believe there is a predator hiding, ready to pounce. Stress is the body's way of helping to deal with the situation. In the emergency situation stress can save your life as your body automatically adapts to stay focused, alert and highly energized. This acute stress response, often referred to as **fight or flight** (or sometimes the 'fight, flight or freeze response'), prepares the body for fending off an attacker or rival or for running away. The response can also result in freezing to the spot, unable to move.

The response is triggered by a threat, excitement, noise, bright lights or temperature and is characterized by physical changes in the body including the release of hormones such as adrenalin and cortisol. Adrenalin regulates heart rate and the flow of blood and air, by altering the diameter of blood vessels and air passages, while cortisol increases blood sugar, suppresses the immune system and increases metabolism. This chemical/hormonal change triggers the physical changes in the body. Once the threat has passed the body returns to its normal state ready for the next time.

The fight or flight response is directly associated with the autonomic system, which controls both the physiological and psychological changes in the body in response to a stressor. We will look at this system in more detail in the next chapter.

General adaptation syndrome

Stressors lead to stress and some form of physiological or psychological reaction. In 1936 Austrian-born physician Dr Hans Selye defined his general adaptation syndrome (GAS) as comprising three stages:

1 the **alarm reaction stage**, where a shock stimulates the body's defences
2 the **resistance stage**, where the body either resists the stressor or adapts to the effects of the stressor
3 the **exhaustion phase**, where if the stressor continues but the resistance or adaptation is lost, the body is overloaded, the alarm stage returns and if the stress is prolonged, damage will occur.

Stress in the modern world

Some see GAS as over-simplistic and have developed their thinking to consider a more interactional approach, considering the individual in more detail. Whereas GAS seems to imply an automatic response, research has shown that individuals balance the demands made on them considering a variety of factors and this approach leads to a definition of stress as more of an imbalance.

Factors associated with the interactive model of stress that affect an individual's response include:

- **cognitive appraisal** – an individual's perception of a situation or event
- **experience** – familiarity, previous/historical exposure to similar events, relevant learning or training and any reinforcement or conditioning (what is seen as success or failure to cope)
- **demand** – perceived demand, actual ability to meet demands
- **interpersonal influences** – background and influencing factors
- **state of stress imbalance** – between actual and perceived demand and the ability to cope.

The interactive model provides a useful foundation for the management strategies detailed in later chapters.

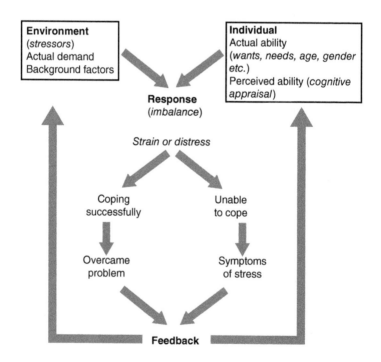

The interactive model of stress

Fight or flight evolved for dealing with physical danger in the modern work environment. Today, the situation is more likely to result in psychological danger, anticipation of events such as losing a job, failing to meet a deadline as well as actual danger from bullying or harassment. The world has moved on from the threat of being eaten by a tiger but as yet our biology has not caught up; it doesn't distinguish between physical and psychological threats – just think back to the last time you went to see a horror movie.

So from a work or organizational perspective, what we mean by stress today is more accurately described as *the negative effects or response to excessive pressure or other types of demands placed on people.*

Stress isn't always bad

Stress can be both positive and negative. Much of this Part focuses on management of the negative aspects of stress. However, the benefits of positive stress or pressure should not be overlooked. Positive pressure can be motivating and create a sense of team that helps get the job done.

The effects of positive stress, such as the 'butterfly feeling' you get in your stomach, link back to the basic biological response of fight or flight and the response to hormones in the bloodstream. In small doses this can help you perform under pressure and motivate you to do your best. Think of feelings you may have had before a job interview, a critical presentation or a looming deadline or target. Positive stress can make you feel pumped up and ready to succeed. Managed effectively in the workplace it can improve performance and bring a team together and improve overall wellbeing.

Like all stress though, people's thresholds vary and beyond a certain point stress stops being helpful and can start to damage the body. If you are continually performing under pressure your body and mind will ultimately pay the price.

The human performance curve shows the relationship between stress and performance and is adapted from the Yerkes-Dodson Law, originally developed in the early twentieth century by psychologist Robert M. Yerkes and John Dodson. The law states that performance increases with physiological or mental arousal, but only up to a point. When levels of arousal become too high, performance decreases. The adapted human performance curve illustrates how the same variation in performance is related to the amount of stress to which an individual is exposed.

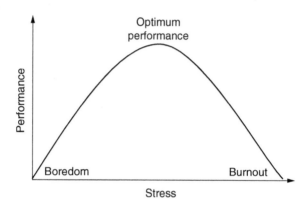

Adapted human performance curve

Stress isn't the same for everyone

Stress can be caused by a variety of stressors, including work situations (e.g. time pressure, fear of redundancy, overwork, bullying, and lack of tools and equipment) or personal experience such as home life or marriage breakdown. No two people react in the same way or to the same degree to a particular stressor. Some people seem to roll with the punches while others crumble at the slightest obstacle.

Earlier we introduced GAS and the idea that adaptation is required to respond to a stressor and that this can be expanded to consider factors relating to the individual – e.g. strength both physically and psychologically, perception and degree of control.

Various psychologists have researched the types and traits of personality or disposition. In Table 22.1 we consider six personality types, their preferred stress state and their vulnerability to the negative effects of excessive stress.

You might recognize some of the personality types in yourself or your work colleagues, although research concludes that most

Table 22.1 Disposition and vulnerability to stress

Type	Definition	Preferred stress level	Vulnerability to stress
Ambitious	Strong desire for success or achievement	High	High
Calm	Tranquil, placid and does not easily become disturbed, agitated or excited	Moderate/ Low	Low
Conscientious	Meticulous and takes great care over everything	Low/ Moderate	Moderate (high during change)
Non-assertive	Difficulty in standing up for themselves	Moderate/ Low	Moderate
Lively	Full of vigour, experiences mental and emotional vigour	High	Low (high if pressure from self)
Anxious	Worried and tense, concerned about possible misfortune	Low	High

people combine traits of more than one personality type so this information should only be used as a guide for individuals. Good managers realize that people are far more complex than any single model can show and will use this information to build an overall picture of an individual and won't jump to conclusions about who fits into which precise category.

Age, gender and a number of other factors influence an individual's vulnerability to stress. The four important factors of control, predictability, expectation and support provide an initial understanding of what controls might be appropriate to combat stress, and we will consider these further later.

Control

If you have the ability to influence events (control the stressor) and meet the specific challenge it is easier to handle stress. This may be a result of your position/level of authority, experience and freedom within an organization. Older people with secure finances may feel they ultimately can walk away or not have to put up with the pressure. This in itself allows them to cope better.

Predictability

An individual is likely to feel greater stress if they are unable to predict the behaviour or occurrence of a stressor. For example, bullying is notoriously unpredictable in terms of knowing what the bully will do next. Predictability is linked with familiarity, knowledge and preparation. An effective technique employed by hospitals to reduce patient stress is to provide an option for patients to familiarize themselves with the hospital surroundings and timetable of events prior to an operation or giving birth. Think about the value of fire drills in preparation for a real emergency situation.

Expectation

People have expectations of their own ability to cope, as well as societal pressures. For example, men have traditionally been seen as breadwinners and so men may be more vulnerable to stress relating to financial pressures. Women on the other hand have traditionally been seen as carers so may appear to be tasked with caring for sick or elderly relatives as well as the stressor of raising a family. These expectations may also be impacted by perception of whether things are, or are likely to start, getting better.

Support

People who feel they have support, including support from colleagues, managers, unions, friends, family or doctors, are less likely to be affected by stress. Those who take comfort from some form of spiritual support, faith or belief system might also find it easier to cope.

Assessment of stress

In order to identify the signs of stress in the workplace and determine the magnitude of its impact, a manager or organization can start by analysing, using existing performance measures such as sickness absence, accident rates, productivity and quality metrics (customer complaints, volume of rework, etc.).

Generally a high degree of stress in the workplace will have a detrimental impact on these measures.

You may also be able to pick up on individuals showing signs of stress such as increased medication, smoking or alcohol use, nail biting or grinding of teeth. People often lose their sense of humour, become touchy or you might sense a general 'negative air' or 'atmosphere' in the workplace. Personal appearance and levels of grooming or personal hygiene may also get worse.

In order to gain a complete picture it is necessary, and in some countries a legal requirement, to make a formal assessment of stress.

Before an assessment takes place it is important to prepare by securing senior management and wider organizational support and buy-in, explaining the potential benefits and that everyone should be involved in the process. This might be seen as a significant change in the organization and we deal with the issues associated with change management in Chapter 27.

The formal assessment process is broken down as follows.

1 **Identify potential stressors**
   Think about the potential causes of stress within the organization, using the information from this book but also think specifically about the type of organization you are in and draw on your own and others' experiences.
2 **Identify who is at risk**
   Gather data, such as any existing performance measures as described above. Get feedback through a survey or questionnaire. Various templates for benchmarking surveys or questionnaires exist and having read the remainder of this book you will no doubt be able to create something that suits your organization.
3 **Evaluate the risk**
   Having collected the data, what does it tell you? Do any existing controls or practices have an impact? Which areas do you need to focus on? It is important to focus on preventing stress but you should also consider mitigation when stress does arise. How is stress identified, escalated and managed?

4 Create an action plan

Create and communicate an action plan showing what will be done, by whom and when. Make sure the actions are followed up and completed.

5 Monitor and review

Periodically check to make sure actions are effective. Regularly review the sources of data, perhaps redoing the survey if you feel it is necessary. You should review at regular intervals but also be aware of any changes within the organization (e.g. downsizing, introducing new equipment or work patterns) that may prompt an additional review or the need for improved controls.

No signs doesn't mean no stress

Regardless of what you have already learnt, a critical thing to remember is people are often good at hiding stress. This may be through fear or embarrassment, or perhaps driven by the culture of an organization. Alternatively it may be an individual's desire not to let the team down or feeling they have everything under control or they may simply be blocking it out.

So just because your organization and the individuals within it may look stress-free doesn't necessarily mean that is actually the case – more often than not the opposite is true, with a calm façade hiding the turmoil beneath. Think of a swan gliding gracefully across a lake: the calm vision isn't the true picture as beneath the waters its feet are flapping away like crazy.

Causes and impacts of stress

While an organization and work itself can cause stress, not all stress is work-related and individuals often bring their own stress into the workplace.

In the late 1960s two researchers, Dr Thomas Holmes and Dr Richard Rahe, identified a relationship between life events and illness. Their results, commonly known as the Holmes-Rahe stress scale, show the relative impact of life events in life-changing units (LCU) (see Table 22.2).

Table 22.2 The Holmes-Rahe stress scale of life-changing units (LCU)

Life event	LCU	Life event	LCU
Death of a spouse	100	Change in responsibilities at work	29
Divorce	73	Child leaving home	29
Marital separation	65	Trouble with in-laws	29
Imprisonment	63	Outstanding personal achievement	28
Death of a close family member	63	Spouse starts or stops work	26
Personal injury or illness	53	Begin or end school	26
Marriage	50	Change in living conditions	25
Dismissal from work	47	Revision of personal habits	24
Marital reconciliation	45	Trouble with boss	23
Retirement	45	Change in working hours or conditions	20
Change in health of family member	44	Change in residence	20
Pregnancy	40	Change in schools	20
Sexual difficulties	39	Change in recreation	19
Gain a new family member	39	Change in social activities	18
Business readjustment	39	Minor mortgage or loan	17
Change in financial state	38	Change in sleeping habits	16
Death of a close friend	37	Change in number of family reunions	15
Change to different line of work	36	Change in eating habits	15
Change in frequency of arguments	35	Vacation	13
Major mortgage	32	Christmas	12
Foreclosure of mortgage or loan	30	Minor violation of law	11

The LCU scores in the table are based on averages from the study. Using the stress scale, a score of 300 or more places an individual at high risk of illness, a score of 150–299 at moderate risk, and less than 150 only at slight risk of illness.

Individual stressors from outside work may overlap with those at work, such as financial problems at home linking with reduced hours or pay and job uncertainty. Old style management that says 'leave your worries at the gate' is no longer acceptable or effective. Forward thinking employers see the benefit in providing a sympathetic response, some flexibility or additional support for individuals with personal stress.

In the workplace stressors can be categorized into several groups.

- job roles, responsibility and control, i.e. the actual requirements of a job role, level of ambiguity in what is expected, any conflict of interest and the degree of autonomy or control
- workload and work pressure, the characteristic of the task, the capacity of individuals, equipment and processes and both the amount and type of work being undertaken
- the work environment, including the physical environment, space, lighting, heating and ventilation
- behaviour, conflict and support (interpersonal factors). These are associated with relationships between staff and management but also the organizational environment, how well or otherwise the organization is managed and its culture. Also included is the approach to harassment and bullying and level of support available, how people are recognized and how poor performance and behaviours are managed along with specific individual concerns
- change management and how the organization handles changes, from installing new equipment to dealing with growth or downsizing including redundancies.

It is clear from this list that some stressors might be easy to change with minimal effort, while others are harder to address and some are impossible. Understanding these causes of stress by definition will inform the type of controls that may be effective, which we will look at from Chapter 24 onward.

Summary

In this chapter you have covered a lot of ground, so well done. You started by understanding the difference between stressors (the causes of stress) and the response (the effects of stress) and went on to learn about the fight or flight response, general adaptation syndrome and how in today's world we use an interactive model for stress, considering the individual as well as the surrounding environment.

You learnt the principle of assessing stress in the workplace and how stress isn't always bad and can, in small doses, help improve performance. You saw that stress isn't the same for everyone and factors such as personality, control, predictability, expectations and the level of support available all play a part in how an individual may respond. You also learnt that stress can exist even if there are no visible signs.

You covered the main categories of stress in the workplace, which we will revisit through the remaining chapters.

Finally you saw how events in our personal life can overlap with work and how these events can vary in intensity and the impact they have on health.

Fact-check [Answers at the back]

1. Which of the following is not an appropriate description of stress?
   a) The natural biological response to a threat or danger ❑
   b) The series of reactions to a stressor: alarm, resistance or adaptation and potential exhaustion ❑
   c) The negative effects or response to excessive pressure or other types of demands ❑
   d) The way weak people respond in a crisis with panic and confusion ❑

2. Which of the following is a true statement about stress?
   a) The signs of stress can always be seen ❑
   b) Some stress can be positive ❑
   c) Everyone reacts the same way when faced with a life-changing event ❑
   d) Jolly people tend to be less stressed than miserable ones ❑

3. Which of the following personality types may be the most vulnerable to stress?
   a) Ambitious ❑
   b) Calm ❑
   c) Conscientious ❑
   d) Non-assertive ❑

4. What important factors might affect the vulnerability of an individual to stress?
   a) Expectation ❑
   b) Predictability ❑
   c) Level of control ❑
   d) All of the above ❑

5. In the interactive model, which of these factors does not have an effect?
   a) An individual's perception of a situation or event ❑
   b) Whether the threat is physical or psychological in nature ❑
   c) Experience, previous exposure or relevant training ❑
   d) Perceived or actual ability to meet demands ❑

6. What might happen to sickness absence, accidents and customer complaints if a workforce is subject to stress?
   a) They are likely to remain unchanged ❑
   b) They are likely to decrease ❑
   c) They are likely to increase ❑
   d) Measuring these kind of things is irrelevant and a waste of money ❑

7. When assessing stress in the workplace what is the first thing you should do?
   a) Put together an action plan ❑
   b) Assess who might be at risk ❑
   c) Gain support and buy-in from senior managers ❑
   d) Send out a questionnaire ❑

8. When might you revisit your assessment of stress in the workplace?
a) Regularly or if the organization is about to or is going through change ❏
b) When human resources ask for a good news story for the company website ❏
c) If the survey results are bad ❏
d) Just before your performance review so you can show your boss how effective you've been ❏

9. Using the Holmes-Rahe stress scale, which of these events has the greatest impact in terms of life-changing units (LCU)?
a) Change in sleeping habits ❏
b) Pregnancy ❏
c) Change in line of work ❏
d) Marriage ❏

10. What might an organization do to support people with stress relating to their personal life?
a) Be sympathetic, show flexibility and provide support ❏
b) Give them a good talking to so they get a sense of perspective and move on ❏
c) Reduce their overtime or cut their hours so they have time to deal with personal matters ❏
d) All of the above ❏

CHAPTER 23

Understanding stress – some basic psychological and physiological aspects

In the previous chapter you learnt what stress is, the different models of stress and how in threatening situations the body reacts. Now we will look in more detail at the way the body responds to stress.

We will consider physical and psychological symptoms and the autonomic nervous system's effect on the body as part of the natural stress response. Then we will learn about some of the medical conditions that may be found in the workforce and diagnosed as a result of personal issues or experiences at work. These conditions include anxiety, depression, phobias and post-traumatic stress disorder. Finally we will see how stress can negatively affect an organization.

The aim of the chapter is not to make you a medical expert but to provide a basic understanding of some of the signs and symptoms of stress and how these link to biological processes in the body. You will be able to use this understanding to see warning signs in yourself and work colleagues and also be able to support those with diagnosed medical conditions in your organization.

Effects of stress

The effects of stress on the individual will vary from person to person but will broadly fall into two categories:

- **physiological effects** – the short-term and long-term effects on the body
- **psychological effects** – how people think, feel and behave (also termed cognitive, emotional and behavioural effects).

The following lists give some commons signs and symptoms of stress. The more you notice in yourself or others the closer you or they may be to a stress imbalance or burnout. Bear in mind that the signs and symptoms of stress can also be caused by other medical problems so wherever possible you should seek or encourage others to seek professional medical assistance.

Physiological signs and symptoms

Physiological signs and symptoms are short-term or long-term health effects, and can include the following:

- headaches
- nervous twitches
- memory problems
- mental ill health
- tiredness or sleeping problems
- frequent colds
- breathlessness
- chest pains, rapid heart beat
- high blood pressure and high cholesterol
- heart disease
- stroke
- feeling sick, nauseous or dizzy, fainting
- a craving for food or loss of appetite
- constipation or diarrhoea
- indigestion or heartburn
- diabetes
- gastric ulcers
- cramps or pins and needles
- arthritis

- sexual problems, lack of libido
- susceptibility to some types of cancer.

Psychological signs and symptoms

Psychological signs and symptoms involve how people may think, feel or behave, and include the following:

- anxiety
- fearing the future
- irritable, short temper or aggressive
- seeing only the negative
- frustration
- depressed, generally unhappy
- poor/irrational judgement
- inability to relax
- feeling overwhelmed
- feeling neglected, alone or uncared for
- breakdown in relationships
- job dissatisfaction
- restlessness, agitation, inability to concentrate or relax
- believing you are a failure, bad or ugly
- lack of interest in others
- loss of sense of humour
- avoiding making decisions or difficult situations
- denying there is a problem
- reliance on alcohol, cigarettes or drugs to relax
- nervous habits, nail biting, pacing.

The autonomic system

We've already learnt how the fight or flight response is linked to the body's autonomic system. In this system two sets of nerves are responsible for the automatic and unconscious regulation of the body's functions. The sympathetic system prepares the body to fight and the parasympathetic system is concerned with protection of the body with both systems acting in balance. For example, the sympathetic system causes rapid heart rate and breathing while slowing digestion, and the parasympathetic system in contrast reduces heart rate and breathing while increasing digestion. As you will see from the summary of autonomic responses in Table 23.1, it is the body's natural response that causes many of the basic signs and symptoms of stress.

Table 23.1 Effects of the autonomic system

Body part/ organ	Effect of parasympathetic system	Effect of sympathetic system
Brain	Reduced neural activity	Increased neural activity, quick decision-making
Heart	Decreased heart rate and output	Increased heart rate and output
Lungs	Breathing slowed	Airways increased, breathing rapid
Liver	Storage of glucose and fat	Breakdown of glucose and fat for energy
Spleen	Retains red blood cells	Contracts and empties red blood cells into the circulation
Digestion	Increased	Decreased
Kidney	Urine production	Reduced urine production
Eyes	Closed, pupils small	Open, pupils dilated
Mouth	Saliva produced	Saliva reduced, dry mouth
Ears	Hearing less acute	Hearing more acute
Skin	Dry, hair flaccid/normal	Sweating, hairs erect
Muscles	Relaxed	Tense
Blood	Normal ability to clot	Increased ability to clot

In addition to these general symptoms, certain chronic conditions may arise, with those listed below being the most common although other disorders exist. Specific advice for individuals will be available as a result of formal diagnosis. Whether you see symptoms of these disorders in yourself or others, professional help should be encouraged.

Depression

Depression is a state of low mood, associated with an aversion to activity and feelings of sadness, worry, restlessness and guilt. Depression may also be related to the presence of factors such as:

- family or personal history of depression
- life-changing events such as the death of a child or spouse
- drug or alcohol misuse
- chronic pain or illness.

A depressed mood is not necessarily a medical or psychiatric disorder in its own right but in some cases may arise as a side effect to some medical treatments or as a result of some infections or illnesses. Depression can also be the main symptom of some psychiatric disorders, including major depression (also called clinical depression), bipolar disorder (also called manic depression) and seasonal affective disorder where episodes of depression follow a seasonal cycle.

Anxiety

Anxiety is a feeling of unease, apprehension, worry and fear. Many people will feel anxiety at some point in their lives, particularly in response to a dangerous situation or disruptive life events as described in the previous chapter in the Holmes-Rahe stress scale. Anxiety is a perfectly natural response but can develop into a number of conditions.

Generalized anxiety disorder (GAD)

Generalized anxiety disorder arises from feeling anxious over a prolonged period of time rather than in response to a specific event. It can cause both physical and psychological symptoms as described above, and can have a significant impact on daily life. Treatments are available, including a variety of therapies and medication.

Panic disorder

Panic disorder is diagnosed when sufferers experience panic attacks on a regular basis. A panic attack is an overwhelming fear or apprehension and may be accompanied by physical symptoms such as nausea, sweating and palpitations (irregular heart beat). Sufferers may experience as few as one or two panic attacks per month while others may experience them at a frequency of several per week.

Attacks can occur at any time and without warning but may also be related to a particular situation or location. Although intense and frightening, attacks do not cause any physical harm. Treatment is usually by psychological therapies and or medication.

Phobias

Phobias are a fear response that is out of proportion to the risk posed by a particular object, animal or situation. People can gain an irrational fear of almost anything: heights, enclosed spaces, flying, spiders, snakes, clowns or the number 13. The level of anxiety may vary between sufferers, ranging from mild anxiety to a severe panic attack. Sufferers will often go out of their way to avoid all contact with the source of their anxiety, meaning it can have a significant disruptive effect on people's lives.

Those with simple phobias, such as fear of snakes, may be treated by gradual exposure to the animal, object or place, and over time, in incremental steps, sufferers can become desensitized. This can be done using self-help techniques or through professional help. Those with more complex phobias such as agoraphobia (fear of situations where escape might be difficult or help may not be available in an emergency), where an individual may be scared of public transport or may not even be able to leave their house, can be treated over a much longer period of time. Treatment will normally involve therapies such as counselling, psychotherapy or cognitive behavioural therapy (CBT).

Post-traumatic stress disorder (PTSD)

PTSD is an anxiety disorder triggered by a specific frightening or distressing event, including:

- wars, military combat
- terrorism attacks or being held hostage
- natural disasters such as floods or earthquakes
- witnessing violent deaths or serious crimes.

PTSD can develop immediately after the trigger event or become apparent weeks, months or even years later. Sufferers relive the event through flashbacks and nightmares and may experience feelings of guilt and isolation and become irritable and have trouble sleeping.

Treatment depends on the severity of symptoms and how soon they occur after the trigger event. Trauma-focused CBT as well as medication and other psychological treatments may be used.

As you might expect, certain types of work may expose people to greater risk of PTSD: those in the emergency services, armed forces or those who work with the potential threat of physical violence such as prison workers, some civil service positions (e.g. welfare and benefits workers) or even teachers of young adults. In addition to the work people undertake in your organization you should consider their working history as certain industries tend to attract those from a particular background as a second career – e.g. those with military service may be recruited by security or defence firms. In such situations you may consider additional training for staff to be aware of symptoms, and proactively consider support provisions.

Obsessive compulsive disorder (OCD)

OCD is an anxiety disorder characterized by ritualistic behaviours designed to fend off the cause of apprehension, fear or worry. Symptoms include excessive hand washing, cleaning or repeated checking. Some sufferers have a preoccupation with sexual, violent or religious thoughts and others exhibit an aversion to a particular number.

OCD is sometimes linked to high intelligence and sufferers often exhibit other personality disorders. It can be treated by a variety of behavioural therapies and medication. In extreme cases surgical options may be considered.

Other biological considerations

A circadian rhythm is any biological process that follows a 24-hour cycle and can be found across the natural world in plants, animals and fungi. Fundamentally, circadian rhythms are hard-wired into our bodies; however, they can be adjusted to the local environment by external causes. In humans the rhythm is most evident in sleeping and feeding patterns but can also be seen in regulation of core body temperature, brainwave activity, hormone production and cell regeneration.

Circadian rhythms are important when it comes to work patterns, particularly shift working or people who travel extensively crossing multiple time zones – e.g. airline pilots and crew. Inability to following usual sleeping patterns can lead to fatigue, disorientation or insomnia.

To mitigate the impact of shift work it is important to avoid rapid shift changes and permanent night shifts. Minimizing the number of consecutive nights worked and offsetting working time with clear days away from work will all help. Individuals can also improve their ability to sleep during the day by avoiding alcohol, heavy foods and exercise prior to sleep.

In addition to circadian rhythms the body may also be affected by other temporal cycles such as seasonal changes including reduced daylight hours. In the workplace there may be practical things you can do to accommodate these variations, such as varying lighting types and intensity.

Understand the signs of your own stress

We often see things in others, while failing to recognize the very same things in ourselves. As an individual it is important to consider what stressors trigger a specific reaction in you and what symptoms the response generates, whether they be physical changes or shifts in our feelings, thoughts or behaviour.

By reflecting and taking time to appreciate our own level of stress we can see early warning signs and ensure that we take appropriate action so that symptoms do not become serious and we manage the situation.

We will consider simple steps that everyone can take to reduce stress and improve their general wellbeing in Chapter 28.

Effects of stress on an organization

In addition to the effect on individuals, stress, irrespective of the cause (either generated by the workplace or brought in by an individual from their personal life) can have a significant impact on an organization. The effects of stress on an organization can include:

● employee loyalty and commitment to work
● employee recruitment and retention
● employee performance and productivity
● accident rates, sickness absence and customer complaints
● customer satisfaction
● reputation, brand and image.

In some situations, where an organization is the cause of stress, employers may also face legal responsibilities and failure to manage stress may result in regulatory action or litigation resulting in prosecution and or compensation claims.

Like individuals, organizations also vary in their vulnerability to stress, with certain occupations or organizations more prone by the nature of the work done. These might include the emergency services; teaching; work that involves a high degree of uncertainty or interaction with public or societal groups who themselves may be under stress, so employees end up on the receiving end of others' fight or flight responses; shift or night workers, where their diurnal rhythms are impacted; those who perform safety critical roles where errors may have catastrophic consequences, such as air traffic controllers.

Remember that if you decide to take action to manage stress, you must prepare individuals and organizations, as you do not want your efforts to backfire and cause additional pressure/demands on others. You will also need to be conscious that not all management techniques are appropriate for all organizations.

Summary

In this chapter you have learnt some of the psychological and physiological symptoms of stress as well as the link between these symptoms and the autonomic system's effect on a variety of organs and parts of the body.

You saw some of the common medical conditions associated with stress, and how circadian rhythms and seasonal cycles can impact the body and what steps may be taken to manage them. You should understand the importance of self-awareness in terms of what triggers stress for you personally so you can manage your own stress levels.

Finally you saw how stress in the workplace can negatively impact an organization through reduced employee loyalty, commitment to work, performance and productivity, increased accidents and sickness absence rates, low customer satisfaction and damage to an organization's reputation and brand. Organizations should also be aware of any specific regulatory requirement associated with the management of stress to avoid potential prosecutions or compensation claims.

Fact-check [Answers at the back]

1. Which of the symptoms below is not a potential physical sign of stress?
   a) Headaches ❑
   b) Indigestion or heartburn ❑
   c) High blood pressure ❑
   d) Believing you are a failure, bad or ugly ❑

2. Which of these psychological signs of stress might you pick up on in the workplace?
   a) People avoiding making decisions ❑
   b) Staff making poor or irrational judgements ❑
   c) Work colleagues denying a problem exists ❑
   d) All of the above ❑

3. With regard to the autonomic system, which of the following is not part of the sympathetic nervous system response?
   a) Decreased digestion ❑
   b) Decreased clotting ability of blood ❑
   c) Increased breathing rate ❑
   d) Increased heart rate ❑

4. Similarly, which of these is not a true statement relating to the parasympathetic response?
   a) Pupils are dilated ❑
   b) Hearing is less acute ❑
   c) Skin is dry, hair normal/ flaccid ❑
   d) Muscles are relaxed ❑

5. Which of the following is unlikely to be a significant factor relating to depression?
   a) Family or personal history of depression ❑
   b) Life-changing events such as the death of a child or spouse ❑
   c) Moderate consumption of alcohol ❑
   d) Chronic pain or illness ❑

6. Which of the following is not an event likely to trigger post-traumatic episodes?
   a) War ❑
   b) Natural disaster ❑
   c) Witnessing a fatal car accident ❑
   d) PowerPoint failure during an important presentation ❑

7. Which of the following is not a characteristic of obsessive compulsive disorder?
   a) Excessive hand washing ❑
   b) Keeping lists as a reminder of tasks to complete ❑
   c) Regular checking or cleaning ❑
   d) Preoccupation with violent or religious thoughts ❑

8. Which of the following temporal events is not recognized as influencing biological cycles?
   a) New Year celebrations ❑
   b) Changing of the seasons ❑
   c) Crossing multiple time zones ❑
   d) 24-hour cycle of day and night ❑

9. Why is it important to identify your own triggers, symptoms and levels of stress?
a) To be an example to others of how to cope ❏
b) To set challenging targets for yourself ❏
c) To see warning signs and take action to ensure that symptoms do not become serious ❏
d) To know when to book your holiday ❏

10. Which of these may be negatively impacted by stress in the workplace?
a) Employee loyalty, commitment to work, productivity ❏
b) Accidents and sickness absence rates ❏
c) Brand and reputation ❏
d) All of the above ❏

CHAPTER 24

Job roles, responsibility and level of control

The old adage that prevention is better than cure holds true for managing stress at work. Now we have learnt what stress is and some of its effects, we can start to look at ideas, methods and practical examples of how to prevent stress in the workplace.

In this chapter we will look at how lack of clarity around job roles, the failure to communicate or have an agreed understanding of what individuals are expected to do and the boundaries of their responsibility can lead to confusion, worry and stress. We will also consider how conflicting expectations can lead to frustration and errors.

We will learn how engaging with employees, allowing them freedom to determine how they work and the opportunity to get involved in decision-making processes can increase motivation and productivity, create a sense of power and ownership and reduce anxiety and stress.

The Dalai Lama once said:

> *If a problem is fixable, if a situation is such that you can do something about it, then there is no need to worry. If it's not fixable, then there is no help in worrying. There is no benefit in worrying whatsoever.*

Role clarity

Role clarity is about communicating clear expectations of what is to be done or achieved and the boundaries of responsibility. This is essential to reducing stress in the workplace.

Without understanding exactly what is expected of you, it is easy to be blamed for something you have done but that management felt you didn't have the authority to do, seemingly being punished for taking the initiative when things go wrong. Alternatively, you may also be blamed if you didn't complete an activity that management thought you should have done – e.g. being challenged as to why you didn't foresee a problem and take the initiative to solve it. Working in these circumstances you seem to be damned if you do something and damned if you don't.

Often you will also find that where there is an absence of role clarity there can be a considerable lag between a problem and its discovery. For example, a contractual or equipment specification change may be made and only discovered by management many months later when a dispute arises or the equipment has been installed and is found to be inappropriate. Inevitably an investigation more akin to a witch-hunt will ensue and all involved will try and point the finger elsewhere.

I am reminded of a simple story that illustrates the point on role clarity very well.

You have heard the story about Anybody, Nobody, Somebody, and Everybody?

An important job had to be done and Everybody was sure that Somebody would do it. Anybody could have done it, but Nobody did it. Somebody got angry about that because it was Everybody's job. Everybody thought that Anybody could do it, but Nobody realized that Everybody wouldn't do it. It ended up that Everybody blamed Somebody when Nobody did what Anybody could have done.

Language can also be a significant issue in role clarity; it is all too easy to write job descriptions or make statements that can be interpreted in more than one way. So it is important to avoid ambiguity and things that can be interpreted or taken out of context.

In Chapter 28 we will look at time management and the importance of prioritization. You can see that without role clarity and a true understanding of who is expecting you to do what, it is hard to assign priorities and allocate time appropriately.

All roles in an organization need to have a formal job description explaining what the role is for, what is expected, boundaries of responsibility and also cover any required knowledge or training. This should be agreed by both parties. Most people get a job description when they start a new job or join a new organization but over time you get asked to take on new responsibilities and the workplace may change, and bits of what you did may transfer to others or disappear because procedures or the technology has changed. A formal job description should never be used as a barrier to taking on or changing your duties but it should be reviewed regularly to make sure it stays current and meaningful.

Role conflict

When we talk about conflict we usually think about disagreements between two parties and this may occur in the workplace. Here we are thinking about conflict within an individual's role. There is a potential for stress when two parts or elements of a job are seemingly incompatible. If you are a parent of small children this is something you have to wrestle with on a daily basis. On the one hand you need to encourage your children to be honest and open and confident that they can confide in you, on the other there is a need to provide discipline when you find out something naughty has been done, thus discouraging the open and honest behaviour you are seeking to instil.

Work examples may include potential conflict between productivity over safety, or company loyalty over care for subordinates. Think of a medical doctor: they have to balance care for the individual patient with getting a certain volume of appointments completed in each day.

The most obvious solution is to deconflict a particular role, by designing jobs and allocating conflicting responsibilities to different people. While this may be practical in some organizations, particularly where the potential of role conflict can have catastrophic effects, such as safety critical roles in the nuclear or aviation industries, for many, role conflict has to remain part of the job and work becomes a balancing act to manage these conflicts.

In addition to role conflict inside the workplace, there may also be conflict from outside. The most common is the balance between work and home life. Parents have responsibilities to their family, perhaps there may be a sick or elderly relative at home or some workers may have more than one job.

Where role conflict can't be avoided and regardless of the source, these factors need to be considered and dealt with in an open and sensitive manner. I am a believer that bad news is in fact good news when delivered early. Knowing about a problem sooner rather than later allows you to deal with it before it gets out of hand. It is therefore important to provide a mechanism where people can express concern or validate their decision-making. One method is through the implementing of a **just culture** (see Chapter 26) where it becomes the organization's normal practice, within defined boundaries, to raise concerns and problems without the fear of punishments or reprisal and all employees have a clear authority to STOP, particularly if a problem relates to safety, quality or spiralling costs.

Being able to stop or raise issues without the fear of punishment or retribution prevents employees masking genuine mistakes or covering up problems.

Motivation

An understanding of motivation is important for any manager to get the most out of their team. It also has a direct link to stress in the workplace. If you feel undervalued, overlooked or stuck in a dead-end job, you are likely to look negatively on things and become susceptible to stress, particularly if you feel powerless to change your situation.

In 1943, Abraham Maslow presented his paper 'A Theory of Human Motivation' in which he described stages of growth through a 'hierarchy of needs'. This hierarchy of needs is often depicted as a pyramid with basic or physiological needs (air, food, water, shelter, etc.) at the base and self-actualization (the state of achieving your true potential) at the top.

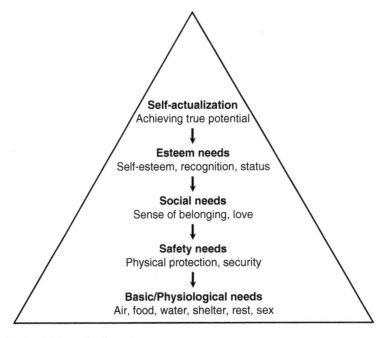

Maslow's hierarchy of needs

Maslow's model has been adapted and updated a number of times and a revised model from the 1990s is shown below.

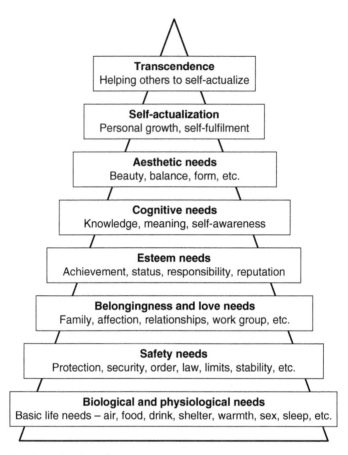

Adapted hierarchy of needs

Frederick Herzberg proposed the Motivation-Hygiene Theory, also known as the Two Factor Theory, of job satisfaction in the late 1950s following extensive research, where he investigated the factors that lead to employee satisfaction and dissatisfaction (see Table 24.1).

He discovered that certain factors were expected to be met in order to avoid dissatisfaction. These hygiene factors need to be present and well managed essentially to maintain a neutral level of satisfaction and have to be addressed before considering the factors that result in positive satisfaction.

Table 24.1 Herzberg's Two Factor Theory

Motivators	Hygiene factors
Challenge	Salary and other benefits
Responsibility	Working conditions
Promotion	Safety arrangements
Interesting or stimulating work	Security
Recognition	Quality of supervision
Achievement	Interpersonal relationships
	Status

The factors having a positive effect are described by Herzberg as 'motivators'.

Herzberg also proposed the idea of job enrichment to improve satisfaction. This involves empowering employees to take greater control of their work through less supervision, freedom to select methods and approach to work.

One surprise from Herzberg's work might be that money (i.e. pay and benefits) is a hygiene factor rather than a motivator. Herzberg himself acknowledged that there was some degree of disagreement over this point but stated, 'viewed within the context of the sequences of events, salary as a factor belongs more in the group that defines the job situation and is primarily a dissatisfier'.

As a manager, it is often easy to try and retain staff by simply paying them more, but this actually has little impact in the long-term, despite what the individuals themselves may say. As with other hygiene factors though, the expectation is that pay is at least in line with the market to avoid dissatisfaction. If this requirement is met, effective managers need to seek to provide true motivators in the work environment.

Level of control

From the work of Maslow and Herzberg, we see that we have certain basic needs and other more complex motivational needs. Lack of, or failure to meet, either of these can lead to stress. Staff should be able to influence decisions and understand the reasons why, when factors are more rigid and less negotiable.

Lack of control can affect morale and self-worth and create frustration, whereas giving people greater freedom and a sense of self-determination over their place of work can encourage them to develop new skills, to undertake more challenging work, use their skills to be innovative and become more productive.

Job enrichment can be achieved by reducing supervision or allowing greater autonomy to employees to decide how they work. This approach should be supported by clear responsibilities and accountability and aligns well with an objectives-based approach to working.

It must be recognized though that some jobs (e.g. those of a repetitive nature) are less adaptable and so alternative methods need to be found to motivate employees. Here, increasing the responsibilities of staff to cover a wider remit will help to provide challenge. Alternatively, job rotation can provide variety which is beneficial both to individuals in terms of job satisfaction and the organization in terms of preventing mistakes. When engaged in repetitive and monotonous tasks employees can become complacent, distracted or blinkered to what is happening, essentially 'switching to auto pilot', which can lead to errors or accidents affecting safety, quality and productivity. Creating a sense of team and allowing for job rotation can ensure people remain focused and mutually supportive with collective responsibility for a series of tasks.

As an example, think of a manufacturing line with several stages, each requiring an operator with a specific skill. By training all the staff on the line to perform all tasks (multi-skilling), collectively the team can own the output from the line and freely rotate between positions to provide working variety. Multi-skilling may require an investment in training but this is usually outweighed by the benefits in motivation and productivity. Multi-skilling also means less reliance on individuals and a greater ability to accommodate leave, absences, etc.

In a previous role I was responsible for ride operations at a theme park. The larger rides would need a number of staff to operate, some managing queues, others batching, loading and unloading guests from the ride, looking after bags and an operator to start, stop and monitor the ride. Many of the positions required repetitive actions and had a safety dimension. Multi-skilling and job rotation proved very effective in ensuring safety was maintained but also by providing variety for employees they remained motivated and as a consequence interacted better with guests, improving the quality of their day out.

Objective output-based working

Objective output-based working means providing less prescription to employees and supports an increased level of autonomy and control. Mutually agreeing a specific work outcome and allowing the employee freedom to determine how to achieve the objective in a specific timeframe addresses many of the motivation factors identified by Herzberg.

A common acronym for effective objective setting is SMART:

- **S**pecific
- **M**easurable
- **A**chievable
- **R**elevant
- **T**imely or **T**ime bound

SMART work objectives provide clarity by defining **S**pecifically what needs to be accomplished, the reasons why, who is involved and any specific requirements, boundaries or constraints. The **M**easures of success define how much or how many and a clear end point, i.e. how you know when you have achieved the objective. They must be **A**chievable, which means providing stretch and challenge to an individual or team but not so extreme as to be unrealistic. Objectives must have a **R**elevance to an individual or team and the organization as a whole, otherwise it is hard to understand the context and value of what is to be done. A clear **T**ime constraint provides a guide as to the level of urgency and the prioritization of tasks.

Regarding the relevance of objectives, this is one area that is often overlooked as obvious, but failure to adequately think through the consequences of an objective can force actions and behaviours that may be counterproductive. An example is objectives for an organization's sales force. While it is obvious the sales team should sell more, if volume is the only measure of success, it will drive sales at any cost, reducing profit margins or even selling at a loss. Also the sales team may sell more than can be delivered, leaving customers disappointed or a workforce burnt out trying to deliver more than they can produce. So relevance needs to be assessed in a broader context.

Employee engagement and consultation

In many situations there are statutory requirements to consult with employees on a variety of matters. Irrespective of external requirements it makes good sense for managers to engage and consult with their staff, ensuring that everyone has a voice in influencing their work practices and environment. The ability to influence decision-making provides a feeling of power rather than powerlessness; as we have learnt, being powerless to impact your situation or surroundings plays a key part in levels of anxiety or stress.

Organizations might wish to create some form of employee forum or consultation group, or utilize existing bodies such as trade unions for this purpose. There are several challenges that need to be addressed for such a group to be effective. The group needs to be truly reflective of the workforce, a balance of management and employees, and adequately representative of different departments, functions and workgroups. Usually representatives should be elected, demonstrating they have the support of their peers, and serve for a defined period of time ensuring they can step down or periodically refresh representation if ineffective.

Representatives need to have time to consult with their peers to be effective, and need to be sufficiently robust to represent views, even if they have personal feelings to the contrary. It is important to keep individual, internal or external politics out of discussions and decision-making. The most important element is to ensure that the group actually has power and that feelings and comments from employees are acted upon, and where this is not possible the reasons why are clearly explained.

Engagement groups should be able to influence both hygiene factors and motivators in the workplace. For example, they may comment on safety and operational procedures, breaks and work patterns, levels of supervision and how pay and benefits are awarded in relation to performance as well as working with management to ensure work is challenging and people receive appropriate recognition.

In Chapter 27 we will look more closely at change management. When an organization is planning significant change, whether downsizing, expanding, implementing new work practices or machinery, employee engagement and buy-in is critical for success. Therefore, the engagement and consultation structures an organization uses day to day can become a powerful vehicle to ensure a successful change.

Manager's action

An effective manager should try to minimize conflict, improve clarity and empower employees. Sometimes you may not be supported by the organization as a whole, but you can set an example within your area of responsibility. You should regularly ask yourself some questions:

- Do you discuss working practices and arrangements with employees, and act on their feedback?
- Do you discuss employees' objectives, progress against objectives and aspirations for the future?
- Do you encourage training and development and provide opportunity for progression?
- Do employees raise issues and concerns early and help identify causes and solutions?
- Do you thank and recognize individuals and teams for their efforts?

Of the above I have found nothing motivates employees more than recognition that they have done well. So say 'thank you' often and sincerely. Two simple words can reduce tension and flood the body of both manager and employee with feel-good chemicals. You will reinforce positive behaviour and build a bank of goodwill which you may need to draw on in the future. So whoever and for whatever reason, say thank you – you will find people are happy and more open, you can follow up with questions about what they have achieved, what they have learnt and what you can do to help in the future.

Summary

In this chapter you have leant how to reduce worry and anxiety for your workforce by setting clear expectations and responsibilities for individual job roles. You saw how to reduce role conflict and ambiguity and how to provide appropriate support to staff where conflict can't be avoided, using open and honest dialogue without fear of punishment or reprisal as part of a just culture.

You have examined the works of Maslow and Herzberg, and how these theories support the idea of allowing employees to have greater freedom and control concerning their work and work environment, and learnt how to set SMART output-based objectives to improve motivation.

Consideration was given to multi-skilling and job rotation to provide variety and reduce errors and to create a sense of team or collective ownership for a series of activities or tasks. Finally you covered some principles of employee engagement and consultation and considered some simple questions you should ask yourself as a manager to ensure you get the most out of your team.

Fact-check [Answers at the back]

1. Why are clear responsibilities important?
   a) To ensure you know who to blame when things go wrong ❑
   b) To provide clarity so everyone knows what's expected of them and can manage their priorities accordingly ❑
   c) To ensure you know you are not paying someone too much ❑
   d) To give Human Resources the correct paperwork ❑

2. If an employee raises a concern regarding role conflict, you should...
   a) Tell your boss immediately to avoid being blamed ❑
   b) Get the employee to swap roles with a work colleague ❑
   c) Give the employee a pay rise and ask them to live with it ❑
   d) Discuss the issues and try to identify potential solutions with the employee's involvement ❑

3. In the hierarchy of needs, which needs should be satisfied first?
   a) Esteem ❑
   b) Social ❑
   c) Safety ❑
   d) Physiological ❑

4. In Herzberg's two factor theory which of the following is not a hygiene factor?
   a) Salary ❑
   b) Achievement ❑
   c) Working conditions ❑
   d) Quality of supervision ❑

5. Which of the following is not a motivator?
   a) Challenge ❑
   b) Interpersonal relationships ❑
   c) Responsibility ❑
   d) Interesting work ❑

6. Which of the following is not an element of SMART objectives?
   a) Specific ❑
   b) Measureable ❑
   c) Robust ❑
   d) Time-bound ❑

7. Why might setting a volume-only sales target for the sales team become counterproductive?
   a) It might drive behaviour that was unintentional, reducing margin or exceeding production capacity ❑
   b) Human Resources says everyone has to have a safety objective as well ❑
   c) We may have to pay the sales team extra commission if they meet the target ❑
   d) It wouldn't be counter-productive, increasing sales is a good thing ❑

8. Why might job rotation improve motivation?
   a) Employees get a greater variety of work and a sense of shared ownership ❑
   b) Employees get to spend more time training than working ❑
   c) Employees get to pick a job that pays more ❑
   d) Employees get to move around so no one knows who's responsible anymore ❑

9. What important factor should be considered in establishing an employee forum?

a) Make sure none of the trouble makers get elected as representatives ❏

b) Make sure you make decisions before the meeting so you can tell everyone what's happening ❏

c) Make sure all departments and functions are represented, including managers and employees ❏

d) Make sure representatives are kept busy to avoid them chatting to other staff ❏

10. What can I do as a manager to improve the motivation of my team?

a) Discuss concerns and issues ❏

b) Encourage training and development ❏

c) Say thank you ❏

d) All of the above ❏

CHAPTER 25

Workload, work pressure and work environment

It is easy to see ourselves as overworked. Sometimes this is genuinely true, other times it is down to personal negative perceptions or our own expectation of what good performance looks like, rather than being driven by management or others in the workplace. It is also easy to confuse activity for productivity. We may spend all our time travelling from site to site, in meetings or writing reports but never seem to get anything of value done.

In Chapter 28 we will consider time management and prioritization, an important skill for managing workload and pressure, in more detail. Now we will focus on how, as a manager, you can build on knowledge from the previous chapter to motivate employees without setting unrealistic targets to improve workload and pressure and will learn to distinguish between activity and productivity.

We will see how you can use Pareto analysis to identify the most significant factors in order to prioritize improvement activity and will consider some lean principles, tools and techniques to help increase productivity and reduce workplace stress by removing waste, eliminating bottlenecks and smoothing work demands.

Finally we will look at how elements of workplace design and the work environment can create or contribute to work pressures and stress and we will investigate how these elements can be effectively managed.

Workload and work pressure

In the absence of clear communication of expectations, people will make assumptions based on behaviour. As a manager you may think it appropriate to always be the first one into work and the last one to leave at the end of the day. This might be required or a self-imposed demand. Either way your behaviour will set an expectation among your team. Others will pick up and mirror your practice making an assumption that because you do it it must be important and therefore if you're going to get on, that is what is expected.

This innocent action now creates an atmosphere where, potentially, people fear to ask for time off or to leave early to attend their children's school theatre production, a dental appointment, etc. Staff may switch to auto pilot where they perceive it is more important to be seen sat at the desk, irrespective of what they are doing. Pressure mounts, resentment sets in and before long the entire office is stressed out.

This example is real, if perhaps a little extreme, and something I encountered first-hand, when a bold secretary came to see me to vent the frustrations of my team. My response was one of shock: of course I don't expect people to be there the same hours as me or miss the Christmas play. Today I make a point of varying my start and finish times so I am not always first in or last out, take an interest in what others are doing out of work and make a point of leaving early occasionally, and the impact is quite stark.

As well as driving psychological expectation, as a manager you also set physical expectations. These might be production or other performance targets, contracted working hours or shift patterns. We learnt in the previous chapter that challenge is an important part of motivation and setting SMART output-based objectives can provide employees with greater control over their working day. This work freedom also helps reduce work pressure as individuals have the power to influence how they work.

When setting SMART objectives other factors you should consider include:

- Are demands appropriate in relation to agreed timetables/ hours of work?
- Is the individual physically capable of meeting the demands?
- Are equipment or processes capable of meeting the demands?
- Are skills and abilities matched to demands – does an individual have the appropriate competencies and training?
- Have any concerns been addressed and how will issues be raised?

Productivity and process improvement

In addition to a particular manager's approach, workload and work pressure are often associated with poor processes and productivity. This might be that work isn't divided equally among staff, creating a bottleneck for certain tasks or individuals, which in turn creates a feeling of overwork, pressure and stress. Alternatively, operational procedures or authorization processes might be unnecessarily complex or have been written without the involvement of those actually performing a task. The slogan *work smarter not harder* is often bandied around by managers but few actually act on this intention. How many times have you or work colleagues said 'This job would be so much easier if we just...'

In the next couple of sections we will learn some basic tools and techniques for improving processes and increasing productivity, thereby avoiding excessive workload and pressure.

Pareto analysis

Sometimes it is hard to know where to start. A useful tool for both managing your time and tackling problems is Pareto analysis. The idea is that 80% of tasks can be completed in 20% of the time and this has clear implications for time management. We can apply the same rule to work demands and productivity, assuming that 80% of productive activity can be completed with 20% of the tasks and the remaining 20% productivity taking 80% of the time or covering 80% of tasks.

Essentially Pareto analysis lets you determine where you will get your biggest impact for the time and money spent on improvement – 'the best bang for your buck!'

Sometimes you need to consider how you analyse your data. Consider the example below, a real situation I dealt with, in which you can see how powerful Pareto analysis can be.

A company runs a set of fast food restaurants in a particular town. Each of the six restaurants occasionally runs out of certain product lines of food. This causes customers to complain, and staff to become pressured as they think they might be blamed by management and will also have to deal with angry customers. They decide to solve the problem and collect data on which restaurants have the biggest problem and what the cause of the problems are, and graph their results.

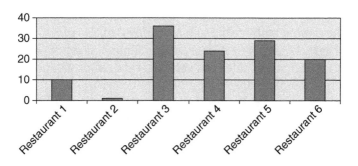

Number of product lines run out by restaurant

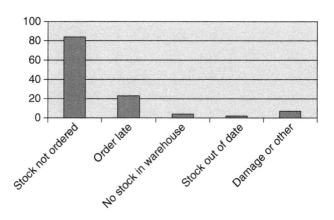

Causes of product lines running out

By simply looking at the number of events in the first graph they might choose to focus on restaurant 3 and deal with over 30 events. However, if they consider the causes across all restaurants they see that the single biggest problem is stock not being ordered. This means they can focus on over 80 events across all the restaurants, getting more from their effort. In the real-life situation, this was investigated and a simple reminder system implemented by the central warehouse. Each day they would ring round each restaurant at the end of the day to check orders had been placed in the electronic system. Problem solved, customers were happy, stressful situations for staff were removed.

Five lean principles

Terms such as Lean, Kaizen, Six sigma or Process improvement can sometimes get bandied around as management buzz words. They have been around for a number of years and all seek to improve productivity. While my personal feeling is that all of these practices can add value, you can take it too far and forget the social and people elements of work which in themselves contribute to productivity. However, the pragmatic application of some of the principles and tools can significantly improve workload and pressure and a summary is provided below.

1. Identify what adds value

Value-added activity changes something for the first time to meet a customer requirement, while non-added activity takes time and resources but does not change anything and/or does not help meet customer requirements. Here we are using the term customer to mean an external or end customer as well as an internal customer such as the next task in a production line, another department or facility.

It sounds obvious but think about your working day and how much of your time is spent on non-value added tasks such as waiting, rework, etc. It stands to reason that if you can reduce non-value added activity you will free up time to focus on other work demands and knowing that you are actually doing work that adds value can motivate you and the team.

It is important to note that some non-value activity may be essential to complete a process, but just because it is essential doesn't mean to say it has to be value-added. Don't take things for granted and don't be afraid to ask 'Why do we do this?'

In a previous job I used to spend at least two full days each month creating a very detailed operations report with dozens of graphs, dashboards and action plans. This was very demotivating and frustrating as I knew no one in head office really took any notice or rarely went beyond the summary front cover. I was wasting my time but someone long ago had decided we needed the report, so it had to be done. One month I decided to put my theory to the test and simply updated the front page and left the remainder of the report exactly as the previous month. No comments came back. When I explained what I had done to head office, the requirement for the monthly report was reduced to one page for all seven of our facilities, freeing myself and my opposite numbers at other sites to focus on other activity.

2. Eliminate waste

There are generally seven types of recognizable waste:

- defects or mistakes
- over-production
- transportation
- waiting or unnecessary approvals
- inventory or excessive stock
- motion
- over-processing.

The challenge is to reduce these in favour of value-added activity. Some examples that apply to stress management include motion and the reduction of physical labour, perhaps relying on mechanical aids rather than manpower, or perhaps unnecessary or burdensome procedures or approvals processes, that create frustration and pressure when work is 'stuck in the system'.

3. Make value flow at the pull of the customer

All too often our work rate or workflow is dictated by activities that occur prior to an activity reaching us, rather than our responding to the request of an internal or external customer. This essentially drives work rate that will find the weakest link and create a bottleneck.

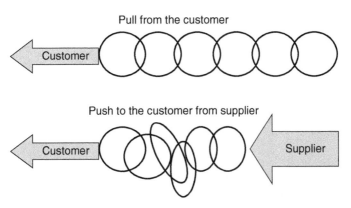

To deal with bottlenecks the temptation is to just add more resource or equipment. However, you might discover that with some simple analysis you can smooth demand across the existing resource, sharing the workload and reducing pressure on individuals.

The following real example relates to the operation of a roller coaster in a theme park that was regularly failing to meet its guest throughput target (the number of people going on the ride each hour). This affected queue times and customer satisfaction, as well as the stress of staff from pressure of failing to meet the target and potentially dealing with unhappy customers who had to queue for a long time.

The ride could theoretically be dispatched every 20 seconds (this is sometimes called takt, the available working time divided by the customer demand). To achieve this takt time of 20 seconds a number of activities or process steps had to be completed simultaneously: guest batching, bag collection, loading, ride dispatch, etc. When measured, each of these steps could be completed in the allocated time, as seen in the diagram below.

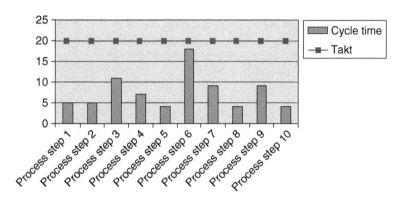

Process steps – ride loading and dispatch

Then we looked at how the ten process steps were divided among the five ride staff, the operator and four attendants, and from the load chart below, you can easily see that the bottleneck was the second attendant.

As you might imagine the second attendant position was one that no one wanted to do as they would always be seen as letting the team down – no matter what they did they were always holding the ride up. Rather than add more resource, we were able to allocate one process step each to attendants

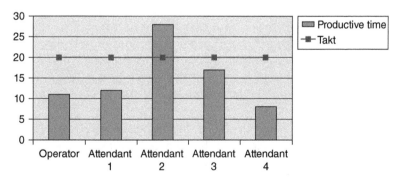

Ride staff load chart

1 and 4 from the second attendant as they were underutilized (also potentially demotivated as they spent time hanging around waiting for the second attendant).

So in the end everyone in the team was used efficiently and could work within the takt time and avoid the bottleneck, as seen in the final chart below, making both staff and customers happy.

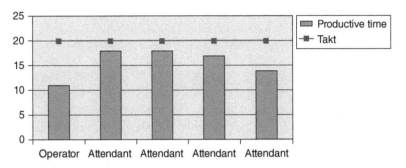

Ride staff load chart – after change

4. Involve and empower employees

When we look at change management in the next chapter we will see how employee engagement is critical to successful change. We also learnt in Chapter 24 how challenge and engagement can improve motivation and create a sense of team, a buzz and energy to make things happen.

5. Continuously improve

Once improvements have been made, revisit them regularly to make sure changes are effective. Customer needs, technology, staffing and the interaction between different processes all change over time and create additional opportunities to improve the way you work to smooth demand, reduce pressure and engage and motivate the workforce.

Workplace design and work environment

We've already looked at Maslow and Herzberg and learnt that basic biological needs and other hygiene factors need to be managed to avoid dissatisfaction. The work environment includes both the physical and psychological surroundings in the workplace. Therefore, designing the workplace, whether the layout of a factory or production line, right down to the way you organize your desk can play an important role in managing stress.

Ergonomics, sometimes called human factors, is the study of how humans interact with their work environment or other parts of a system. It plays an important role in workplace design to ensure that unnecessary demands or stress aren't placed on the body or mind.

Ergonomic evaluation looking at physical demands of a workplace is particularly important when jobs involve significant physical effort, sitting or standing for long periods as well as close-up or detailed work.

Ergonomics can also take into account psychological aspects. Think about the design of computer software and the frustration created if it is not 'user-friendly', the continual repetition of tasks that may lead to mistakes or poor warning signs and signals. For example, a warning light that flashes green is counterintuitive, as we usually associate red lights with danger or abnormal situations.

When considering ergonomics, the need to design workplaces so that elements can be tailored or adapted to suit the individual should be considered. This can cover everything from adjustable seating and workbench height to environmental factors such as heating, lighting, etc. After all, everyone is slightly different when it comes to their height, size, physical capability and personal preference as to what is comfortable.

The training of staff is also important so that they understand and utilize correct work methods. These might include lifting techniques, posture for standing or seating to reduce the impact of work on the body, or instructions on the use of systems and equipment.

In general, workstations or areas should be designed to:

- ensure the right tools and equipment are available
- allow for easy access of most frequently used items/tools
- avoid repetitive motions
- avoid bending, stretching, reaching and stooping
- avoid the need for transporting product by hand (use shoots, rollers, conveyors, etc.)
- be easily adapted, adjusted or modified to accommodate individual needs
- allow access for maintenance tasks and repair.

Processes tend to operate better when activities are arranged sequentially. Depending on available space this can be achieved using lines, circles or U-shaped designs. Some reorganization of the workplace can be done easily and cheaply – try using scale plans and moving furniture and equipment about to see how it might work before physically moving anything. Remember to engage with everyone who uses the workspace or area to get everyone's input and views. Clearly, if more significant change is required and at significant cost it is always advisable to get some professional support in the design process.

Most organizations take care of the basics of life through provision of shelter, toilet facilities, water and space to store, prepare and eat food, although in some cases provision of these essentials can be a challenge (think about those working in remote outdoor areas such as pipeline engineers, surveyors, forestry workers, etc.)

Other considerations should include:

- **lighting** – the use of daylight verses artificial light, intensity, suitability for the type of work, local bench or task lighting for detailed close-up work, changing level for night work or seasonal variations
- **heating or cooling** – variation dependent on the physical nature of work activities, ambient temperature of work environment and individual preferences

- **ventilation** – volume of ventilation to provide regular changes of air. This may be impacted by use or presence of chemicals, dust, vapours or even bad odours
- **noise and vibrations** – control of loud or excessive noise but also consider low level background noise such as equipment humming or office chatter (piped music can be both a blessing and a curse)
- **personal space** – sufficient to move about, stretch and complete work activity
- **maintenance** – consider the impact of poorly maintained or outdated tools and equipment

Playrooms and power naps

Some progressive workplaces can take design of the work environment to the extreme, making it more like home than the workplace. Playrooms encourage staff to take time out to relax from their usual work activity, play video games when things get too much and they need a release, or have a power nap. Evidence suggests that this can boost productivity, particularly in the afternoons.

Softer work surroundings such as lounge-like meeting rooms can provide a relaxed environment particularly appropriate for creative industries where innovation and problem-solving are a key part of day to day work. The relaxed environment makes it easier to think and brainstorm ideas.

This type of approach is not for everyone and is particularly popular with industries such as internet-based or software companies, marketing organizations or organizations attracting highly skilled younger workforces with a different perspective on work.

Summary

In this chapter you have learnt how management behaviour can set expectations among the workforce that can contribute to work pressure and stress; communication and clarity are required to manage these expectations.

You considered the difference between activity and productivity and how the use of some simple tools can help identify bottlenecks and smooth workload. You learnt how using Pareto analysis can help you determine which areas are a priority for improvement and you covered the five principles of lean thinking.

You saw how workplace design can reduce stress by considering the order of tasks, ergonomics, and some simple rules to ensure ease of use and reduction of physical effort. You learnt how environmental factors such as lighting, heating and noise also play a part and considered the need to design for individual adjustments.

Finally, you saw how some organizations take workplace design to the extreme, creating playrooms to stimulate creativity and innovation.

Fact-check [Answers at the back]

1. As a manager, how might always being the first in and last out of the office negatively impact staff?
   a) It might drive expectation that staff should do the same and avoid leaving early or being seen as not spending enough time at work creating pressure or stress ❑
   b) Staff will resent you being good at your job ❑
   c) The office cleaners will not be able to clean your office ❑
   d) No negative impact; employees should follow their manager's example ❑

2. Which of the following is not a correct statement about Pareto analysis?
   a) It suggests 80% of tasks can be completed in 20% of the time ❑
   b) It suggests 80% of productivity can come from 20% of the tasks ❑
   c) If everyone worked at 100% efficiency you could reduce your workforce by 80% ❑
   d) Data may need to be viewed more than one way to see the biggest issue ❑

3. Which of the following are important lean principles?
   a) Identify what adds value ❑
   b) Eliminate waste ❑
   c) Continuously improve ❑
   d) All of the above ❑

4. Of the items listed below, which one would not be considered as waste?
   a) Waiting or unnecessary approvals ❑
   b) Maintenance activity ❑
   c) Transportation ❑
   d) Defects or mistakes ❑

5. Which negative impact might result from operating at a pace dictated by an internal or external supplier?
   a) Bosses will see who isn't pulling their weight ❑
   b) Bottlenecks may occur that create work pressure for certain individuals or tasks ❑
   c) Internal suppliers will be able to reduce their work rate ❑
   d) None of the above ❑

6. Why might continuous improvement be of value?
   a) To ensure everyone is always busy ❑
   b) To ensure that a new manager has an opportunity to put their stamp on the workplace ❑
   c) To ensure those not adapting to better ways of working are performance managed ❑
   d) To ensure changes are still effective and changes in customer need, process or technology are considered ❑

7. Why might effective workplace design reduce workplace stress?
a) Changing the workplace is always seen as a positive thing ❏
b) Good design can reduce the demands placed on the body and mind ❏
c) Having chairs that adjust means people can work longer hours at the computer ❏
d) Good design can impress customers when they visit the organization ❏

8. Which of the following is an appropriate definition of ergonomics?
a) The study of human biology ❏
b) The study of how humans interact with their environment ❏
c) The study of human temporal behaviour patterns ❏
d) The study of business finances ❏

9. Which of these is not a valid consideration when assessing lighting levels in the workplace?
a) The amount of daylight coming from windows and skylights ❏
b) The ability to control/switch lighting on and off to suit individuals needs ❏
c) The level of detailed or close-up work undertaken ❏
d) Ensuring that lighting levels are the same across an entire office, building or site ❏

10. What might be the benefits of designing a more relaxed working environment, including installation of softer meeting areas or playrooms, into the workplace?
a) More effective use of rest breaks to improve productivity or to encourage creative thinking and innovation ❏
b) Employees will spend less time working and will therefore be happier ❏
c) It will make use of redundant office space ❏
d) None of the above ❏

CHAPTER 26

Behaviours, conflict and support

So far we have looked at a variety of topics. While each chapter stands alone you will hopefully by now have started to see how all the elements overlap to form an effective programme that will help you manage stress in the workplace.

In this chapter we will look at how behaviours play a vital role in supporting the more procedural or physical elements of managing stress. We will look at submissive, assertive and aggressive behaviours as well as considering some classic psychological experiments that demonstrate the role authority can play in changing behaviours for both better and worse.

We will consider how management can set behavioural expectations and manage them like other performance objectives. Building on existing knowledge we will look at empowerment in more detail and consider a just culture model. Then we will examine types of internal conflict, workplace bullying and harassment as well as appropriate actions and methods of providing support.

Behaviour

Much research has been documented regarding submissive, assertive and aggressive behaviour and character traits. Table 26.1 summarizes some of the attributes relating to these behaviours.

As you might imagine, those who behave in a more submissive way may be at greater risk of bullying or harassment and may therefore benefit from assertiveness training. Likewise those exhibiting more aggressive tendencies would also benefit from coaching to consider the impact of their behaviour. As we saw in Chapter 22, we need to consider what we have learnt in context and avoid making judgements about individuals based on one set of observations.

In addition to personality traits such as submission, assertion and aggression, level of authority can have a significant impact on the behaviour of those with and those subject to authority. The following two experiments show just how easily behaviours can be influenced and modified in response to authority.

Table 26.1 Attributes of submissive, assertive and aggressive behaviour

Attribute	Submissive	Assertive	Aggressive
Perceived value of other	High	High	Low
Perceived value of self	Low	High	High
Approach	Submits or defends, others first, concedes easily	Respects others, both equal, negotiation	Attacks others, self first, stands firm
Speech and language	Apologetic, hesitant and avoids the real issue	Clear, concise, honest, open and positive	Threatening, accusatory, demanding, interrupts
Other visible cues	Head down, no eye contact, fidgeting	Eye contact on same level, open, balanced and relaxed	Staring, standing over or above others, hands on hips, waving and pointing

Milgram experiment

Stanley Milgram, a psychologist at Yale University conducted a study in the 1960s in response to war trials following World War Two. The study sought to examine obedience, a common defence in the trials with the accused maintaining they simply followed orders from their superiors. Milgram wanted to see how far people would go in obeying orders if it involved harming another human.

The experiment involved two volunteers (who thought they were participating in a learning study), one taking the role of a learner and the other a teacher. Finally, there was an experimenter, played by an actor and dressed in a white coat, representing a figure of authority.

The learner was strapped to a chair with electrodes, behind a screen and asked to memorize pairs of words. The teacher then tested the learner by reading one half of the pair of words and asking the learner to recall the other paired word. The teacher was told to administer an electric shock each time a mistake was made, and the level of shock increased each time, starting at 15 volts (a slight shock) and progressing to 450 volts (a severe, potentially fatal shock). No shocks were actually given but a sound recording was linked to the shock switches so the teacher heard what he thought was the learner being shocked each time.

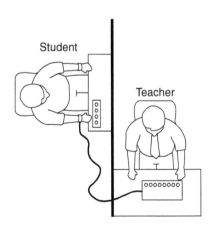

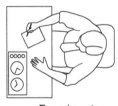

Experimenter

Layout of the Milgram experiment
© Barking Dog Art

When the teacher refused to administer a shock and turned to the experimenter for guidance, he was given a standard series of instructions:

1 Please continue
2 The experiment requires you to continue
3 It is absolutely essential that you continue
4 You have no other choice but to continue

The experiment was repeated numerous times and all the participants continued to 300 volts, and 65% of participants continued to the highest level of 450 volts. The experiment showed that people are likely to follow instructions given by an authority figure, even to the extent of killing an innocent human being. Society ingrains our obedience to authority from a young age, obeying parents, teachers, police officers and others in authority.

The Milgram experiment has been repeated in many countries since and although the percentage of teachers prepared to administer the maximum shock does vary, the overall findings remain consistent. The experiment has been criticized for its approach and methodology, even of psychological abuse to the participants.

Stanford Prison or Zimbardo's experiment

This experiment was a study conducted by Phillip Zimbardo in the basement of the Stanford psychology building in 1971, where he had created a mock-up of a prison. He aimed to study the psychological effect of being a prisoner or prison guard.

Twenty-four male students were selected and assigned roles as guards and prisoners in what was supposed to be a two-week study. Guards were dressed appropriately and given wooden batons, while the prisoners were subjected to standard processing including fingerprinting and mug shots, and were then assigned numbers which were displayed instead of names on their prison uniforms. Prisoners had to remain in their cells overnight but guards could leave when they had completed their shifts.

In a short period of time the participants had adapted to their roles to such an extent the guards started to enforce authoritarian measures and even subjected some of the prisoners to psychological torture. Prisoners accepted abuse passively from the guards and even harassed those other prisoners who tried to prevent it. Two prisoners left the experiment and the entire study was abandoned after only six days. In his finding Zimbardo concluded that the situation rather than the individuals' personalities caused the participants to behave as they had done – comparable with Milgram's result.

We have seen from the results of both Milgram and Zimbardo that behaviour is heavily influenced by authority and situation. It is therefore important that organizations set clear expectations for behaviour and actively manage the behaviours of the workforce. We started to consider this in the previous chapter concerning the management behaviour of being first in and last out of the office each day, creating expectation and work pressure among their staff.

Just culture

Some organizations drive a culture of fear and blame, by seeming to react negatively when things go wrong, making examples of people when a mistake is made, irrespective of whether there was a malicious intent or not. Fear of speaking out, stopping work or being seen to have made a mistake drives behaviours of covering things up, concealing the truth and lying. This inevitably means the issues will escalate and get worse until they become so significant they are no longer concealable. In fact, fear and blame cultures have been shown as significant factors in many serious industrial disasters, with multiple opportunities to have prevented fatal consequences if someone had only spoken up.

A just culture is one that recognizes normal human fallibility (we all make mistakes) and seeks to install mutual trust between an organization and its employees. So when something goes wrong the focus is on learning and prevention of recurrence rather than blame and punishment. However, a just culture does not mean no blame, rather a proportionate response. Where deliberate or wilful acts cause damage, harm or loss, individuals can expect to be appropriately managed.

A just culture requires a significant level of organizational maturity and for management to take it seriously, ensuring that those who do admit to mistakes or errors receive positive recognition and even reward for speaking up. When it comes to conflict and bullying, a just culture makes it easier for victims to raise concerns knowing they will be heard and creates an environment where others witnessing poor behaviour can speak out on behalf of the victim.

Managing conflict and bullying

Conflict in an organization may arise for a whole host of reasons: disagreements about operational requirements, change, simple misunderstandings and deliberate acts with malicious intent. In order to manage conflict or poor behaviours, organizations should set clear expectations so that everyone is aware of what is acceptable and what is not. Having considered what an organization believes to be acceptable and unacceptable, this should be communicated to all staff. It should be made clear what constitutes bullying or harassment along with the consequences of engaging in such behaviour. Managers should lead by example and promote positive behaviours in others to avoid conflict and ensure fairness.

Physical violence, sexual advances, verbal abuse or derogatory comments relating to gender, age, race, religion, sexuality or disability might be obvious behaviours that should be managed. However, other more subtle forms of bullying may occur – e.g. failing to pass on information relevant for work, discriminating between individuals when allocating work tasks, or providing reward and recognition may also be considered forms of bullying.

Certain occupations, such as the emergency services, security guards or those handling complaints, are also susceptible to conflict and bullying from external sources such as customers or members of the public. Their needs should also be considered and appropriate behavioural standards communicated through signage, etc. to clarify that certain behaviours will not be tolerated.

Once expectations have been set, it is important to ensure unacceptable behaviours are reported and resolved. The type of resolution will be dependent on the severity of the unacceptable behaviour. In circumstances where there is simply disagreement or misunderstanding this can be cleared up with discussion, a sharing of views and potentially an agreement to disagree. Perhaps where comments have inadvertently caused offence or in response to an isolated malicious incident, more robust communication of the required standards may be required or some form of formal mediation between parties. More serious issues might be managed through a formal disciplinary process, including independent investigation of the facts and action, ranging from formal verbal or written warnings up to and including summary dismissal. In extreme cases, where a criminal offence may have been committed such as physical assault, it will be necessary to involve the police or other law enforcement agencies.

Employee welfare services

In addition to clear expectations and processes to manage unacceptable behaviours, organizations should consider what support services may be offered to employees. As we have learnt, good managers provide flexibility and support to those suffering from stress, regardless of the cause, whether it is work-related or not. We have already considered how those occupations with susceptibility to disorders such as PTSD should be assessed for the need for additional workforce support.

In addition to internal support for employees, many organizations provide access to external advice and support services. These usually involve some form of hotline or contact number so that employees can discuss matters in confidence and with someone independent from the organization or employer. They can then receive direct advice or be directed to other service providers for support. Services typically include counselling, health and wellbeing, legal and financial services.

Communicating clearly what support is available and how to access these services is essential, as is the need for maintaining complete confidentiality.

Managing behavioural performance

Behaviours can have as much impact on the success of an organization as any other factor. It is therefore essential that behaviours are managed in the same way as other deliverables or results. Managers should provide regular, objective feedback on both what individuals are delivering and their behaviours. Managers should also not be afraid to use disciplinary action including dismissal for poor behavioural performance. Even where an individual is seen as indispensable because of their results (e.g. the leading sales person with twice as many orders as the next best), if this person's behaviours are incompatible with those expected by the organization then removing this person is not only the right thing to do but inevitably the whole organization breathes a sigh of relief. and it It becomes apparent that others can step up and fill the gap – or more often realize that although the leading sales person historically got the credit their behaviours masked the work others were already doing, so the loss is minimal overall.

The performance matrix has been used in two organizations where I have worked and has proved effective in both, particularly when linked to pay and bonus awards. Rating employees by their results and behaviours allows for meaningful discussion and prompts action if issues exist in either area.

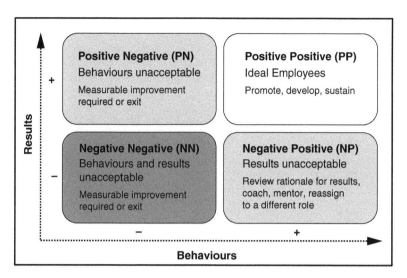

Performance matrix for results and behaviours

Summary

In this chapter you have learnt the importance of behaviours and how these can be effectively managed. You saw how both the Milgram and the Stanford Prison experiments showed that authority can have a significant effect on behaviour, that driving a fear and blame culture can cause issues to be covered up and grow into significant problems. You considered how a just culture might aid in identifying and addressing problems early, allowing for management intervention and proportionate response.

You learnt how conflict, bullying and harassment can take many forms, some more obvious than others, and that certain people or occupations are more likely to suffer from the behaviours of others. You considered some key principles in managing unacceptable behaviours and supporting employees and gained an understanding of the pivotal role managers have in leading by example.

Finally you saw that behavioural expectation should apply equally to all and can be performance managed in the same way as other more tangible results.

Fact-check [Answers at the back]

1. Which of the following is not one of the three behaviours/character traits discussed at the start of this chapter?
   a) Assertive ❑
   b) Submissive ❑
   c) Subversive ❑
   d) Aggressive ❑

2. Which of these are attributes of those with assertive behaviours?
   a) Respects others, high value of self and others, clear, concise and honest ❑
   b) Attacks others, high value of self, low value of others, demanding and accusatory ❑
   c) Concedes easily, low value of self, high value of others, hesitant and apologetic ❑
   d) None of the above ❑

3. What form of support might be appropriate for someone with submissive behaviours?
   a) Assertiveness training ❑
   b) Coaching to consider the impact of their behaviour ❑
   c) Self-defence classes ❑
   d) Formal disciplinary action ❑

4. What do both the Milgram and Stanford Prison experiments show us?
   a) Students are easily manipulated ❑
   b) Those in authority do what needs to be done to get results ❑
   c) Authority and situation can significantly influence behaviour ❑
   d) All of the above ❑

5. What are some of the key elements in developing a just culture?
   a) Discipline and punishment ❑
   b) Mutual trust, acceptance of human fallibility ❑
   c) No blame for anything ❑
   d) Encouraging staff to tell management about their work colleagues ❑

6. Which of the following may be considered bullying?
   a) Physical abuse ❑
   b) Withholding important work information, unfair allocation of work activities ❑
   c) Malicious comments concerning gender, race, sexual orientation and religion ❑
   d) All of the above ❑

7. Which of the following is not a means to deal with conflict in the workplace?
   a) Coaching or mediation ❑
   b) Formal disciplinary, verbal or written warnings, dismissal ❑
   c) Transferring victims to an alternative department ❑
   d) Notifying local law enforcement agencies where appropriate ❑

8. Which of the following is not an important consideration for employee support services?
a) Assessment of the most appropriate services considering the workforce needs ❏
b) Communication of what services are available ❏
c) Publicity for those who have used services ❏
d) Clear means of access to support services ❏

9. What management action might be taken for those exhibiting poor behaviours but excellent business results?
a) Formal performance management, leading to exit if no improvement ❏
b) Promotion ❏
c) Assign to a different role or department ❏
d) None of the above ❏

10. What management action would not be appropriate for someone who shows good behaviours but poor business results?
a) Understand reasons for poor results ❏
b) Promotion ❏
c) Consider reassignment to a different role more suited to skills ❏
d) Coaching or mentoring ❏

CHAPTER 27

Change management

Change is a fundamental part of modern life and the pace of that change seems to continually increase. In the workplace change can happen at the organizational level through downsizing, mergers or acquisitions, privatization, contractualization or demographic change. Change may also happen at the job level with new equipment, changes to shift patterns or in reaction to short-term demands.

Change management is worthy of a book in its own right and indeed many hundreds if not thousands already exist – not to mention countless millions of internet articles and other reference materials.

In this chapter we will be focusing on the people side of change and how an understanding of people's reactions to change can lead to greater buy-in and reduced stress for management and workforce alike. We will learn how organizations and their employees have unwritten psychological contracts with each other and why people resist change. We will look at some of the many models for change, understand how engagement with stakeholders can ensure understanding of why change is needed, and how considering the views and opinions of those affected by change can deliver a better solution that staff have already invested in, making the change process easier to implement and more likely to be sustained in the long term.

Resistance to change

Ask yourself why we resist change. Perhaps it is because of a fear of the unknown, security in the way we know, others may be resisting so people follow the pack, or some aren't convinced the change will work and don't see where the personal benefit is for them. Perhaps too much else is going on or people think it will pass like other changes that have appeared.

All these feelings are completely normal and understandable, but are often overlooked as managers simply try to force through predetermined solutions to timescales seemingly plucked from thin air. When it comes to change, it has been said that a majority of managers spend 10% of their energy selling the problem and 90% selling the solution. However, if the problem isn't properly understood then the solution won't be either.

The psychological contract

The psychological contract is an informal, unwritten arrangement built over time between an organization or employer and its employees. It represents inferred or implied obligations based on experience and future expectation. The concept of the psychological contract is especially relevant to organizational change, in particular the move for outsourcing jobs from

Table 27.1 Change in workers' psychological contract

Old contract	New contract
Stability	Change
Predictability	Uncertainty
Permanence	Temporariness
Standard work patterns	Flexible work
Valuing loyalty	Valuing performance and skills
Paternalism	Self reliance
Job security	Employment security
Linear career progression	Multiple careers
One-time learning	Lifelong learning

public to private sector, and helps us understand and plan to accommodate the reactions of the workforce.

Jamais Cascio, a writer and ethical futurist, began designing future scenarios in the 1990s. He believes that business trends drive change in order to adapt to market conditions, globalization and demands for technology to maintain competitiveness. He also suggests that change causes a shift in the psychological contract that binds workers to an organization.

Change as a transition

We can help our understanding of how change affects people by considering a few of the many models for change. Kurt Lewin proposed just such a model in 1947, and although the world has changed much since then, arguably most other models are derived from the basics of his theory of three stages of change:

1 **unfreezing** – getting an organization and its people ready for change, motivating and making decisions
2 **change or transition** – implementing a new way, people are unfrozen and move towards the new approach
3 **freezing** – establishing stability in the new way

In the mid-1990s significant progress was made in change management, primarily in response to the frustrations of large organizations who continually failed to deliver sustainable change. Most of this work focused very much on the people side of change, rather than the top down methods historically used. William Bridges developed an alternative three-phase model to describe the transition.

Time

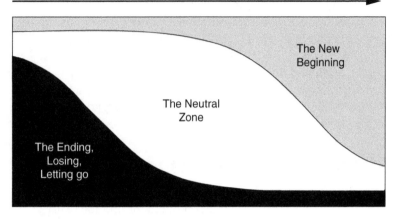

Three phases of transition

1 The first phase is an **ending**, where people are letting go. It is important to agree and sell the change, understand the impact and help people to come to terms with the loss.
2 The second phase is the **neutral zone**, where the new way isn't fully implemented and some are still working to the old way. In this phase realignment and re-enforcement are required to show progress and deal with resistance.
3 Finally there's the **new beginning**, where the change is beginning to work, energy needs to be harnessed to keep momentum going and successes need to be visibly rewarded.

Kotter's eight-step change model

In 1995 John Kotter, a professor at Harvard Business School, introduced an eight-step approach for leading change.

Step 1 – Create urgency

For change to be effective a majority of people must want it – it is important to create a sense of urgency through logical discussions on the need for and the detail of the change. People will start to talk about the change and, like a snowball rolling down a hill, the sense of urgency will build and grow.

Step 2 – Form a powerful coalition

In any organization there are usually one or two key players to whom everyone looks for leadership. They might not be the most senior hierarchically, but obtaining their visible support can make the difference between success and failure.

Step 3 – Create a vision for change

People need to see what you are trying to achieve. While there may be various ideas and solutions floating around in the early days, it is important to link these into a single vision that is straightforward, easy to understand and remember.

Step 4 – Communicate the vision

The vision needs to be communicated frequently and become embedded into everything that is done. It is often easy for messages to get swamped or overshadowed in large organizations and so be relentless. Remember it is not just about what is said, people are far more likely to be influenced by what is done and others' behaviour.

Step 5 – Remove obstacles

Empower people to make the change and continually monitor for barriers, whether they are systems, processes or people. Recognize and reward those who are making progress and manage those who aren't, and help them understand the need and process for change.

Step 6 – Create short-term wins

Create short-term targets and milestones and celebrate these successes. Success motivates people and encourages others to adopt the change. Incremental successes will also make it harder for those resisting the change as they will not be able to point to a lack of progress as justification that the change isn't working.

Step 7 – Build on the change

Real change takes time and continual re-enforcement. Declaring the job is finished too early may mean people revert back to old ways rather than continuing with new ways.

Step 8 – Anchor the change into the organization's culture

Make the change stick for good. Continue to integrate the change activity into the everyday life of the organization. Link it to reward and continually communicate ongoing successes.

Change and the personal transition

Looking back at the early models for change, we saw that individuals and whole organizations go through a variety of phases. Following research into service organizations, John Fisher's work in the noughties (early 2000s) has resulted in a very helpful model of how individuals deal with change, the process of transition curve. Although consistent in its elements, the journey will be unique for each individual – some may adapt quickly, others may never fully adapt or accept change. As you read on, consider change you have witnessed or experienced and you will no doubt be able to correlate Fisher's findings with your own experience.

Anxiety

We learnt about anxiety and the feeling of unease or apprehension in Chapter 23. In the transition process people may be unsure or feel a lack of control or visibility of a change.

Happiness

In this phase employees might feel relief that someone is doing something, satisfaction that change is coming and that things will be different from before, perhaps with feelings of anticipation and excitement. There is a risk that expectations will be raised as assumptions are made concerning what will happen and the impact. Some will think about opportunity for progression, promotion, etc. Others may think that an exit route is coming – 'they're bound to make me redundant' – and already start to spend their severance package. Thorough engagement at this stage will minimize impact.

Denial

Here people carry on regardless, 'put their head in the sand' refusing to accept that the change is happening, sticking to the old ways and ignoring anything that contradicts their view of the world.

Fear

This is a realization that things will be different in the future and everyone will need to act differently.

Threat

It dawns that the change is going to have a fundamental impact. Old choices will no longer stand. Staff may be unsure how to act in the future. Old ways are gone but new ways aren't established yet.

Anger

Anger may exist in the early stages of the transition. At first others might be blamed for forcing a change that wasn't wanted. Employees might also start to reflect on their own actions and think they should have kept control or known better. This anger at oneself can lead to guilt and depression.

Guilt

This is a realization that previous behaviours were inappropriate and that they may have had a negative impact. Being part of the problem causes a sense of guilt and sometimes shame.

Disillusionment

Disillusionment may set in if staff realize there is a fundamental difference between the individual and the organization. They become increasingly withdrawn and almost switch off, becoming dissatisfied. Recovery is possible but if the difference is too great exiting may be the only solution.

Depression

Awareness that old behaviours, actions and beliefs are no longer compatible with what employees are now expected to do or be. There may be confusion or lack of motivation as what was done and past behaviours are viewed in a negative way.

Hostility

Here, some might continue to try to make things work that have already proved a failure and others have moved on from, but they maintain the belief that it will somehow come good if they continue to plug away and ignore the new way of working.

Gradual acceptance

People start to see some of the early wins and successes of the change and start to see how they will fit into the new order. They are starting to make sense of change and acknowledge that they on the right track. There is light at the end of the tunnel.

Moving forward

Things are getting more positive and are starting to feel comfortable. Everyone is becoming more effective and understands the new environment.

Behaviours during change

We have seen above how change has distinct phases and that people go through a personal transition at a pace specific to the individual. It is important to note that while people may be at various points along the transition their behaviours may be modified by other factors – e.g. it is possible to be actively supportive of change even though you are suffering anxiety about what exactly might happen.

In the engagement and satisfaction model you will see how people may respond to a particular change in terms of their level of satisfaction and level of engagement. This model enables us to consider an appropriate management strategy for certain behaviours. Being in any one zone is perfectly normal and all are manageable; people will change their behaviours over time or in relation to different change activities.

Both axes in the engagement and satisfaction model are continuous so you will get extreme behaviours in each group. However, at the centre you tend to find those who are indifferent, those who may be easily swayed in any direction. If they see the change is happening and successful they are likely to join in, so show them the plan and keep them informed of progress. Don't be afraid to explain the dangers of 'sitting on the fence' and failing to commit one way or the other.

In the top right hand quadrant, Zone 1, you will find those who are satisfied with the change and engaged in the change process. These people can be enthusiastic and energetic and want to spread the word. Tactics for managing

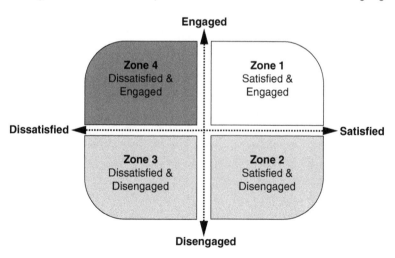

Engagement and satisfaction model

this group include using them to win over others and giving them plenty of support and authority to help progress the change. Make sure they are recognized, rewarded and kept motivated.

At the opposite end of the scale you have those in Zone 3. They are dissatisfied with the change and disengaged or passive in their response, failing to get involved. They may be cynical and may play a political game, agreeing in public but creating problems, spreading rumours behind closed doors. In order to manage people in this zone it is crucial to understand why they are unsupportive and tackle them on their objections. Don't dismiss their input as they may well have seen the change from a different perspective and come up with issues that you hadn't previously been aware of. Show them the change can and is working and seek their involvement.

In the bottom right are 'the saboteurs' – those who are dissatisfied with the change and are actively engaged in their opposition, potentially trying to derail the process. Sometimes their actions may be overt, other times more subtle, such as slowing up decision-making. You will need to show you understand their concerns but be able to put your case as to why you think differently. Try persuasion to bring them round to your way of thinking and try to resolve their concerns. Avoid stooping to their level and tactics, rise above them. Ultimately you may have to confront them – the change is here and if they can't engage and help make it work then perhaps they don't have a role to play in the organization. This conversation is tough but often bears fruit. If they know you are serious they may change their view and if not, it may be best for both parties if they move on. Often everyone breathes a big sigh of relief when the issue is dealt with. The important thing is to have robust adult conversation.

Finally, in Zone 4, you find those who see things as inevitable. They are satisfied but unwilling to engage fully. This group needs lots of engagement: ask them a lot of questions, gauge their views and use their expertise. Recognize and reward them but don't take their support for granted.

Timing of change

It is important to briefly mention the timing of change – get it right and you may make things easier, get it wrong and it could be a whole lot worse.

Arguably there is never a good time to change and you can always find reasons why not to do something today when you can put it off till tomorrow. However, this shouldn't stop you giving proper consideration to objections and or alternate time scales. You will need to consider other change activity: announcing that you are going to make redundancies, implementing a new computer system and relocating your manufacturing plant 50 miles up the road all at the same time, might be seen as over-adventurous and detrimental to your organization. Perhaps the computer system and relocation overlap and it makes sense to deliver them at the same time, but redundancies, particularly if these relate to efficient savings from the other projects, might be better postponed.

When working in theme parks I had to undertake a major reorganization of staff, including a significant outsource of facilities management activity. I considered long and hard the timing; we could wait till the winter maintenance period when the park was closed but risk not being ready for the start of the following season, or get it over and done with while the park was open and risk impacting customers now.

After speaking with key employee representatives, we went for the peak summer season, and the restructure went without a hitch. By listening to key staff I learnt that most were expecting something anyway and that they wanted it over and done with, and that on the whole most people were so energized dealing with the day to day excitement of the park during the summer that the reorganization was not their priority. Waiting for winter would mean uncertainty for longer and the change would happen when people were already low after the season had finished, their focus switched to menial tasks of cleaning, painting, etc. and they would probably be miserable due to the bad weather and short daylight hours.

Gauging the right time is more of an art than a science and nobody gets it right all the time. Remember to listen to others, and even if you don't agree make sure people understand your reasoning.

Examples of change

In my career I have witnessed and been involved with both good and bad examples of change. Good examples include the process improvement work in the theme park reorganization I have mentioned already, while the following case study serves as a lesson in what not to do.

I was working for a US aerospace company based in London, with a sister facility in Frankfurt, Germany. One Friday a senior executive flew into Frankfurt, called a staff meeting and through a translator basically said, 'We're closing you down with immediate effect, don't come to work on Monday and the London office will manage everything including the disposal of the building'.

Clearly this came as a shock, to the German workforce but also to my team in London as we had no prior knowledge either. The senior executive flew straight back home and left us to pick up the pieces. He had failed to understand some of the basic legal rights of the workforce as well as any understanding of the implications for all concerned. While legal challenges progressed and transitional plans devised, the German workforce continued to operate the facility for a number of weeks, openly hostile to the team from London.

Law, culture, language and customer loyalty had all been misunderstood. In the end the facility was closed, many customers were lost or moved to a new company set up by former German employees and the final cost came in at an order of magnitude more than planned, which essentially much negated the business case for the closure. Interestingly, no criticism was ever made of the executive, only of those working in Germany and London!

Summary

In this chapter you have learnt some of the reasons why we resist change, that individuals behave differently and that this variety of reactions is perfectly normal, to be expected and can be managed.

You saw a variety of models for change: Bridges' three-phase transition, Kotter's eight-step change model and Fisher's process of transition curve, each of which provides clues as to how change can be implemented effectively. You considered engagement and satisfaction to characterize types of reaction and behaviours to change and some of the management techniques appropriate for each group.

Finally, you saw how the timing of change is critical and many factors need to be considered at the planning stage to make sure bad timing doesn't create additional management issues.

Remember change management is not an exact science, but considering the principles covered in this chapter will make the process more bearable for all concerned.

Fact-check [Answers at the back]

1. Why might people resist change?
   a) Fear of the unknown or lack of security ❏
   b) Comfortable with the status quo ❏
   c) Too busy to care ❏
   d) All of the above ❏

2. Which of these is not a true statement about managing change?
   a) A variety of behaviours and reactions to change is perfectly natural ❏
   b) Those negative about change simply don't understand it ❏
   c) People may change their reaction and behaviours through the change ❏
   d) All types of behaviours are manageable ❏

3. With regard to Cascio's work, which of the following is part of the 'old psychological contract'?
   a) Predictability ❏
   b) Change ❏
   c) Employment security ❏
   d) Lifelong learning ❏

4. Which of the following is not one of the three phases of transition proposed by Bridges?
   a) Unfreezing ❏
   b) The neutral zone ❏
   c) The beginning ❏
   d) The loss or ending ❏

5. Thinking of Kotter's eight-stage change model, which of the following is a true statement about forming a coalition?
   a) Coalitions must always be with the most senior people ❏
   b) Coalitions will only work if you offer concessions to the other party ❏
   c) Visible support from key people can make the difference between success and failure ❏
   d) All of the above ❏

6. Why are Steps 7 and 8 of Kotter's model so important?
   a) Failure to reinforce or embed change may result in people reverting back to old ways ❏
   b) The true benefits of the change may not be realized ❏
   c) New people to the organization simply adopt new ways as part of everyday working ❏
   d) All of the above ❏

7. Which is not a true statement about Fisher's personal transition model?
   a) The more senior a person is the quicker they transition ❏
   b) Each individual takes a unique journey through the transition ❏
   c) Some people may miss stages of the transition; others may never accept change ❏
   d) Some people may feel guilt over the way they have previously acted ❏

8. Which of the following is a classification of reactions/behaviour to change?
   a) Zone 4: Dissatisfied and disengaged ❏
   b) Zone 3: Disorganized and empowered ❏
   c) Zone 1: Satisfied and disengaged ❏
   d) Zone 2: Satisfied and endangered ❏

9. What management tactic should not be used for those who are dissatisfied but engaged?
   a) Have robust adult conversations ❏
   b) Avoid adopting their tactics ❏
   c) Try persuasion to bring them round to your view ❏
   d) Give them a role to lead the change ❏

10. Which of these is not an important consideration when planning the timing of a change initiative?
   a) The presence of other change initiatives ❏
   b) Customer demands ❏
   c) Being seen to make a quick impact in a new job ❏
   d) Proximity to holiday times or cultural festivals ❏

CHAPTER 28

Personal responsibility and actions

No matter who you are or what you do, life can be stressful. So far we have learnt about stress, its symptoms and what organizations can do to reduce and manage stress. At an individual level it is important to understand the specific triggers or activities that cause you stress and, using the information we covered in Chapter 23, be able to recognize the signs of your response to stress and finally to understand what control strategies are effective for you.

In this chapter we look at some simple steps you can make to take responsibility for managing your own stress levels regardless of the type of organization you work for and the attitude of that organization towards effectively managing stress.

Much of what is discussed in this chapter may seem very simple and to some extent just common sense: manage your time, get regular exercise, and watch your diet and how much you drink or smoke. As is often the case, the simple things can be some of the hardest to do; they get overlooked by other more exciting options or it simply takes too long to embed them into our behaviours. So read on, and congratulations if you already do some or all of these things but be open to trying something new.

Make it a habit

Small changes in lifestyle and the choices you make can have a big impact, and quite often these changes are incredibly simple, such as take more exercise, eat more healthily, drink less alcohol. But we often struggle to maintain our discipline and soon revert to old ways of behaving. We've looked into behavioural change and although actions appear straightforward you need to make a positive effort to embed them in your daily life so that they become habitual. I took up running a few years ago and the first few weeks were really tough – making the conscious effort to get up early, stretch, warm up and run, warm down, all before hitting the shower and starting my normal daily routine took real will power. After a few weeks, with positive support from my wife and focusing on the positive benefits of losing weight and having more energy during the day, it became easier to the point where the daily run was as much a part of the routine as the shower, no longer requiring thought or effort. The same will be true for any of the suggestions in this chapter.

Be positive

At some low point in your life someone will no doubt have said to you 'Don't worry, there's always someone worse off than yourself'. On hearing this, a usual response is that people don't understand what you're going through or it may even spark a stronger response, as although probably true (statistically it is highly unlikely that you happen to be the human being who genuinely has got the worst possible life) it doesn't actually help.

That said, you might want to consider this quote from Marcus Aurelius, Roman Emperor A.D. 161–80:

If you are distressed by anything external, the pain is not due to the thing itself, but to your estimate of it; and this you have the power to revoke at any moment.

When stressed we often can fall into negative feelings or 'mind traps' that can lead to self-criticism and become self-perpetuating to the point where you eventually believe that your negative perception of yourself is in fact reality. By being aware of these thoughts, when they arise you can help yourself break the negative spiral. Common negative thoughts include the following.

Seeing extremes

The thought that 'one mistake' will result in total failure. Everyone makes mistakes and on the whole most are easily recovered. Unless you have been wilfully negligent most organizations have a formal policy of helping you improve and at least a verbal and formal written warning before it comes to the boss letting you go.

Over-generalization

If you find yourself saying 'this always happens', just pause to consider the real evidence. When emotions run high it is all too easy to shoot from the hip and ignore the facts. Think of the average married couple – at some point over a 40-year partnership one or other party will forget a birthday, anniversary or dinner date. Inevitably the focus is always on the one time you forgot rather than the 99 times you remembered and had a great time.

Rejecting the positive

You receive a compliment with a small note for improvement on the end – e.g. your boss says, 'That was a great project, delivered on time and on budget and the team really appreciated your leadership, well done. Next time I'd appreciate a bit more communication to me of potential risks to the programme.' All you hear is that the boss didn't think you communicated with them enough.

Learn to listen, acknowledge the good done and accept positive praise. If you manage others there's a lesson here, for you. Keep praise separate from criticism as people tend to focus on the latter.

Jumping to conclusions

You respond to information by making assumptions based on your perception of yourself. For example, you hear a rumour that the department is going to be reorganized and some people will be made redundant, so you instantly think this will be you. Just consider the evidence and you might actually see how a critical skill or knowledge makes you far more indispensable than your colleagues.

Time management

Rather like change management there is a plethora of programmes and self-help books to help you better manage your time. Most are based around the need to:

- create an appropriate work environment
- set priorities
- perform tasks or activities against the set priorities
- minimize the time spent on non-priorities.

We touched on some organizational elements of time management in Chapter 25 when we looked at workload, work pressure and the work environment (e.g. value and non-value added activity, Pareto analysis and workflow analysis) but you can apply some simple rules to make your personal time management more effective.

Prioritize

Prioritization is key to time management. I use a very straightforward questioning system based on the 4Ds: Do it, Defer it, Delegate it or Drop it.

Does this activity need to be done by me and does it need to be done now? If the answer is yes to both questions it has to go in the **Do it** pile. Sometimes you have to really challenge yourself: do you have some unique knowledge, skill, experience or authority that means it has to be you?

Think about the time pressure and who this is being driven by. You might be being chased for a piece of work but you know that it is going to sit on someone else's desk for two weeks because someone else is on vacation or the next approvals committee isn't for a fortnight. If it has to be done by me, but the time pressure isn't critical then the work goes into the **Defer it** pile. I will do it, just not now. Clearly, as time moves on 'defer it' items eventually make their way into the 'do it' category.

If someone else can do it, either now or later, then **Delegate it.** You will need to provide some guidance on the level of urgency as the person you delegate to may need to prioritize your requests with others from different sources. Make sure they understand their accountability and leave them to get on with it. Be prepared to let them make the decision to delegate it further but hold them to account for any deadline agreed.

Finally, if is not important for you to do and no one is going to be chasing anytime soon simply **Drop it.** A word of caution – make sure the originator of a task or activity knows that you have dropped it. You don't want it to come back and bite you in six months' time because they made an assumption it was still on your radar.

Effective meetings

When it comes to time management, I have found the best way to free up more time is to have effective meetings. I used to spend a significant proportion of my time in meetings – meetings that seemed to have no purpose, or that felt like repeats of other meetings I'd already attended, and ones I'd leave not knowing whether or not a decision had actually been made.

Poor meetings can create uncertainty, blur responsibility and accountability and lead to confusion, particularly for those who weren't there. It is also worth remembering that they cost money. Next time you are in a meeting, consider the hourly rate of everyone round the table, add it together and see what it is costing per hour – you are likely to be shocked.

Every meeting should have a chairperson to take control, and all attendees should follow some simple rules.

Responsibilities of the meeting chairperson
- Start on time
- Make sure all phones and unnecessary IT equipment are off
- Have a time-bound agenda – no agenda, no meeting
- Confirm the purpose/objective of the meeting
- Check attendees can make a contribution
- Control the discussion and keep to time
- Summarize actions
- Conclude with a discussion on what went well, opportunity for improvement and what needs to be covered next time
- Record the outcome, log and circulate minutes/records of actions
- Finish on time.

Simple rules for all attendees
- Be on time
- Be prepared (read reports/papers circulated in advance and have any questions ready)
- Know the agenda
- Contribute effectively (if you can't contribute, don't attend)
- Help solve problems
- Be respectful of others' opinions
- Keep to the point (don't get side-tracked by discussions that aren't on the agenda)
- Make notes
- Follow up actions.

Like any other form of behaviours, these rules for meetings need to be adopted and linked to performance reviews.

Say no

Everyone is an adult and in order to prioritize and limit the workload you have to learn to say no. Think back to the common mind gaps: how often do you say to yourself, 'I can't say no or I will get into trouble'? If you say yes to tasks or activities most managers or colleagues assume you have given it conscious thought and have decided you can accommodate the request.

People in authority often don't see stress, particularly if people are good at hiding the signs. They may think you are very capable and because you keep saying yes keep giving you more to do. Say no, and when you have said no once you will find that people understand and will respond by saying 'Ok, no problem, I'll get John to do it instead' or they might give you additional information and provide assistance in determining what the priorities are. Try saying no but following up with 'but I can if you help me by taking on a task for me or by helping me to prioritize your request against all my other demands'.

Working from home

A regular time management action I take is to avoid commuting. Over the past decade I have changed jobs a number of times and have commuted for anything up to two hours to get to the office. Time in the car, on a bus or train can be helpful and allow for thinking time or act as a break between work and home life but on the whole, in the absence of a need for face to face contact, it can be a waste of time and money just commuting 'to be in the office'. Even if you don't have the space to work from home you might consider other local places to work from – e.g. the local library, or nearby offices of a subsidiary organization. These days the technology exists to work from home – the challenge here is discipline, and you might find it helpful to consider the pitfalls of working from home that can make it counterproductive.

First, make sure the technology works. Remotely connecting to work systems can be fraught with problems if you don't have the right equipment and technical support. Second, make the work environment right. Home can be very distracting – home comforts such as the lounge to relax in with your tea or coffee, raiding the fridge and 'five-minute' breaks to watch TV, walk the dog, etc. can all become a drain on your productive time. Working from home can also work the other way with constant access to work encroaching on your family or home life.

Create a clear work place and stick to clear work times, avoiding distraction and the blurring of the work–life boundary. If necessary you might want to create an artificial commute, say a short walk round the block just to mentally separate your time in the home office from time with the family.

Personal health and wellbeing

In addition to positive thinking and better time management, general wellbeing and personal health have an important part to play in both combating stress and mitigating the psychological and physiological effects. Certain illnesses, health problems and even our genes may predispose us to particular stress responses so taking care of our mind and body is essential for successful management of stress, but also as part of a happy, long and fulfilled life.

Activity and exercise

Life is getting more sedentary: we are collectively spending longer in cars, sat at desks or in front of the TV or a variety of other electronic devices. Studies have shown that those with higher levels of activity in their lives live longer than those less active and have a better quality of life, improving heart and lung functions and bone health while reducing blood pressure and the risk of a variety of health conditions. Physical activity includes time spent on leisure activities such as walking/ hiking, swimming, dancing, games and sports; transport activities like walking and cycling; and daily tasks such as physical paid work, household chores and community activity.

Activity is split into aerobic exercise (that which increases heart and breathing rates and involves low to moderate intensity over longer periods) and anaerobic exercise which helps build muscle with short periods of high-intensity activity.

The World Health Organization (WHO) has issued guidance on appropriate levels of physical activity for three age ranges: 5–17 years, 18–64 years and 64+:

- Children aged 5–17 should complete at least 60 minutes of moderate- to vigorous-intensity activity daily.
- Adults aged 18–64, should complete at least 150 minutes of moderate-intensity aerobic physical activity throughout the week or do at least 75 minutes of vigorous-intensity aerobic activity throughout the week or an equivalent combination.
- Aerobic activity should be performed in bouts of at least 10 minutes' duration.

- For additional health benefits, adults should increase their moderate-intensity aerobic physical activity to 300 minutes per week, or engage in 150 minutes of vigorous-intensity aerobic physical activity per week, or an equivalent combination.
- Muscle-strengthening activities should be done involving major muscle groups on two or more days a week.
- In addition older adults, with poor mobility, should perform activity to enhance balance and prevent falls on three or more days per week. When older adults can't do the recommended amounts of physical activity due to health conditions, they should be as physically active as their abilities and conditions allow.

When we talk about exercise we might think about signing up to a gym or contemplate investing in lots of training equipment or a personal trainer. While these are fine, you can start simply and for free. Likewise we may complain we just don't have the time but again you can start to make a real impact with some minor changes to your routine. Try taking the stairs rather than the lift, go for a walk in the park or round the block instead of spending lunch time sitting in the staff room or at your desk, and get off the bus a stop early and walk into work.

In addition to the physical benefits, taking up a physical hobby or sport that can be done with others or in a social group or club can improve mental wellbeing and create a vital social network of friends and support.

Diet

A healthy diet consists of the right mix of foods and the right amount. For the average person, a balanced diet consists of 33% fruit and vegetables, 33% carbohydrates from bread, pasta, rice, etc., 15% milk and dairy products, 12% protein (meat and fish) and 7% fats and sugars. Salt intake should also be limited as this has an effect on blood pressure.

In terms of amount this is best represented by the energy supplied by the food in calories. Recommended levels for calorie intake are 2,500 for men and 2,000 for women, although these are averages and the energy needs of individuals will vary dependent on age, lifestyle and size. Larger people and those with physically demanding work or leisure activities will require more calories and a more tailored diet.

Alcohol

Alcohol is a drug and it affects the body in a variety of ways. Over time and with prolonged exposure, like other drugs it can become addictive. As with certain foods that pose a health risk, it is a case of everything in moderation.

Certain professions, usually those putting particular stresses on staff through high expectation or pressure to perform, are seen as drinking professions – e.g. journalism, legal professions and corporate/investment banking – and there is often significant peer pressure for work colleagues to drink, particularly after work.

Individual governments and health agencies provide guidance on the level of alcohol consumption deemed 'safe' for both men and women. There are a variety of values, which reflect the level of uncertainty from research regarding what levels may have an adverse effect on health. Likewise local agencies will set alcohol limits for driving and other activities which are legally enforced so it is always advisable to check local data sources, particularly if travelling or working overseas.

Relaxation

Relaxation is a very personal thing, whether snuggling in an armchair with a good book, a long hot bath, lying in the sun on a summer's day, having a massage, aromatherapy or any one of a variety of formal meditation and/or breathing techniques.

Care should always be taken to make sure you take a break from work. Holiday entitlement is there for a reason. Even if you don't go away and stay at home, the break gives you time to unwind. Make sure you take an 'unplugged' break – the temptation to access work in the evening or while on holiday is made all the easier by the plethora of electronic devices that give us instant access to e-mails, work networks, etc. Try to avoid this when away from work; if it is essential you maintain contact with the office when on holiday, allocate specific times to work so you can focus the remainder of your time on you, your family and friends.

Summary

You should now know that in order to cope with stress in your own life you need to:

- recognize the existence and the signs of your response to stress
- understand the specific triggers or activities that cause you stress
- understand what control strategies are effective for you.

In this chapter you have considered how you can place demands on yourself through negative feelings and 'mind traps', how you might reduce work pressures and demands through better prioritization by deciding to Do it, Defer it, Delegate it or Drop it as well as looking to reduce commuting by working from home and to make the most out of meetings.

Finally you learnt about the importance of your personal health and wellbeing, considering the importance of regular exercise, a balanced diet and reducing alcohol intake as well as the need to understand the best way for you to unwind and relax.

Fact-check [Answers at the back]

1. Which of the following is a mind trap that can cause you to create demands on yourself?
a) Seeing extremes ❏
b) Over-generalizations ❏
c) Jumping to conclusions ❏
d) All of the above ❏

2. Which of the following statements about 'saying no' is likely to be true?
a) Your boss will fire you ❏
b) You'll never be asked to undertake a new challenge again ❏
c) People will understand, will ask someone else or help you prioritize their requests ❏
d) Your work colleagues will think you are not pulling your weight and shun you ❏

3. Which of these is not one of the 4Ds for better prioritization?
a) Do it ❏
b) Delegate it ❏
c) Deny it ❏
d) Drop it ❏

4. Why might ineffective meetings contribute to stress?
a) They use up time that could be spent on other priority tasks ❏
b) They may create confusion or lack of clarity of who is doing what ❏
c) You might feel uncomfortable/ embarrassed if invited to contribute to a discussion not relevant to you and where you have no knowledge of the subject ❏
d) All of the above ❏

5. Which of the following is not good practice for the chairperson of a meeting?
a) Start on time ❏
b) Confirm the purpose or objectives for the meeting ❏
c) Let the meeting overrun if the discussion is lively ❏
d) Summarize actions ❏

6. Why might working from home have a negative impact on your stress levels?
a) You can avoid unnecessary time spent commuting ❏
b) You might blur the boundary between home and work and end up working in the evenings and at weekends ❏
c) You can focus on work without the continual interruptions you get in the office ❏
d) You are still contactable throughout the day, should someone need to speak with you ❏

7. Which of the following is the recommended level of exercise for an adult?
a) At least 150 minutes of moderate-intensity aerobic physical activity or at least 75 minutes of vigorous-intensity activity throughout the week or an equivalent combination ❏
b) At least 60 minutes of moderate- to vigorous-intensity activity daily ❏
c) At least 90 minutes of moderate-intensity aerobic physical activity or at least 60 minutes of vigorous-intensity activity throughout the week or an equivalent combination ❏
d) No more than 120 minutes of vigorous-intensity aerobic activity throughout the week ❏

8. Which of the following is a true statement about diet?
a) You can eat as much fat and sugar as you like providing you do more exercise to compensate ❏
b) Your ideal calorie intake will depend on age, size and lifestyle ❏
c) A balanced diet should contain at least 33% protein from meat and fish ❏
d) An average calorie intake for a woman is 2,500 per day ❏

9. Which of the following is not an important consideration concerning the intake of alcohol?
a) Local legal blood alcohol limits for driving and other activities ❏
b) The special offers on during happy hour at your local bar ❏
c) Whether you are taking prescription medication ❏
d) Peer pressure from work colleagues ❏

10. What is the best way to relax?
a) Taking a foreign holiday ❏
b) A long hot bath ❏
c) Having your in-laws to stay for the weekend ❏
d) Find out what works for you ❏

7 × 7

1 Seven key ideas

- Stress isn't always bad and isn't the same for everyone; its signs and symptoms are often hidden.
- Lack of clarity on job role, responsibilities and objectives drive a significant proportion of work-related stress.
- Pareto analysis (also known as the 80–20 rule) can be applied to many events, i.e. roughly 80% of the effects come from 20% of the causes. Put another way, 80% of tasks can be completed in 20% of the time, or 20% activity creates 80% of the value.
- The work environment (light, temperature, noise, ergonomics, etc.) can have a significant effect on behaviour and productivity.
- People's motivation is determined by how well their needs are met, from basic survival needs (food, water, safety, etc.) to social, cognitive and esteem needs (knowledge, belonging, self-actualization, etc.).
- The timing and communication of change is more important than what the actual change is.
- Our minds tend to distort and generalize information to fit our own view of the world, meaning we can fall into 'mind traps' that reinforce a particular belief or behaviour creating a downward spiral we feel is beyond our control.

2 Seven best resources

- http://lean.org The Lean Enterprise Institute strives to answer the simple question of every manager, 'What can I do on Monday morning to make a difference in my organization?'

- http://mind.org.uk Mind, the mental health charity, provides information and support for a variety of mental illnesses.
- http://www.hse.gov.uk/stress/index.htm The Health and Safety Executive, the UK's government regulator for health and safety, provides free information and tools to manage stress at work.
- Mo Shapiro, *NLP In A Week* (John Murray Learning, 2016). The acceptance and use of NLP in organizational management is increasing and this book (among others) provides a good introduction.
- Stephen Covey, *The 7 Habits of Highly Effective People* (Simon & Schuster, 2004). A highly influential management guide.
- http://www.businessballs.com/ Website offering free and fun career help, business training and organizational development.
- http://en.wikipedia.org/wiki/If Rudyard Kipling's poem 'If' offers some helpful advice on life!

3 Seven inspiring people

- Frederick Herzberg (1923–2000) for his early work on motivation and job enrichment.
- John Fisher for his model of personal change – The Personal Transition Curve.
- Richard Bandler and John Grinder for their founding work in Neuro-linguistic Programming.
- James Reason for his work on managing human error and organizational safety culture.
- John Kotter for his work and publication on change management.
- William Edwards Deming (1900–93) for his 'System of Profound Knowledge' and leading the way for others in the field of lean thinking and process improvement.
- Elisabeth Kübler-Ross (1926–2004) for her pioneering studies and her theory of the five stages of grief.

4 Seven great quotes

- 'God give us the grace to accept with serenity the things that cannot be changed, the courage to change the things that should be changed, and the wisdom to distinguish the one from the other.' Reinhold Niebuhr (1892–1971), American theologian
- 'Life is not a matter of having good cards, but of playing a poor hand well.' Robert Louis Stevenson (1850–94) Scottish novelist and travel writer
- 'Many companies have long contended that stress in the home causes productivity loss in the market place ... and it does. But research now reveals that stress on the job causes stress at home. In other words, they feed off each other.' Hilary Hinton 'Zig' Ziglar (1926–2012) American author, salesman and motivational speaker
- 'To achieve great things, two things are needed: a plan and not quite enough time.' Leonard Bernstein (1918–90) American composer and author
- 'The mind can go either direction under stress – toward positive or toward negative: on or off. Think of it as a spectrum whose extremes are unconsciousness at the negative end and hyperconsciousness at the positive end. The way the mind will lean under stress is strongly influenced by training.' From *Dune*, Frank Herbert (1920–86) American science-fiction writer
- 'Stress is caused by being here but wanting to be there.' Eckhart Tolle, spiritual teacher and author
- 'Stressed spelled backwards is desserts.' Loretta Laroche, motivational speaker, author, humorist

5 Seven things to avoid

- Judging people based on their behaviour: we are all human, subject to mistakes and are heavily influenced by our environment.
- Ambiguity in roles, responsibilities and objectives.

- Command and control, unless there's a real emergency; people respond better when allowed to determine their own approach to deliver an objective.
- Your personal stressors, or at least plan your coping mechanisms in advance.
- The 'mind traps' of seeing extremes, focusing on the negative and overgeneralization.
- Creating conflicting demands and conflicts of interest (e.g. productivity and safety), or at least provide a means to escalate concerns when they arise. Ensure everyone understands what is expected of them and where boundaries lie.
- Change for the sake of it. Make sure there are clear benefits to any change and that the costs of the change both financially and emotionally have been properly assessed.

6 Seven things to do today

- Say 'no'. Most people will simply accept you are busy and go elsewhere. Even if they don't, the consequences will never be as bad as you think.
- Engage and take time to understand staff problems and concerns. Everyone is an adult and everyone is human and besides you might learn something to your advantage.
- Say 'Thank You.' Nothing motivates employees more than recognition that they have done well. Two simple words can reduce tension and flood the body with feel-good chemicals. You'll reinforce positive behaviour and build a bank of good will which you may need to draw on in the future.
- Prioritize and help others prioritize. Use the four Ds:
  - Do it – it has to be you and it has to be now.
  - Defer it – it has to be you but you can do it later.
  - Delegate it – it can be someone else (make sure they know if it needs to be now or later).
  - Drop it – no one needs to do it any time soon.

- Allow individuals control over their work. Set clear objectives and allow individuals and teams to determine how they are delivered. Consider multi-skilling to allow for job rotation and balance the work load.
- Set clear expectations for behaviours and manage them in line with other performance measures. Do not tolerate bullying or harassment, make sure employees are aware of what this means within the organization and the consequences of such behaviour, how they can raise or report concerns, access help and support services.
- Make time for yourself to relax and do the things you enjoy. Keep fit, eat well and get some sleep.

7 Seven trends for tomorrow

- The pace of organizational change will continue to increase – embrace it. Appreciate that others will go through their own journey. Create urgency, get buy-in and create alliances, communicate continuously, celebrate short-term success, reinforce positive behaviours and embed the change.
- The boundaries between work and home life will eventually blur and overlap. Always be clear on what you are doing, for whom and why. Amongst it all make time just for you.
- Technology will continue to provide new ways to share and access information. Information is only of value when you do something with it.
- Time is becoming a scarce commodity. You will need to learn the skills of influence and persuasion to get others to allow you to use it.
- You will be challenged to spend an increasing amount of time in meetings. Meeting are for decisions not discussions.
- Technology, fashions and trends will be superseded quicker and quicker; if you try and keep up with them all, you will lose both your time and money. Be selective on when you become an early adopter and in other areas get comfort

from periods of continuity and stability. A great lifestyle isn't the same thing as a great life.

- The world will continue to find 'others' to blame for mistakes, failures and anything negative. By taking responsibility for yourself, your behaviour and actions and feelings, you can never be a victim.

References

Arnsten, A. F. (1997). Catecholamine regulation of the prefrontal cortex. *Journal of Psychopharmacology*, *11*(2), 151–62.

Arnsten, A. F. (1998). Catecholamine modulation of prefrontal cortical cognitive function. *Trends in Cognitive Sciences*, *2*(11), 436–47.

Arnsten, A. F., and Li, B. M. (2005). Neurobiology of executive functions: catecholamine influences on prefrontal cortical functions. *Biological Psychiatry*, *57*(11), 1377–84.

Asch, S. E. (1951). Effects of group pressure upon the modification and distortion of judgments. *Groups, Leadership, and Men.* 222–36.

Bandura, A. (1999). Moral disengagement in the perpetration of inhumanities. *Personality and Social Psychology Review*, *3*(3), 193–209.

Baumeister, R. F., Bratslavsky, E., Finkenauer, C., and Vohs, K. D. (2001). Bad is stronger than good. *Review of General Psychology*, *5*(4), 323.

Brown, K. W., and Ryan, R. M. (2003). The benefits of being present: mindfulness and its role in psychological well-being. *Journal of Personality and Social Psychology*, *84*(4), 822.

Brown, K. W., Ryan, R. M., and Creswell, J. D. (2007). Mindfulness: Theoretical foundations and evidence for its salutary effects. *Psychological Inquiry*, *18*(4), 211–37.

Carlson, D. S., Kacmar, K. M., and Wadsworth, L. L. (2002). The impact of moral intensity dimensions on ethical decision making: Assessing the relevance of orientation. *Journal of Managerial Issues*, 15–30.

Chiesa, A., Serretti, A., and Jakobsen, J. C. (2013). Mindfulness: Top–down or bottom–up emotion regulation strategy? *Clinical Psychology Review*, *33*(1), 82–96.

Chugh, D., Bazerman, M. H., and Banaji, M. R. (2005). Bounded ethicality as a psychological barrier to recognizing conflicts of interest. *Conflicts of Interest: Challenges and solutions in business, law, medicine, and public policy*, 74–95.

Corbetta, M., and Shulman, G. L. (2002). Control of goal-directed and stimulus-driven attention in the brain. *Nature Reviews Neuroscience, 3*(3), 201–15.

Creswell, J. D., Way, B. M., Eisenberger, N. I., and Lieberman, M. D. (2007). Neural correlates of dispositional mindfulness during affect labeling. *Psychosomatic Medicine, 69*(6), 560–65.

Dane, E. (2008). Examining experience and its role in dynamic versus static decision-making effectiveness among professionals. In *Academy of Management Proceedings*.

Eisenberger, N. I., Lieberman, M. D., and Williams, K. D. (2003). Does rejection hurt? An fMRI study of social exclusion. *Science, 302*(5643), 290–92.

Epley, N., and Caruso, E. M. (2004). Egocentric ethics. *Social Justice Research, 17*(2), 171–87.

Goleman, D. (1996). Emotional Intelligence: why it can matter more than IQ. *Passion, Paradox and Professionalism, 23*.

Hallowell, E. M. (2005). Overloaded circuits: Why smart people underperform. *Harvard Business Review, 83*(1), 54–62.

Herndon, F. (2008). Testing mindfulness with perceptual and cognitive factors: External vs. internal encoding, and the cognitive failures questionnaire. *Personality and Individual Differences, 44*(1), 32–41.

Hölzel, B. K., Lazar, S. W., Gard, T., Schuman-Olivier, Z., Vago, D. R., and Ott, U. (2011). How does mindfulness meditation work? Proposing mechanisms of action from a conceptual and neural perspective. *Perspectives on Psychological Science, 6*(6), 537–59.

Hoyk, R., and Hersey, P. (2010). *The Ethical Executive: Becoming aware of the root causes of unethical behavior: 45 psychological traps that every one of us falls prey to*. Redwood City, CA: Stanford University Press.

Jones, T. M. (1991). Ethical decision making by individuals in organizations: An issue-contingent model. *Academy of Management Review, 16*(2), 366–95.

Kabat-Zinn, J. (1994). *Where Ever You Go There You Are*. London: Piatkus.

Killingsworth, M. A., and Gilbert, D. T. (2010). A wandering mind is an unhappy mind. *Science*, *330*(6006), 932–32.

Lieberman, M. D., and Eisenberger, N. I. (2008). The pains and pleasures of social life: a social cognitive neuroscience approach. *NeuroLeadership Journal*, *1*, 1–9.

Milgram, S. (1963). Behavioral study of obedience. *The Journal of Abnormal and Social Psychology*, *67*(4), 371.

Neisser, U., and Becklen, R. (1975). Selective looking: Attending to visually specified events. *Cognitive Psychology*, *7*(4), 480–94.

Ochsner, K. (2008). Staying cool under pressure: insights from social cognitive neuroscience and their implications for self and society. *NeuroLeadership Journal*, *1*.

Pashler, H. J., and Johnston, J. C. (1998). Attentional limitations in dual-task performance. *Attention*, 155–89.

Rest, J. R. (1986). *Moral Development: Advances in research and theory*. Santa Barabara, CA: Praeger.

Rock, D. (2008). SCARF: A brain-based model for collaborating with and influencing others. *NeuroLeadership Journal*, *1*(1), 44–52.

Ruedy, N. E., and Schweitzer, M. E. (2010). In the moment: The effect of mindfulness on ethical decision making. *Journal of Business Ethics*, *95*(1), 73–87.

Schneider, S. C., Oppegaard, K., Zollo, M., and Huy, Q. (2005). Socially responsible behaviour: Developing virtue in organizations. *Organization Studies*.

Shapiro, K. L., Raymond, J. E., and Arnell, K. M. (1994). Attention to visual pattern information produces the attentional blink in rapid serial visual presentation. *Journal of Experimental Psychology: Human perception and performance*, *20*(2), 357.

Shapiro, S. L., Carlson, L. E., Astin, J. A., and Freedman, B. (2006). Mechanisms of mindfulness. *Journal of Clinical Psychology*, *62*(3), 373–86.

Smith, E. E., and Kosslyn, S. M. (2013). *Cognitive Psychology: Pearson New International Edition: Mind and Brain*. Pearson.

Teasdale, J. D. (1999). Metacognition, mindfulness and the modification of mood disorders. *Clinical Psychology and Psychotherapy*, *6*(2), 146–55.

Tenbrunsel, A. E., and Messick, D. M. (2004). Ethical fading: The role of self-deception in unethical behavior. *Social Justice Research, 17*(2), 223–36.

Tencati, A. (2007). Understanding and responding to societal demands on corporate responsibility (RESPONSE): Final Report.

Wager, T. D., and Smith, E. E. (2003). Neuroimaging studies of working memory. *Cognitive, Affective, & Behavioral Neuroscience, 3*(4), 255–74.

Wolff, S. B. (2005). *Emotional Competence Inventory (ECI) Technical Manual*. The Hay Group. Retrieved 31 January 2010.

Zimbardo, P. G. (1973). On the ethics of intervention in human psychological research: With special reference to the Stanford prison experiment. *Cognition, 2*(2), 243–56.

Zollo, M., Casanova, L., Crilly, D., Hockerts, K., Neergaard, P., Schneider, S., and Tencati, A. (2007). Understanding and responding to societal demands on corporate responsibility (RESPONSE): Final Report.

Answers

Part 1: Your Mindfulness at Work Masterclass

Chapter 1: 1a; 2c; 3b; 4d; 5b; 6a; 7c; 8c; 9d; 10a

Chapter 2: 1d; 2c; 3a; 4d; 5c; 6a; 7b; 8d; 9a; 10d

Chapter 3: 1b; 2d; 3c; 4b&d; 5d; 6c; 7b; 8c; 9d; 10a

Chapter 4: 1b; 2d; 3a; 4d; 5b; 6c; 7d; 8b; 9c;10a

Chapter 5: 1b; 2d; 3b; 4d; 5c; 6a; 7a; 8d; 9c; 10b

Chapter 6: 1c; 2b; 3d; 4a; 5c; 6d; 7b; 8c; 9a; 10c

Chapter 7: 1c; 2b; 3c; 4a; 5d; 6c; 7c; 8a; 9c; 10d

Part 2: Your Confidence Masterclass

Chapter 8: 1b; 2c; 3a; 4c; 5b; 6b; 7d; 8d

Chapter 9: 1b; 2c; 3b; 4c; 5a; 6c; 7d; 8a

Chapter 10: 1c; 2b; 3b; 4c; 5a; 6b; 7c; 8a

Chapter 11: 1c; 2b; 3b; 4d; 5b; 6c; 7c; 8c

Chapter 12: 1c; 2d; 3b; 4b; 5b; 6c; 7b; 8d

Chapter 13: 1a; 2d; 3c; 4b; 5c; 6a; 7c; 8b; 9c; 10b

Chapter 14: 1a; 2c; 3b; 4b; 5c; 6b; 7a; 8b

Part 3: Your Assertiveness Masterclass

Chapter 15: *Individual responses*

Chapter 16: 1a; 2c; 3d; 4c; 5c; 6c; 7c; 8a; 9d;10d

Chapter 17: 1d; 2d; 3d; 4d; 5d; 6c; 7b; 8c; 9c; 10c

Chapter 18: 1b; 2d; 3c; 4c; 5c; 6c; 7c; 8b; 9c; 10d

Chapter 19: 1d; 2d; 3c; 4d; 5d; 6b; 7c; 8d; 9d; 10d

Chapter 20: 1d; 2c; 3c; 4b; 5b; 6b; 7b; 8b; 9b; 10b

Chapter 21: 1b; 2c; 3 *individual response*; 4c; 5 *individual response*; 6a; 7a; 8 *individual response*; 9b; 10 *individual response*

Part 4: Your Managing Stress At Work Masterclass

Chapter 22: 1d; 2b; 3a; 4d; 5b; 6c; 7c; 8a; 9d; 10a

Chapter 23: 1d; 2d; 3b; 4a; 5c; 6d; 7b; 8a; 9c; 10d

Chapter 24: 1b; 2d; 3d; 4b; 5b; 6c; 7a; 8a; 9c; 10d

Chapter 25: 1a; 2c; 3d; 4b; 5b; 6d; 7b; 8b; 9d; 10a

Chapter 26: 1c; 2a; 3a; 4c; 5b; 6d; 7c; 8c; 9a; 10b

Chapter 27: 1d; 2b; 3a; 4a; 5c; 6d; 7a; 8a; 9d; 10c

Chapter 28: 1d; 2c; 3c; 4d; 5c; 6b; 7a; 8b; 9b; 10d